FISHY TALES

FISHY TALES

Living Memories of New Hall

1930–2012

THE CANONESSES OF
THE HOLY SEPULCHRE

First published in 2012 by the Canonesses of the Holy Sepulchre
Howe Close, Colchester, Essex CO4 3XD
to celebrate the 370th Anniversary
of the founding of the Community and its School

www.canonesses.co.uk

A catalogue record for this book is available
from the British Library

ISBN 978 0 9574063 0 8

Cover photograph by Chris Beech, Van Cols Ltd
Text typeset in Garamond by Antony Gray
Printed and bound in Great Britain by
TJ International, Padstow, Cornwall

Contents

Fishes in front of New Hall during the 1920s

These are fishy tales . . .

This is a book of memories. Memories by their nature are subjective and oftentimes two people will remember the same event in entirely different ways. As publishers of this book we make no claims to its being an accurate historical record of life at New Hall. It is merely a collection of memories. Bear with us if you find inconsistencies.

Henricus Rex Octauus Rex inclit' armis
Magnanimus struxit hoc opus egregium

Preface

This book of memories has been put together as part of the celebrations to mark the 370th year since the foundation of the English Community of Canonesses of the Holy Sepulchre and their School in 1642.

The School, which began its life in Liège, continued in two temporary dwellings in England until at the end of the eighteenth century it finally found its home at New Hall in 1799. It has remained there since then and will continue there, we hope, for many generations to come.

Our aim in compiling this book was not only to celebrate our 370 years of existence but to provide a lasting record of life at the School in the words of those who have lived in it over the last 80 years. This is not a dry and academic history of New Hall, it is a collection of living memories and loving recollections of a place that has in different ways shaped the lives of the many individuals who have passed through its doors.

Following the Prelude, which is composed of a number of pre-1930s reminiscences drawn from the Archives, each section of the book covers a decade and is prefaced by a short outline of what was happening both in the School and in the world during that time. We hope that by providing this historical context we will enhance the reader's appreciation of the different personal contributions.

We have had a dedicated team of volunteers working on the book, and the result is a compelling and entertaining collective account of the School's evolution over eight decades told through the reminiscences of those who were there.

The book itself is not the only product of this venture. It has already brought people back in touch with one another, has reignited friendships and has uncovered many potentially lost memories. We hope that this impetus will be a catalyst for many more discoveries and renewals, that some ghosts may be laid to rest and that those key values that have always been at the heart of the Community and School will find renewed life and focus.

Henry VIII's Coat of Arms in the Chapel

Our final words must be of thanks: to all those who delved deep to retrieve their memories and then had the courage to write them down, to members of staff at New Hall and to those who worked for many months to produce this book. It is an immense achievement, arising out of a challenge, a struggle and a lot of fun!

The Book Team

S. Moira (O'Sullivan), S. Teresa (Lenahan), Henrietta Bond, Juliet Glass, Joan Jones, Rachel Kellett, Pauline McAloone, Claire Merry (née Fisher), Claire van Helfteren (née Golding)

Prelude

Excerpts from the Archives

The grammar, spelling and punctuation have been left largely unaltered to retain the authenticity of the writing. Thanks are due to S.M.Magdalene, who has done much work to preserve and find these archival stories for us.

Cattle grazing in front of New Hall, circa 1920,
before the East and West Wings were added (circa 1925)

Extract from the book *The Things of a Child* by **M. E. Francis**

M. E. Francis, daughter of Margaret Powell, writes about her mother's memories of New Hall. Margaret's lifelong friend, Eleanor Walmesley (who became the Honourable Mrs Henry Petre, of Springfield Lawn, Chelmsford), was the great-grandmother of Elizabeth Gough, who showed this book to the Community in October 2011. This extract tells of the antics of three young girls, 'the ringleaders' – Miss Powell, Miss Walmesley and Miss Weld – and their 'accomplices' at New Hall, circa 1840.

We were interested to hear of the lessons my mother did, and the friendships which she made, one in particular which lasted while life

North View of New Hall, circa 1920

endured; but we were, above all, delighted to hear of the talent for mischief which she soon developed when thrown among companions of her own age . . .

There was a secret hiding-place, entered by a hole in a hayloft, which was the scene of many stolen meetings of the leading spirits of that school. It proved a harbour of refuge after hairbreadth escapes from the vigilance of the authorities, and a safe council chamber where mischievous schemes could be hatched at ease . . .

It was my mother, however, who stole the jam tarts in company with her special friend, dear Ellen . . . The regime of the school, though plentiful and wholesome, was of an extremely simple order – roast meat and a plain pudding appearing regularly at the principal meal. That pudding was the source of much dissatisfaction among the young people, for it was nearly always composed of rice. One of the Seven, who chanced to be a poet, delivered her companions from a state of things which was at length felt to be unendurable. When the Refectory Sister came to remove the dish one day, at the allotted time, she found

its contents untouched; everyone's plate was empty, everyone was looking sadly at the tablecloth, but the pudding itself was decorated with a piece of paper bearing the legend: 'I wish the mice / Would eat the rice / And then the pudding would be nice.'

As a result of this indirect appeal the obnoxious viand was banished from the menu. Nevertheless the repasts continued to be plain – very plain – and it was with great indignation that the girls discovered that when the authorities entertained guests a very different order prevailed. They could see trays passing backwards and forwards groaning beneath the weight of succulent roast fowls, delicately browned cutlets, above all, pastry – pastry of the flakiest and jammiest description.

A council was summoned in the secret hiding-place. 'I'll tell you what it is, girls,' cried my mother. 'If they don't give us proper things to eat, we'll take them.'

'Yes,' chimed in Ellen, who was always in the forefront of things, 'we'll steal them.'

'Ellen and I will do it,' resumed my mother. 'We'll just wait in the passage till the trays come out and snatch them.'

'Yes,' agreed Ellen eagerly. 'Old Simmy Monica is so fat, she'll never be able to catch us.'

When 'Simmy Monica' – the name was a corruption of Sister Mary Monica – what schoolgirl could be bothered to pronounce so many syllables? – was waddling out of the guest-room with her tray that evening, she was surrounded by a variety of flying forms; eager little hands swooped into the dish, and then with a whisk of skirts and a patter of hurrying feet, the culprits disappeared.

But before the stolen dainties could be partaken of at ease in the hiding-place, the conspirators found themselves suddenly summoned. Hastily were the luscious morsels consigned to the pockets of their white muslin frocks, and with flushed countenances they presented themselves in the big parlour. To their surprise the Superioress received them with a benign countenance. Two or three high ecclesiastics were still at table; the headmistress was also present. 'Now,' said Reverend Mother, smiling, 'shall we have that little recitation?' The highest of the high ecclesiastics nodded approval, and the seven wicked sinners with beating hearts and bulging pockets were marshalled in a row and desired to begin.

So great was my mother's inward turmoil that she never could remember how she got through her share of the scene from *Athalie* which was the piece in question. She was only conscious of her pocket, which seemed to be growing bigger and heavier every moment, while one horrified glance at Ellen's dress revealed the fact that the jam was slowly oozing through the transparent folds. Their eyes met and the words froze on my mother's lips. But the lofty and benign ladies in their flowing robes seemed to be quite unaware that anything was amiss.

Art class in the early 1900s

When the welcome permission to withdraw was given, and the girls filed past the headmistress, she did indeed lay a detaining hand on Ellen's arm. 'What is that stain upon your skirt, my dear?' Ellen glanced down at the spreading smear, and then back at the mild, enquiring face. 'I think it – it – it looks like jam,' she faltered.

Hurriedly did the guilty seven hasten to their lair, quickly did they devour their booty. The jam tarts were excellent; indeed, the sense of having successfully accomplished so notable an achievement was certainly exhilarating, but the pangs of conscience began to make themselves felt. At length the question was voiced: 'Was it a sin to steal jam tarts?'

'Simmy Monica saw us do it,' said someone, 'so it wasn't exactly stealing.'

'She'll tell, and then we'll hear what they think,' said somebody else.

But 'they' never said anything; no one was scolded, no disapproving remarks of a general nature such as attended most school delinquencies were made. Simmy Monica apparently had not told. The dreadful proposition was next mooted: 'If it was a sin, ought not the guilty ones themselves to confess it?'

Ellen was finally heroic enough to volunteer to lay the case before the chaplain. 'If he says it was really a sin, I'll nod to you when I come out,' she said, 'and you can all own up too. But if he says it was no harm, I'll shake my head.'

The culprits waited anxiously during the absence of the valiant Ellen, and could hardly breathe when she presently reappeared: her face was wreathed in smiles and she wagged her head violently from side to side.

The seven sinners scampered away to the hiding-place and there eagerly questioned her. 'Did he say it wasn't a sin? Did he say it was no harm?'

'He didn't say anything at all,' declared Ellen. 'I saw his shoulders shaking, and he covered his mouth with his hand. I think he was laughing. I told him, of course that we didn't think it fair that they should have all the good things in the guest room while we were put off with such horrible puddings . . . '

Extract from the book *An Irishman and his Family: The Story of Lord Michael Morris*
by **Maud Wynne**, circa 1873

Maud Wynne was one of Lord Michael Morris's daughters – he had 11 children, four of whom came to New Hall: Maud, Sarah, Fanny and Eileen.

The extract below is summarised. Maud was seven years old when she left Ireland for the first time to go to an English convent school where an elder sister was already being educated. She was not on speaking terms with her mother at the time, as her mother had required her to say she was sorry for 'some wickedness' before she would speak to her again, and the child left it so . . .

The convent school in Essex had been a palace of Henry VIII's. Anne Boleyn had lived there many years, and Henry VIII's arms still surmounted the door of the nuns' chapel, and Anne's ghost is still supposed to haunt one of the walks. In front of the large gravel sweep were some of the finest cedars of Lebanon in England, and at one side was a wide beech avenue, where in summer we walked up and down, learning by heart. But the day my father brought us to the school we had none of these attractive anticipations. There the three of us sat in the parlour, bare, bleak and polished, awaiting the Reverend Mother. One is always kept waiting when visiting convents, I can't think why . . .

All at once there was a shuffling noise outside in the wooden passage, and a tiny stout nun, dressed apparently in numerous black petticoats and veils, danced into the room with twinkling eyes, laughing mouth with the makings of a small moustache, and very white teeth. This was Reverend Mother. She hastily shook hands with my father, laughing all the time, and kissed us heartily on both cheeks . . .

Elder sister said, 'We had better go,' and opening the door, hand-in-hand she brought the others along innumerable bare and highly polished corridors where they slipped about miserably in new boots, until finally they reached the school end of the building. And so into the 'little kitchen' where they met Sister Elizabeth, otherwise Sister

Lizzie, but known by all as Slizzie, the head lay sister who looked after the smaller children. Slizzie was loved by all . . .

At the first introduction the little sister maintained her usual stolid silence, and the elder had to leave her to join her own class and contemporaries. Directly she had disappeared the young one felt it was time to do something on her own, and she lay down on the floor of the little kitchen, rolled, kicked, yelled and finally cried. Slizzie did her best to comfort her with tea and toast, but not getting much forwarder, finally carried the bundle of misery up to bed, to a dormitory with several other little beds, parcelled off in squares surrounded by white dimity curtains. Slizzie herself slept in a corner square with blue curtains . . .

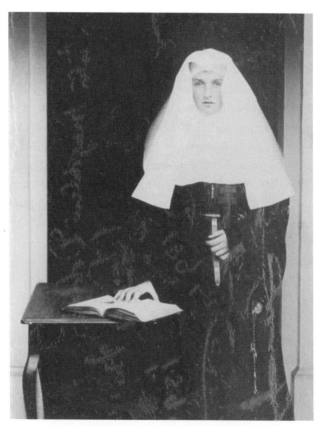

Fanny Morris dressed as an 'Innocent' (1890) when Fishes became members of the Community for the day

The school of about eighty girls was divided into four classes and the two lowest were the Brats Classes, so a 'Brat' she became. The other girls, including elder sister, were 'Fishes', the name coming from a tradition from Henry VIII's time. It seems that New Hall was renowned for the very excellent carp in its pond, and Anne Boleyn, when wishing to pacify her fiery-haired master, would send some fish up to London. As they were superior to ordinary fish, the servitor at dinner would whisper in the King's ear 'New Hall fish', hence the derivation of the name which still carries the supposed superiority in the minds of all at New Hall . . .

MARY McDONNELL

Reminiscences of the niece of S. Ann Teresa Purcell
New Hall circa 1898

It speaks well for the School when I think how short a time it took me to settle down and not only to settle down but to look on it as the next place to home. The Nuns were our mistresses but also our friends. We loved them, and looking back now from a grown-up's point of view what strikes me most was the great influence they had over us. Individual girls had their favourite Nun called their 'Angel', who talked to them and encouraged them. This influence was not used as some people think (even Catholics) to foster vocations, but what was continually impressed on us was to please our parents, to make ourselves pleasant when we went home and to lead useful lives.

I never remember a girl in my time being rude to a Nun. We were of course unruly, idle and we led the lay governesses awry. Dear me! How we teased them! I remember one poor thing we suspected of wearing a wig. This had to be cleared up so we arranged a cord and pin over her usual desk from our class table, and the girl who went to do 'French readings' attached the wig and when the governess rose and walked away we held on to the cord and the wig remained amidst much applause.

When I arrived I remember how kind everyone was. One Nun had known my grandmother; another remembered my Mother when a schoolgirl like myself. My Aunt who was a nun made me feel quite at home, was very kind to me – though later on she used to be extra strict to show that there was no partiality.

When I went to New Hall the 'improvements' had not begun. We slept in large dormitories, our beds being screened off with white linen curtains, and many were the games we had between those curtains. We ran downstairs in the morning to a primitive lavatory with a shelf above, upon which reposed sponges. I remember a walk I took on that shelf, from basin to basin, when I was not quite so heavy as I am now. Afterwards all this was changed and we had cubicles with dressing tables with drawers in front of them and hot and cold water laid on.

We were very well fed. Indeed I look back with wonder at the amount we got through. I have before my eyes wedges of mince pies and tarts of which I wonder I survived to tell the tale, and as for New Hall 'tartine' and gingerbread, they have a worldwide celebrity.

Christmas time was our great holiday. On Innocents' Day the two youngest of the 'Brats' were dressed as Rev'd Mother and Mother Sub Prioress and assisted by six of the big girls dressed as Novices ruled the house and ordered the Nuns about, making them do 'penance' such as singing comic songs, etc. Then came Kingstide for which we had prepared for ages, studying parts, dressing characters and painting elaborate programmes for our audience.

Dormitory – The Blue Room

We were supposed to speak French three days a week and if we did not we were given a badge which if we had in our possession at certain hours cost us a penance, so we were always trying to pass it on to another delinquent. Such French as it was but it gave one a 'fluency' which I have found very useful in later life.

Except when we went for long walks with the Chaplain for a treat, we never left the Convent grounds. This was no privation as there was an avenue a mile long and lovely grounds shaded by lovely trees of all sorts, from the sentinel Cedars in front of the house to the splendid

Innocents, 1898

oaks, the tulip tree and the hornbeam with the stone griffin underneath, on which we took many a ride, down to the trees overhanging the great garden . . . by climbing which we could make a raid on the fruit which tasted ten times sweeter acquired in that manner to when we ate it in the Refectory.

Reminiscences would not be complete if I did not allude to the Chapel so dear to us all, to the Choir where the Nuns said the Divine Office where one heard nothing but women's voices some young and fresh some faint and worn in God's service, and to the old clock whose tones were so familiar but, alas, is getting worn out like the rest of us. How trivial things seem as one looks back to incidents and scenes once all important, now one only smiles at what once made one laugh or cry. But there is one point on which I keep my youthful enthusiasm and that is my old school and if anyone asks me where to send a child there is no hesitation in my answer.

DOROTHY SMYTH-PIGOTT

New Hall 1905–1907

My Mother had only time to hand me over to the Portress and catch the late train back to London. The rather silent nun led me through long dimly lit passages, handing me over to a lay sister (dear Sister Helen) at the door of a little room. 'In you go,' she said cheerfully. 'You have got to be fumigated,' and the next moment I was standing in the dark, inhaling obnoxious fumes and gasping for breath. Luckily it was not in my nature to panic, it just seemed to me a dirty trick to push me in there about five minutes after my arrival! However the friendly little sister let me out and led me across a long room to the second class where a kind and most gracious Nun (dear Sister Mary Joseph Falls) greeted me, but to my horror, straight away and without a pause began to question me as to what I knew! 'Yes Sister,' I said with my mind on the retreating cab and the possibility of catching up with it at the gates, if I was fast enough. 'Now then dear,' said the patient Nun, 'what have you been studying lately in English history?' Gulping down fumes which still lingered in my throat and chest I answered nervously, 'The Tudor Period, all my life it has been the Tudor Period.' At that moment I was saved from general collapse by the ringing of a bell, and we moved into the Refectory.

My chief recollection of the first meal was the lovely little silver mugs which I was later told had been brought from Liège. Then a Nun came round with a card which she held up to each child and either received a bow or was

Dorothy Smyth-Piggott

ignored. Of course I looked down nervously at my plate. Afterwards I was told she was counting how many would be going to Communion next day. By this time (suffering from acute indigestion from the mixture of supper and fumigation) I found that the School had moved into the Pink Room, formed into two lines and performed a sedate dance and I was expected to join in. Nearly reduced to tears, the dance over, I was greeted by a lovely little Nun with the most beautiful manners, Sister Mary Dismas Weld.

Recreation seemed to consist of walking round and round the room, then settling down in a bow window around the Nun. We sat down and were read to, and as we got up and turned towards the altar, I noticed that some of the girls had black bags slung around the back of their necks. Someone led me up to the Top Dormitory and as I lay in bed aching with misery I was kept awake all night by the ticking of many clocks. Each Fish had one opposite their cubicles on a piece of furniture which ran down the middle of the room . . .

The next day I had another talk with Sister Mary Joseph and was admitted to the Great Class. A very severe looking Nun, Sister Mary Josephine, knocked on the classroom door and asked for Dorothy Smyth-Piggott. Without preamble she ordered me to follow her to the Music Room. 'Play,' she said with no encouragement in the timbre of her voice. I sat down quite confidently to my one accomplishment and began to play a little Chopin and as I settled comfortably to my task I was suddenly brought to a halt by the voice of Sister Mary Josephine,

'You do not come up to my standard,' she said, 'I shall send you to Miss Byford.'

Well on this first day, as I stood in the Music room at New Hall, I resolved to make a break for freedom from this curious place where girls wore black bags on their back and clocks that ticked in the night. I would make a bee line for the Avenue, and mother would rescue me at Chelmsford! However, when I returned to the Great Class I was informed that Reverend Mother wished to see me. The door eventually opened and the tiniest little old lady, Reverend Mother Julia Butler, came slowly into the room and sank on to a chair; there was a long pause. She looked intently at me and I looked back at her, and at last she said, 'I never interview a new Fish but as I was Form Mistress to your Grandmother and Great Aunts Arundell I thought I would have a look at you.'

During the two years and a bit that I was at New Hall, she used to send me down little parcels of cake and sweets, and once, when she heard I was terrified of thunderstorms, she sent me down a medal of St Christopher. Sister Mary Philip told me I must never let the Fishes know about these kindnesses. But [I] had made up my mind not to run away. Rev. Mother had somehow given me hope.

At this period in 1905 the School was at its lowest ebb numerically, I do not think we mustered more than eight in the Great Class, about

The Pink Room – destroyed during World War II – which became the Refectory and then the Library

sixteen in the second class, and the little ones in the third class. Later when I learned to love New Hall I revelled in the intimacy of our small numbers and our nearness to the Nuns.

We were called at six, and washed in icy water (in the winter). Mass at 6.30, Breakfast at 7.15, Dinner at 11.30, Tea at 3 and Supper at 6. My introduction to a bath at New Hall in 1905 remains in my memory! The Sister led me into a partitioned area in a large room. Three cubicles contained a bath apiece. A white coat hung on the wall of each. 'What's this coat doing here, Sister?' I asked. 'You put it on to bathe in,' she said as she closed the door. Black bags hanging round girl's necks, clocks in the night, white coats in the bathroom, a nun who did not grasp the fact that you were a budding musician . . . I learnt to love the 'black bag' which turned out to be our Communion hood. My Great Aunt, Isabel Arundell, who married Sir Richard Burton, the explorer, was buried with her New Hall hood.

Very soon after my arrival I was told to join Daisy Thunder with her sister, Magdalen Sales, on their Sunday walk, and that was how I first met my dear friend. I think S. Mary Philip asked her to try and soften up this tiresome frozen Fish. Anyhow I was often asked to join the two which cannot have been much fun for poor Daisy but S. Magdalen Sales was just what I needed at the time with her gorgeous Irish humour and warm sympathy.

I still remember S. Antony's graceful walk as she glided up and down the top Dormitory. And S. Helen who used to wash my hair in a tub in front of the erstwhile 'little kitchen' fire. As she poured soap and water into my ears and eyes we would talk about Lulworth Castle (now a ruin) and the Welds and Weld Blundells, who she had been with before coming to New Hall. White veiled S. Mary Christina used to flit through the Pink Room carrying a huge round alarm clock on her way to teach in the music room.

All I ever learnt in the Great Class was at the feet of S. Mary Joseph. Our education was glorious for those who were fortunate enough to do the Grand Tour of Europe. S.M.Joseph had scrapbooks containing all the chief painters and their work, architecture etc, and when in 1906 throughout the summer holidays my eldest brother took me touring in Europe he told me he was surprised at my appreciation and knowledge of the arts.

Apron holding – a privilege

S. Ignatia Joseph used to sit with me in the Bow window of the Pink room and try, poor dear, to teach me German. I loved her and though she assured me I was wasting her time and languages were not my forte, I insisted on carrying on. Dear little S. Mary Catherine was most amusing and of course French was my second language having had French Governesses up to the time I went to School so we carried on with ease.

Miss Byford was a Royal Academy trained teacher who I found extremely comforting to learn from. I was shocked but not surprised to hear after I left School that scrambling in Snowdon one day with her Father, she slipped, hesitated and fell to her death. Dear Miss Byford.

Almost directly after arriving at New Hall S. Anne Frances was professed. Fr. Bernard Vaughan preached the sermon and his text was 'You have not chosen Me, but I have chosen you,' etc. As the Novice pronounced her vows, the priest held the Sacred Host over her. I believe this has been discontinued but I could not get over it, it was so utterly beautiful. I was lucky enough to have the stall nearest the parapet surrounding the Choir and had a perfect view.

We crowded round the Nuns and in my day it was a privilege for two senior Fishes to walk each side of the recreation Nun and hold on to her habit [apron]. The thought that they rose at 4.30am, laboured all day and remained patient with the Fishes impressed me enormously. I loved all our funny little customs such as nests in the hay on the Feast of St Aloysius, the May processions to the Pavilion when we handed our Hymn Books to our favourite Nun. And above all being dressed in the Habit and white veil and sharing the day with the nuns in the Choir and Refectory, work room and a visit to the Nuns cells, on the Feast of the Holy Innocents. In those days we seemed to have beautiful summer weather and often sat out on benches in the Beech Walk at evening study, with the pigeons cooing around us. It was Mass with daily Communion, with our cold fingers tucked into our hoods, and surely daily Compline and an evening visit to the Chapel on our own and the gorgeous holy atmosphere of New Hall all around us that crept into every corner of my being, and though I had only been two years at New Hall the severance from it was like a surgical operation.

Studying in the Beech Walk

S. ANN (Young)

The Harvest Supper 1908 – Sister Ann Young retold these memories aged over 90

When all the harvest was in, about the end of October, all the men and boys came to a 'Royal Banquet' which was held in Perry's shop. Painter, plumber, shoe-mender, and many other workers for house and farm (men only) were available to help clear it, put up trestle tables, benches etc. and quite transformed the dismal place. The only lighting was gas and candles. Boys came up the steps to the 'Turn' outside the kitchen (which turned round on

Joseph Perry – one of the dedicated Estate Staff who served New Hall

small wheels), rang a hanging bell and spoke through a little hole in the Turn; on no account was anyone allowed to go into the kitchen or even see inside it. The hot plates were all piled up and the boys carried them down, all the vegetables and joints were all piled up round the old pewter platters and the joints had special ones as they were so big. Two pigs from here were slaughtered for the feast.

Nothing was to come back, anything that was left over was to be shared out and taken home. The older men went down to the cellars to draw the beer from the barrels, no boys allowed down there. At the end of supper Canon Heery the Chaplain joined them to drink the Community's health in hot Gin and for this they rang the bell at the Turn and a 2 gallon can of hot Gin was put in; great cheers went up from the Banquet. They all dispersed by midnight.

MARGOT JACKSON

New Hall 1909–1915

It was, I think, 1909 that my sister and I first went to New Hall. We had never been away from home before. The whole of my school years, there were only three classes, first or Great Class, then second, and then third or Little Class. There were no more than twenty-four Fishes in the school our first term, and the highest number ever reached was thirty-six.

In the Great Class, which was in charge of S. Mary Joseph, I remember the following: Vera Shreward-Brown, Grace Binchey, Edie Craigie-Halkett, Frances Boland, Maud Crillier, Rita Stockdale and Cissy Noakes with long auburn hair to below her waist. In the 2nd class, in charge of Sister Christina Magdalene, were Nina Boland, Muriel Coventry, Carmel Nagle [see Archive memoir on pages 46–7], Lil and Maureen Tidmarsh, Aline Coventry, Agnes Nicholl, my sister Joan and myself. In the 3rd class in charge of Sister Mary Dismas [Angela Weld] were Pauline Nagle, Beatrice Innes, Cissy Nicholl, Mary McKeever, Hilda Harold-Barry and two or three others whose names I do not remember.

The Second Class in 1914 (Margot Jackson is 3rd on left)

The first ordeal on arrival at the beginning of each term was 'fumigation'. This took place in Cook's room (now I think part of the First Mistress's room). Here, placed on the floor, was a large shovel with glowing hot coals, which were sprinkled with lumps of sulphur. Sister Helen, then School Sister, waited at the Ambulacrum door for each arrival and hurried them into this room full of white clouds of sulphur fumes. The door was then firmly shut while Sister stood outside. We coughed and choked with streaming eyes and nose for almost two minutes. This was supposed to kill the germs we might have caught in the train on the journey or elsewhere during the holidays. We banged on the door and shouted to be let out and when Sister finally opened the door, we burst forth like wild animals from a cage. Although my sister and I came by car, for we lived only twenty-four miles away, we also had to go through fumigation. I do not remember how long this rule persisted, certainly the first year or more of my school life, but it was suddenly stopped to everyone's great relief and joy.

The first Mass at which Holy Communion was given was at 6.30am and those going were called at 5.50am. If one went to first Mass, one hung a hood on the cupboard door outside the cell and Sister would then call us. I must perhaps explain the hoods, which I believe came over from the first school in Belgium. These were made of thick black corded silk – a long strip pulled up with and tied under the chin and then rolled up in front to form a loose hood. Some of us rolled up the front to show the face, and others rolled it up no more than two or three inches so that nothing at all could be seen of the face – very convenient for shutting out distractions caused by one's next door neighbour on the same bench.

Breakfast was immediately following the first Mass, about 7.15am, and we went straight to the Refectory on coming out of the Chapel. Our breakfast consisted of enormous slices of home-made bread and butter and our own jam from home, except on Fridays, and tea out of an enormous tin tea-pot.

After Mass or after study, as the case might be, there was class until 11 o'clock when a few of us had 20 minutes break out of doors, if fine, with one of the younger Nuns, or sometimes a Novice. We all had a slice of bread and butter which was left on the window-sill in the passage outside the Refectory. Those who did not enjoy this break

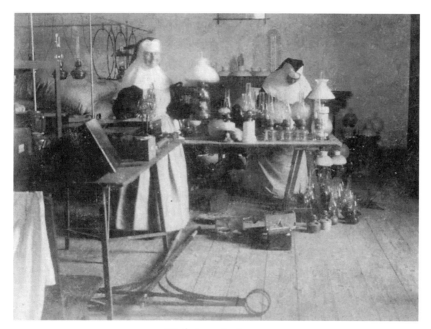

Lighting the lamps

privilege (which was for the supposedly delicate) had either music lessons or piano practice in the practising-room.

Baths were twice a week – Friday evenings and Saturday afternoons. The water was always boiling hot and one could hear the rumbling in the tanks . . . this noise terrified me, for I imagined the tanks might burst. There was no electric light in those days and Sister Helen did not bring in the lamps until dusk. It was very eerie up there alone, and I used to say numbers of Hail Mary's that she would come quickly with the lamps and run a little hot water off so that the bubbling noise would stop for a while.

Our uniform in winter was navy-blue serge skirt and a separate serge bodice with high neck, relieved by a small white embroidered stock-collar. In summer, we wore the same skirt and white cotton blouse. Over the uniform both Sundays and weekdays, we wore black serge aprons with bibs held up by straps over the shoulders. These were always removed for Chapel.

Saturday afternoon until 4 o'clock there was no class, but the time was filled by 'Saturday Duties' . . . Sister Helen examined our heads with a fine comb, just 'in case'. At some time or other, I believe a Fish had come back with her hair in an unsuitable condition, hence what we called 'head scraping'. Finally, Confessions in the Sacristy, after which we felt fully equipped for the coming week . . .

At 4 o'clock in the 2nd class there was 'Letter from Memory' and Composition alternate weeks. In the Great Class, we had a special subject with Sister Mary Joseph. Our letters home were written on Sunday. Compline followed at 5 o'clock. On Sundays there was always sung Mass and either sung Vespers or Compline and Benediction.

At midday 'Rec' we had to walk for at least twenty minutes or play games: rounders and basketball in winter and tennis in summer. Most of us disliked going down the Avenue, it was so cold and exposed to icy winds. At night, 'Rec' began with 'Lancers' or quadrilles, after which we all sat around the Nun taking 'Rec' in the bow windows of the Pink Room.

In summer, at both midday and night 'Rec', we went up to the Plot. The May Processions took place during night 'Rec' and the Fishes waited by the 'Little Gardens' [now built over by classrooms, etc.] until the Nuns appeared, when we would go forward discreetly and offer hymn-books to our favourite nuns. Proceeding up the 'Beech Walk' we

Tennis a hundred years ago

sang the Litany of Our Lady until we reached the Pavilion [now where Beaulieu stands] when hymns to Our Lady were intoned. Then we collected our hymn-books and recreation proceeded until time for night prayers in the Pink Room.

The long benches were pulled to the centre of the room from St Aloysius's Altar so that we sat facing each other during a short reading and facing the altar for prayers. The First Mistress sat at the end where her chair and table had been placed. After prayers, we walked up in a line to say 'good-night' to her and receive her blessing.

Silence in the dormitories was absolute at all times, also in the passages. My first year, there was silence in the Refectory (except for tea) when the First Mistress read from a suitable book once the clatter of plates had subsided. We had good food and plenty, the famous New Hall tarts were a particular feature. They were served in large, round tins about 14 inches across, one for each table. We often had two helpings – apple, gooseberry and rhubarb – according to the season, with custard sauce. These were varied with roly-poly, fig suet pudding or baked sultana roll. On Fridays we had slices of fried fish or salmon pie, the latter really delicious. The vegetables were home-grown in the Great Garden and the bread and butter also homemade. We drank water out of unpolished silver goblets – I think these were brought over with the Community from Liège.

There was one occasion when the Second Class dormitory was invaded by bats – the workmen had disturbed the bats resting in the crevices. About a dozen of these little creatures suddenly appeared and caused havoc among us for they clung to our cell curtains and dropped on our beds or hanged themselves into the hanging oil-lamps and made them flicker. Silence went to the winds until Sister Helen appeared and found out the reason for so much noise. I suppose Sister put out the lamps and opened windows and the bats disappeared.

The exams at the end of the summer term were always a great ordeal for me and for others too, no doubt. In particular, the Music Exam presided over by Sister Mary Josephine and the nuns who taught piano. I felt quite ill beforehand for several days and when the actual time came, my knees knocked together and my fingers seemed to lose all feeling and so, of course, I played nothing but wrong notes and came off very badly. The other frightening exam was the Inspection on

The Pavilion – located where Beaulieu was built (now the Prep School)

religious subjects. Canon Shepherd of Chelmsford took this exam and we had to be word-perfect in the Catechism. There were also written points on Christian Doctrine. The exams lasted two weeks before the end of term and I felt like a piece of chewed string when all was over.

'Place Day' was a very nerve-racking experience, taking place in front of the whole Community and School. It was, of course, greatly mollifying when prizes were given and I happened to be one of the recipients – a surprise and joy that enhanced even the holidays.

In my last year, I managed to be received into the Sodality of the Children of Mary (Enfant was the word we used), obtaining a white badge, which I still possess. The Enfants' Chapel was where the television room is now! Why, I wonder, have all the lovely Sodalities been swept away?

HAROLD BREWSTER

Delivery Boy 1937

Saturdays and Bank Holidays was our chance to earn some pocket money. As a boy of eight or nine, my task on Saturdays was to clean the cutlery. A knife board and some brown scouring powder, a damp cloth and plenty of rubbing, the task was endless. Every few minutes I would run up the front path to see to see if Mr Church, the postmaster, was looking for a delivery boy. Telegrammes to New Hall was my favourite. 6*d.* for 1 or 9*d.* for 2, this was big money for a child in those days. With the post-office pouch strapped safely round the waist, clean hobnailed boots, hair neatly combed I was off at the trot. Down the A12 to the Buckshorns crossing, turn left over the narrow stream, back under the Viaduct and along Payne's Lane, crossing the railway again, then follow the footpath to the Boat House and Potash Cottage . . . As a child, I had heard stories of this being Henry VIII's boat-house and lake, but apart from one small meadow which was very soggy, with a

Courtyard showing kitchen entrance, circa 1930

lot of rushes and occasionally kingcups and peggles growing, I could not imagine a lake there.

After the railway crossing at Payne's Lane, we could clearly hear the Nunnery Clock, which chimed very frequently; I believe it was every seven minutes. We were told this was to call the Nuns to prayer . . .

From the Boat House, we followed the tracks past the Bull's Lodge, then into the back entrance of New Hall, past the pond very gingerly (having heard the old wives' tales of ducking witches in the bygone days), through the farmyard, under the arch, up the stone steps, a tug on the bell, and we would be greeted by a kindly Nun through the hatch. Whilst waiting, we were given a large homemade brown biscuit and a glass of milk or hot cocoa; this was a real treat for children in those days. With mission complete I was wished a safe journey home.

On several occasions I met a Victorian lady, exercising her little bull-terriers in the New Hall grounds. Miss Dolan. I believe she was

The journey Harold Brewster would have taken delivering the telegrams to New Hall: along the old A12, through the lodges and past the 'Black Boys' . . .

. . . over the old level-crossing at Payne's Lane (before the Avenue was re-routed) and on down the Avenue to New Hall

a Shakespearian actress and taught the young ladies at the Convent school; she lived in the cottage opposite the Bull's Lodge entrance . . .

From 1933 to 1934 I was a frequent visitor to New Hall as a butcher-boy, delivering meat about three or four times a week. I remember the stone staircase from the butcher's cellar, leading to the kitchen, with all the part-cured bacon hanging on the walls either side of the staircase. I well remember Sister Veronica. There were times when I helped her prepare the meat when I was late delivering; also the slate troughs and brown earthenware vessels which were used to pickle their home-produced pork and cure the bacon. I remember asking Sister Veronica if she had a secret recipe, with special herbs to cure bacon, it always smelled so nice, up the staircase among the bacons. I have very happy memories of my visits to New Hall, a hard-working and kindly Community.

S. MARY BERNARD (Russell)

This account, which is thought to have been written by Sister Mary Bernard Russell, describes the building programme begun at New Hall in 1923 and the consecration of the new buildings in 1925.

On 11th September 1923, the first sod was cut. When the necessary excavations were made to lay the foundations of the new building several interesting discoveries were made, walls running east and west, north and south, and among the debris were found some old glazed tiles, portion of a carved stone and some bits of marble.

In order to interfere as little as possible with the historic front of New Hall so dear to us, the new School was to be added on to the North aspect. In the first instance it was intended to start with the Hall or Gymnasium, but the architect eventually decided to start operations by pulling down the School shoe cupboards and to build in their place the beautiful passage we know as St Aloysius Corridor. This formed the Southern base of a Quadrangle, flanked on either side by two corridors (East and West wings) on to each of which three spacious classrooms (connected by folding doors) would open, and the fourth side of the Quadrangle was to be occupied by a fully equipped Gymnasium.

Over the East and West wings were to be private bedrooms for the Staff and senior students and above the Gymnasium a spacious Art Room was to be added. Moreover a number of new bathrooms and lavatories were to be installed upstairs and down. The first bricks were laid on October 1st. The Procuratrix at this time was Sister Mary Dismas (Weld) to whose zeal and enthusiasm we owe much of the success of our ambitious project.

More foundations were discovered under the new Refectory and Fisher House.

On 17th November the Foundation Stone was laid by the Right Reverend Arthur Doubleday, Bishop of Brentwood. The Bishop, in his purple silk and wearing the 'Chenille Cope', intoned the Veni Creator in the Sanctuary and sang the Collect. The Procession was formed, the children leading followed by the Lay Sisters, Novices and Nuns, the

Winifred (Aunt Win) Dolan's cottage – now Wharton, the Principal's house

school Staff, Mr and Mrs Duffy, the Architect Mr Myers and his wife and daughter, the Litany of the Saints being sung.

The sun shone but a strong wind blew the Nuns thin Veils over their heads. Boards had been put down over the mud which had been churned up by the building operations. The Bishop blessed the stone which was let down by a chain, and having placed in it relics and medals, including one of St Ignatius, with a silver Trowel handed to him by Reverend Mother, and an ebony Mallet handed to him by Mr Clogg the builder, [the Bishop] laid the stone. After that the Bishop gave an address, speaking of the work of education carried out at New Hall for the last 125 years. The procession returned in the same order, the Ave Stella Maris being sung.

An empty niche above the Foundation stone awaited a statue of St. Thérèse of Lisieux till its arrival on 28th April 1924 when it was duly installed in the presence of the Nuns, School and Staff.

As the building progressed so did our ambition grow. It was decided to ask the Bishop's leave to build new music rooms and fill up the space outside 'Cook's' room, to enlarge the Children of Mary's Chapel. On 9th May this leave was given with the result that on the West wall of the Ambulacrum – which was an outside wall – three rooms were built, the one nearest the School door having a bow window to match the last bow window of the existing Front. Over these rooms a fine linen room and practising-rooms were built and the Children of Mary's chapel extended to coincide with the increased length of the Ambulacrum below. The Statue of Our Lady which stood over the Chapel door was removed and placed over the School door, outside the window of the Children of Mary's Chapel.

On 23rd September 1924 the children returning from the summer vacation occupied the new School for the first time. Then at last came the great day when on 23rd June 1925 His Eminence Cardinal Bourne declared the new School officially open. It was a great occasion. There was a large attendance of guests: clergy, parents, Old Fishes.

Perhaps the following account, written by Sister Antony Magdalen at the time, will be of interest to future generations.

On Monday morning we had all the Office earlier than usual and then the people began to arrive for the Pontifical Mass. The children

Ambulacrum

were packed into one side of the Chapel and the Secular Chapel the other side was left for visitors – some of these were seven in a bench! There were also a few priests as well as the seculars who were not in the procession. At the Communion rails were 10 Priests in Cottas, and in the Sanctuary 20, counting the Cardinal and Bishop. It all went simply splendidly and the Cardinal was delighted. It was certainly a very fine sight as he had on his Cappa Magna which he only wears on the grandest occasions and it was an enormous train spread out behind him and reached right across the Sanctuary and down into the Chapel. The Bishop has the same but purple of course and I think it is made of cashmere, whereas the Cardinal's is moiré.

The Mass took exactly an hour and everything went without a hitch. The luncheon was in three rooms: the Stonyhurst contingent in the Library; the Cardinal, Bishop, the Archbishop of Bombay (he only arrived in time for lunch), the two Abbots and a select few at our table in the Pink Room . . . I think about 100 were fitted in altogether. All the food was put out on to the tables beforehand and about 6 lay Sisters served together with 14 hired waitresses . . .

Meantime the company had gathered in the Gymnasium to witness a performance of *A Midsummer Night's Dream* by the schoolchildren. Everyone thought it was a wonderful performance for children. The Hall was packed; any Nuns who went had to go in the Gallery.

A description of the new Gymnasium may not be out of place here. In 1923 Reverend Mother's sister, by that time a member of the visiting staff and resident at New Hall cottage and who for many years had been an actress on the London Stage, asked to be allowed to produce a Shakespeare play in its entirety. So *As You Like It* was given in the Pink Room with four oil-lamps for footlights and paper scenery from French & Co. in the Strand. It was such a success that the following year *Twelfth Night* was performed under similar circumstances. When the new School was built Miss Winifred Dolan [Aunt Win] was entrusted with the supervision of a proper stage duly equipped for the production of Shakespeare's plays. She secured the services of a retired stage carpenter who had for years acted as Head of that branch of the staff at Drury Lane Theatre and for a time with Madame Sarah Bernhardt.

What 'old Joe Packer' did not know about stage-craft was not worth knowing. He built all our scenery, coming down year after year for six weeks at a time to make the scenery, for the next production. It was he who introduced Mr Crow to us, a leading scenic artist well known for his brushwork in the London theatres. He too came down annually for three weeks at a time to paint the beautiful scenery for seven of Shakespeare's plays and for 'The New Hall Pageant' (produced for Reverend Mother Aloysia Magdalen's Golden Jubilee in 1934).

Friends of New Hall generously subscribed each year a certain sum towards expenses. The total sum raised and expended was £700.

The stage occupies the full width of the West end of the Gymnasium and includes a Scene dock for storing scenery. The Drop Curtain painted by Mr Crow is a beautiful piece of work, heavily draped curtains surrounding a vignette in the centre of New Hall. The body of the hall is, of course, the Gymnasium equipped with all the modern apparatus; its size may be visualised when its seating capacity is 300.

When we returned from Newnham Paddox after the War, Mr Crow came in to overhaul all the scenery and to see how it had withstood the blitz. It was found to be unharmed and in excellent condition. He had been a true friend since 1925 and was ever ready to give of his best. Shortly after this visit he was killed outright in a motor-car accident (1947).

A Midsummer Night's Dream, As You Like It, Twelfth Night, The Tempest, Richard the Second, Much Ado About Nothing, The Merchant of Venice and *Macbeth* so far are the Shakespearian productions seen on this stage, but other plays too numerous to mention have also been staged – such as *The Admirable Crichton, The Mikado, The Bishop's Candlesticks, Little Lord Fauntleroy*, and many Nativity Plays, etc. The age-long tradition of New Hall's interest in Drama as an important element in education is well maintained.

In 1925 the pupils took part for the first time in public examinations. A few, at first, entered for the Oxford School Certificate and London Matriculation. Later on the whole of the Upper V did the same, and now the VI class sits for the Higher Certificate and University Entrance Exams. Pupils were also entered for the Associated Board of Music Examination in all grades and others entered for the Royal Drawing Society Examinations, gaining many awards.

About this time lacrosse was substituted for hockey; netball and tennis also being played. Matches were regularly arranged with other schools.

In 1947 Inspectors from the Board of Education visited the School for three days with the gratifying result we gained the recognition of the Board. In 1946 a third House was added to those of St Thomas More and Blessed Margaret Pole, viz. St John Fisher.

The Chapel (the paintings went during World War II)

WINIFRED IVY MATHEWS

Science Teacher 1925–1927

Early in September 1925, I arrived at New Hall to begin my teaching career. We each had our own room in one wing of the then new building facing the senior girls' rooms on the opposite side of the quadrangle. These rooms were above classrooms. Joining the two wings at the far end away from the main building was the school hall, also used as gymnasium and above the hall, the art room. We soon found one problem which was that the wash bowls in our own rooms were not connected to the drainage system and instead pails had to be used to collect the waste with rather disastrous consequences on some occasions.

I understood that the cost of these new buildings was about £32,000 and that these buildings together with the appointment of additional members of staff were essential for the school to meet the requirements of the then Board of Education. In my second year there was a General Inspection and leading to that there were many preparations, making use of advice obtained from various sources. Two Nuns from the Holy Child Convent and Training College in Cavendish Square, London, visited the school and gave us valuable help.

The Science Laboratory was very small. There was no gas supply and spirit lamps had to be used, which was adequate for teaching Botany but the examination syllabus for the Oxford Board required some General Science and this did present difficulties.

Sister [Mary Winifride] refers to the drawing paper I got for the examination. An emergency arose when it was discovered that the School had not got the necessary paper. Sister gave me particulars and asked me to see if Miss Hunter, who rode a motorbike, would go to Chelmsford for it. She would not go unless I went with her so I had to travel on the pillion seat, something I had never done before or since. Down the Avenue, we had to stop at the level-crossing gates. As she started again, there was a sudden lurch forward, leaving me behind sitting on the ground much to the signalman's amusement. Fortunately, we got the paper and all was well for the examination.

There were two resident Chaplains, Fr Nicholson SJ and Fr Butler SJ who led two Masses each morning, at 7am and 9am. Divine Office was said or sung by the Nuns and on Feast Days and every day in May there was Benediction. On Saturdays there were Confessions in the Community part of the Convent for the girls and in the Chapel in the evening for the public. On one occasion Miss Meek, who used to spray the rooms with disinfectant especially during an epidemic, went into the Chapel. Seeing nobody there and thinking confessions were over she went to spray the confessional. Frantic gestures on the part of Fr Butler saved the situation.

Certain features of New Hall intrigued me, like the convent clock which not only struck the hours, the half hours and the quarter hours but also the seven minutes past the hour and the half hour and the next hour. I believe this timing was connected with the times for Mass and Divine Office.

There were the Griffins on the roof of the main building, which one girl climbed to and sat on, and had been severely reprimanded. This, however, was before my time.

The School uniform was very impressive especially when a party of girls was seen in the Avenue going for the Sunday walk with one of the Nuns. The bright scarlet tunics and blazers with the distinctive Cross

Fr Reuben Butler at New Hall from 1925 to 1959

of the Holy Sepulchre showed up well against the background of greenery. Exceptions for this uniform were allowed for girls with auburn hair who wore brown tunics and blazers. The blouses were made of tussore silk. On Sundays there was a change from the black head-veil worn at Mass on weekdays to the white veil.

After Sunday Mass the tuck shop was opened and it was very popular. My weekly buy was sixpennyworth [old money] of chocolate peppermint creams. On Sunday evening we occasionally had a concert in the School Hall. There was a Jesuit Priest who used to visit and sing Negro Spirituals.

Miss Dolan, Reverend Mother's sister, lived with her friend Mrs Hemming at the cottage in the convent grounds. She taught Drama and one of the outstanding productions was *A Midsummer Night's Dream* which had been performed the year before I arrived. She often invited Staff to her cottage and gave us China tea and toasted buns.

At another cottage in the grounds, which may have been Ann Boleyn's, lived Dodson. He was the Convent chauffeur and drove a large open saloon car. This was the only means of transport available for Convent use. Staff used bicycles or otherwise had to walk to the main road and get the bus to Chelmsford. There were only three a day. Taxis were expensive – the charge was six shillings and sixpence [old money] from Chelmsford Station to New Hall – but were used when funds allowed.

I left in December 1927 and so ended the first chapter in my teaching career. However the influence of New Hall and the happy memories I have of my stay there will never be forgotten.

CARMEL NAGLE (later S. Mary Celestine, Sisters of Charity)

1905–1910
Account recorded at New Hall in 1976

I was a delicate child and aged eight, after an operation, the surgeon was insistent that I be moved farther away from Belfast Lough. So I came to New Hall with my sister after the summer holidays.

My sister was afraid that I might laugh at the nuns' habits – but she need not have worried. From the first day I thought it was very interesting with the white surplice and red two-armed cross.

I settled in very quickly in the Third Class. Sister Mary Dismas was my teacher. Sister Helen took good care of all of us and Sister Anthony was in the linen room, and when I moved up to the Second Class, Sister Mary Christina Magdalen was the teacher. I never got to the First Class because my younger sister who had joined me and I were brought home just before the war.

I remember being told that New Hall 'Fishes' could always be recognised by their high sense of humour and their ability to walk backwards! Certainly the high sense of humour was well inculcated in us and walking backwards came quite naturally as we walked down the Avenue and back at recreation time, if we could not get near enough to hold on to the apron of the nun any other way.

Now these are very far-away recollections. We have lived through the two World Wars and after the first one I entered the Sisters of Charity in Dublin and having lived in several different houses I am now living in Bristol for the second time and expect to remain here for the rest of my days, as my years now number 80!

S. ANTONY MAGDALEN (Frances Russell)

1894–1898

Sister Antony Magdalen – Frances Russell – was 90 when she wrote the memoir summarised here. She came to New Hall from County Cork, in 1894 when she was 14.

The School was divided into three Classes, the Great, the Second and the Third or 'Brats' class (the term in those days did not convey disrespect). Each class had two Mistresses, one to teach English subjects and act as Home Mother, the other to teach French. The subjects taught were History (English, Greek, Roman), Grammar, Arithmetic, Poetry, to be learnt during free time, and a composition in English or French on alternate weeks. All Classes worked at double box desks lit by paraffin lamps.

Several old Liège words were still in use: 'pussy', meaning dust; 'puzzle', to dust with a long brush; the enclosed space round the organ was the 'doxsal', meaning the place to sing from; the bread and butter sandwiches for breakfast were 'tartines'.

All Fishes were 'proclamated' with a special Nun, their 'Angel', permitting some privileges, for example private conversations, and after leaving, sometimes retaining contact with the odd letter; some remained friends for life. S.M.Joseph (Falls) was S.A.M's 'Angel' whom she revered and was grateful for her guidance.

On the Feast of St Stanislaus each class went in turn to see his picture in the Noviceship, to pray there and either 'tread on the Vocation board or not, according to taste' . . . On the Feast of the Presentation there was always Presentation Tart, two layers of pastry with jam in between. On the feast of St Aloysius it was new potatoes, peas, strawberries and games in the hay. Feast Days were free and the Fishes left to their own devices with a Nun always in charge. Long walks were possible, sometimes in the company of Fr Heery; one such walk encompassed Danbury Church, going through Boreham House park which had deer in it.

Canon Heery 1885–1925 (Chaplain) in the outer back courtyard

There were still Fishes who did not go home for Christmas and the great excitement was the Feast of the Holy Innocents. New uniform was worn and the Fishes all went to the Community Workroom for 'Court'. Reverend Mother stood while the Fishes 'processed' in, the last two being the two youngest dressed in the full habit as 'Reverend Mother' and 'Mother Sub Prioress'. The youngest, the 'Reverend Mother', made a speech asking for the privileges and ended by saying, 'I promise to take great care of the Community while you sit by the fire and warm yourself.' The four Fishes who were leaving school and had been there the longest were dressed as Novices. All meals were in the Nuns' refectory and groups of Fishes with their Angels went to a room for quiet conversation, the day ending with 'nun-night' in the Community workroom.

The ensuing 'Grey week' was a quiet time involving a few lessons but mainly preparing for the plays at Kingstide, one in French followed by a farce in English. The next day one or two lighter English plays, and on the third evening the Great Play. It all involved dressmaking, casting, learning, and rehearsing and was very hard work.

The following term began sadly with the death of a pupil; only the previous year three pupils had died of diphtheria, this entailed the closure of the School while the drains were examined and renewed, all were in good condition but every precaution was taken. The winter of 1894–5 was exceedingly severe, the house was not well heated and whatever the cause there were six Community funerals between November and April.

Term ended about July 14 and the school returned early September. 100 marks were given to all who came back on the right day, many did not. The Easter holidays were a sore point as some went home and those that did not did lessons.

The last year was spent in the Great Class with S.M. Joseph Falls as Class Mistress. The subjects were, Latin, General History, English Literature, History of Italian and Dutch painters and of Architecture, Chemistry and Logic. Arithmetic was not taught as it was supposed to be finished within the Second Class. An excellent grounding in Christian Doctrine was given and old Fishes used to attend some of the lessons . . .

Isabella Arundell, wife of Richard Burton, visited us at this time and Sir Evelyn Wood came with the hunt.

Well-behaved seniors were admitted to the Sodality of the Children of Mary, and Frances [later S.Antony Magdalen] was made Child of Mary in 1896, her act of Consecration written out by S.M.Joseph and the Certificate signed by Canon Heery.

One of her worst adventures happened subsequent to this. Frances and Edith Keily heard about a fire–escape in one of the maids' bedrooms which they felt they had to investigate. Sure enough a trap door was discovered under the bed. On opening it there was a horrendous crash and another trap door opened and a rope ladder with iron hooks, metal fittings and wooden treads descended into the maid's room in the Sacred Heart Dormitory, which was occupied at the time. The maid could have been seriously injured. Frances was told she was within an ace of losing her medal, a very great disgrace.

Queen Victoria's Diamond Jubilee was celebrated in 1897, the School had a holiday with meals under the Oak tree which was subsequently destroyed by enemy action in 1943; it was where the New Wing is now.

Reverend Mother Aloysia Austin Butler celebrated her Silver Jubilee of Election and her Golden Jubilee of Profession in 1898. At the same time the Community were preparing to celebrate the centenary of their arrival at New Hall in 1798. The Old Fishes had decided to celebrate the triple event by donating a new Our Lady Altar to replace the rather ugly one already *in situ*. She remembers being given a postcard-size picture of the ivory Crucifix which is now in Howe Close. For the centenary celebration there was a large gathering of Old Fishes, and three days of celebration with Cardinal Vaughan coming on the last day. The Fishes did a series of tableaux depicting scenes from the history of the Order. There was one of the Holy Sepulchre with four Nuns dressed in the full habit kneeling before it and Frances was one of them to her great delight.

This brought an end to Frances's school career. But she says:

I cannot leave this part of my life without a very special mention of one to whom we all owed much for her loving care, S. Elizabeth, the School Sister known and loved by many generations as 'Duckie'. I always feel a very special connection with her, a link in the chain to Liège. S. Agnes Brown, the last of the Liège Community who was in the Black Cap (i.e. a lay Sister postulant) when they left, outlived

50

them all by many years. In her old age and at her death, Duckie helped to look after her. Later it fell to me to be Infirmarian when Duckie was old and ill and to look after her. Her death was very beautiful. She was suffering from gangrene in both legs and the last morning when I came back to her after the Doctor had gone this conversation took place:

'Well what does the old boy say?'

'He thinks you may be in Heaven today . . . '

She was nearly blind and her eyes for months past had looked dead and glazed, but suddenly they cleared and became bright and fixed on some point above our heads for some minutes. And then they closed.

The Tudor Griffin (also referred to as 'the dragon')

The 1930s

What's going on in the world during the 1930s

Abdication / Depression / Unemployment / Hitler / Rationing / Benny Goodman and his Orchestra / Dorothy flies over the rainbow / Scientists split the Atom

1930 The planet Pluto discovered / Construction of the Empire State Building / Youth Hostels Association opens first hostel / Amy Johnson flies solo from England to Australia / Debut performance of Noël Coward's comedy

'Somewhere Over The Rainbow'

Private Lives / Film of *All Quiet on the Western Front* / Arthur Ransome *Swallows and Amazons* / Agatha Christie's first Miss Marple novel

1931 Al Capone imprisoned for Income Tax evasion / The Highway Code is issued / Whipsnade Zoo opens its doors / Dogger Bank earthquake felt across Britain / First film version of Bram Stoker's *Dracula* / Virginia Woolf *The Waves* / Abbey Road Studios opened in London by Sir Edward Elgar / Flanagan and Allen sing 'Underneath The Arches'

1932 First experimental television broadcast by the BBC / Introduction of Book Tokens / Forrest Mars produces the first Mars Bar / Aldous Huxley *Brave New World* / Duke Ellington 'It Don't Mean A Thing (If It Ain't Got That Swing)' / Marlene Dietrich in *Shanghai Express* / Paul Muni in *Scarface* / Thomas Beecham forms the London Philharmonic Orchestra

Left: Fishes outside Boreham Church circa 1930

1933 Adolf Hitler becomes Chancellor of Germany / First Nazi Concentration Camp is established / Prohibition ends in USA / First sighting of the Loch Ness Monster / H. G. Wells *The Shape of Things to Come*

1934 Percy Shaw patents the 'cat's eye' / Bonnie and Clyde shot by police / Parker Brothers' game Monopoly goes on sale / Fred Perry Wimbledon Champion / Paul Whiteman 'Smoke Gets In Your Eyes' / Laurel and Hardy *Babes in Toyland* / Shirley Temple *Bright Eyes*

1935 Maiden flight of Hawker Hurricane fighter aircraft / Publisher Allen Lane founds Penguin Books / James Chadwick receives the Nobel Prize for discovery of neutron / Ramblers' Association founded / Fred Astaire dances *Cheek to Cheek* / George Gershwin's *Porgy and Bess* / Alfred Hitchcock's film of *The Thirty-Nine Steps*

1936 King Edward VIII abdicates / Nazi Olympics held in Berlin / Spanish Civil War begins / BBC is open for business / First flight of the Supermarine Spitfire of Battle of Britain fame / Jarrow March / Vera Lynn 'Up The Wooden Hill To Bedfordshire' / Billie Holiday 'Summertime' / Fats Waller 'It's A Sin To Tell A Lie' / Noel Coward's 'Has Anybody Seen Our Ship?'

1937 Golden Gate Bridge opened / Hindenburg Disaster / George VI's Coronation / 999 calls are introduced into Britain / Marx Brothers *A Day at the Races* / Robert Colman in *Lost Horizon* / Disney's *Snow White and the Seven Dwarfs* / First BBC coverage of Wimbledon and live football

1938 Chamberlain says there will be 'Peace for our time' / Kristallnacht / Bíró brothers file a British patent for ballpoint pen / Tommy Trinder film debut *Almost a Honeymoon*

1939 First commercial flight over the Atlantic / helicopter invented / Germany invades Poland / Britain declares war on Germany / National Service introduced / Beginning of petrol rationing / Glenn Miller 'In The Mood' / First broadcast of radio comedy *It's That Man Again (ITMA)* / Judy Garland stars in *Over the Rainbow* / *Gone with the Wind* achieves 10 Academy Awards.

What's going on at New Hall during the 1930s

The 1930s brought major and minor changes and ever louder rumblings of war. The events of a decade which saw three Kings of England and a new Pope in Rome reverberated in the School. Daily, the Fishes attended Mass and Benediction and prayed for Peace.

There were some august visitors to New Hall in this decade: Queen Mary popped in on her way to Chelmsford, Cardinal Hinsley paid a visit and Archbishop Alban Goodier SJ, who had friends in the Community, came on several occasions.

The School's relationship with the Community was warm and open and there were a number of times when the Fishes were allowed into the Enclosure, although, in the 1930s, the nuns were still strictly cloistered.

There was an increased demand for the pupils to be prepared for a career and they were encouraged to study hard in order to pass the Oxford Local Examinations, which were current at the time; in 1932

Nuns arriving for the 1932 Education Conference

A School picnic in the 1930s

the London Matriculation and Cambridge School Certificate were added. Joy Carey was the first New Hall Fish to go up to Oxford.

Two members of the Community attended the first Conference of Convent Schools and subsequently, in 1932, New Hall hosted the second conference with 270 participants. One of the members of the original Conference was S.M.Veronica Boland, who worked indefatigably and successfully to bring the School into the modern age.

The Pageant of New Hall was performed for the first time in 1934. It was written for Reverend Mother Aloysia Magdalen's Golden Jubilee of Profession by her sister, Miss Winifred Dolan (Aunt Win).

Annual epidemics and the weather often interfered with Prize Day and made the three days of plays, which were an integral part of the end of the summer term, a bit problematic.

In 1939, on the announcement that Britain was at war with Germany, gas masks were issued to all the Fishes and the first siren sent them all scurrying to their shelter.

S. ANTONY MAGDALEN on the visit of Queen Mary

Extracts from a letter of S. Antony Magdalen's to her Mother in 1938

June 17th 1938

It was a very great event – even one all fitted into five minutes or so! Reverend Mother received various instructions as to behaviour – no cheering, no one to speak a word except R.M herself, and only when spoken to, no one to be presented except herself. This from the Lady-in-Waiting, Hon. Margaret Wyndham, not sure if she is Miss or Lady, who said the Queen would not get out.

The grass in front of the house was not only mown but shaved! At 12.15 everyone in the house except the bedridden assembled on the grass in front, the sisters, the nuns, the staff, school, maids & men, those who had been in the war wearing their medals. Several photographers and reporters were about. There were police at the gate.

They were late, driving very slowly – first a police car with the Chief Constable, then the royal car, followed by another with the

Queen Mary visits the School, 1938

suite and then another with police. The Queen's car was very big, black with red leather inside with three sets of seats behind each other. She was in the middle one at the right hand side, and her seat was raised and rather forward so that you could see her quite plainly, even at a distance.

R.M stood in front of us (the nuns) on the edge of the grass. The Queen then began beckoning R.M. forward. At the same moment the lady beside her jumped out and came to meet R.M. and said very loud, 'Her Majesty Queen Mary – Rev. M. Prioress.' R.M. then went up and the Queen at once shook hands with her and began talking, 'What a beautiful place you have here. How long have the nuns been here?' and she seemed very surprised to hear we came in 1798 – she repeated it. Then, how many children had we? What kind? R.M. said daughters of professional men, army and air force and so on. Then, 'Do all the nuns teach?' R.M. said no, some were heads of department, bursar, infirmarian, laundry, etc. She said, 'Oh I see.' R.M. presented the visitors book (a new one). She asked R.M. to send her a photograph of the house, then she said she was 'awfully' sorry to stay such a short time but they were late and she shook hands again and away they went.

She was all in white with an ermine coat and white toque, a lovely diamond pendant. She is 71. The Lady beside her must have been Lady Byng. In the seat behind the Queen were the Earl of Athlone and Princess Alice.

ELIZABETH EDWARDS (née Gough)

Pole and Fisher 1934–1940

I visited the Community recently to take them a book which contained information about my great-grandmother's years at New Hall. During that visit I was shown a copy of the school register and there on 28 September 1934 was my entry, signed by S.M. Veronica. I was 10 years old.

My great-grandmother's time at New Hall was so different from mine but the essential spirit of New Hall has been constant and recognisably evolved into what I found 100 years later. I loved my time at New Hall.

When I started the number of pupils was in the low fifties. My first recollections of the School have to be climbing into the uniform, stockings and other things I hadn't been in the habit of wearing before, like those red knickers with separate white 'linings' . . . To show you were washing and changing your clothes it was compulsory to send a minimum of three handkerchiefs and two knicker linings into the laundry every week. If you didn't you got an order mark, which was bad for the House. So the Prefects checked. If you had nothing, they'd encourage you to scrunch up a lining or handkerchief to make up your laundry. A conduct mark was really bad, as you had to stand up and apologise in the weekly House meeting.

Soon after I started at New Hall, S.M.Benedict took her vows. I was one of her bridesmaids because her family lived close to mine. It was on the festival of St Theresa. I had a beautiful deep-rose-pink satin

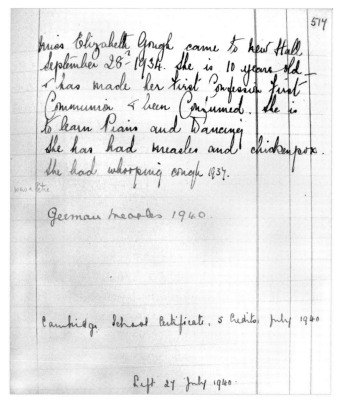

Elizabeth Gough's entry in the School register

dress, and found the ceremony both incredibly moving and also so sad. I remember being terrified that if you had a vocation it would lead to a wedding without a bridegroom.

Some schools have a reputation for Music, Sport or Art but for New Hall in the early thirties it was Drama, following a series of Shakespeare plays which had been widely praised. The sister of Reverend Mother, Miss Dolan, was a well-known classical actress, and had retired to live quietly at New Hall. By the time I arrived Miss Dolan no longer took an active part, but the tradition lived on, and she came in to coach us in the less ambitious productions we put on. In my case, she played Elizabeth Bennett to my Mr Collins in a little sketch called *Mr Collins Proposes*. I'm sure Miss Dolan must have been responsible for the wonderful stage we had – a reconstruction in miniature of a proper theatre, with a raked floor, footlights, wings, overhead gantry for lighting and even a trapdoor. There was a Green Room and an immense collection of costumes had been accumulated.

At New Hall I overlapped with Bridget O'Connor – many people will remember her later as S.M.Christopher. She was in the year above me but stayed on after the others left. It was 1939, war had just started and the future was dark and uncertain. At New Hall it was literally dark as well, not just because of the black-out curtains but because of the dimmed lights behind them. I was in my final year as a Prefect and we had a new First Mistress, whom none of us knew – all rather unsettling. Into this background Bridget, merry and bright, didn't seem to fit. She wasn't so much academic as artistic. She didn't join in our lessons, but we supposed she might be painting or drawing somewhere. She seemed beyond the rules. Given her personality she was a bit of a loose cannon. If we were ponies in one paddock, she was a racehorse in another field! I wonder now if she was grappling with her call to a vocation, something I could have readily understood and sympathised with, but we were not close enough then – later in life we were.

When I first arrived there were maids who did the chores but when war broke out we had to help with the housework. I vividly remember sweeping the passages and that then somebody came along behind you with a padded polishing thing.

The school had its own farm so in the early war years food was plentiful and excellent. We had fresh milk, butter and cream. There

One of Aunt Win's 'famous' plays

were pigs killed every Thursday in winter, so we had fresh pork. (We never saw the slaughter because the farm was out of bounds.) We also had wonderful homemade bread and rolls and plenty of fruit and vegetables, strawberries and raspberries. I recall a pudding we called 'Putty and Varnish' which was a plain suet roll with treacle poured over it. It was black treacle – not syrup – which some people hated but I rather liked. There was also chocolate tart for treats, with jugs of thick cream.

With the start of rationing all food supplies had to be pooled, so our diet changed. I remember the day a perfectly shaped oblong yellow brick appeared on the table and we thought, 'Oh good, bought butter!' It turned out to be margarine and horrible.

In the spring term of 1937 we had an outbreak of whooping cough and chicken pox – both at the same time. I was with the 'chicken whoopers' as we were called. It was really most exciting, because we were sent to the High Nursery at the top of the Convent. It was thrilling because we'd never been to 'the other side' before. This was an isolation dormitory where we were looked after by a nurse and food was sent up from the kitchen by lift. There were no lessons but we were allowed to get up and play games. It was fine because you didn't feel sick – although you were constantly being sick. I was there for at least three weeks. Once your temperature had been down for three days you were sent home to recover fully. One delicate girl developed pneumonia and I heard that there was a real drama when the doctor was called out but couldn't get across the level-crossing with the oxygen. Fortunately she recovered, but it was a close thing.

In the summer of 1940 we were evacuated to Newnham Paddox, which was in Monks Kirby, near Rugby. The house was owned by the Denbigh family who were Catholic, and they had a little church in the grounds. The first things to be packed were our books, and we stowed them ourselves individually into our desks and tied the lids down securely with strong cord. It was days before we saw them again, and I don't know what we did for schoolwork, but somehow we managed to sit and pass our School Certificate Examinations only a few weeks later.

We travelled in coaches and I know that journey must have been a real shock to the older nuns, many of whom hadn't seen the outside world for 50 or 60 years, When they first arrived at New Hall it would have been in carriages pulled by horses. Some were frail and ill, so goodness knows how they coped with that journey. But it must have

Farm Sister feeding the cows

been extremely well organised because I remember very little of it. We woke up in our beds at New Hall, got into buses and went to bed on mattresses in the ballroom of Newnham Paddox, with portraits of the Feilding ancestors looking down on us.

The experience at New Hall that had the most effect on my later life was being taught to play the organ by Mother Mary Cecilia. (My grandmother demanded that I was taught as soon as my legs were long enough.) With this modest skill I did many organ 'stand-ins' in different places in the course of a peripatetic life as an army wife. One memorable occasion was Christmas Eve in the Malayan jungle, in a clearing by the camp, playing carols for the troops crowding round the piano.

I had four children and recently moved to Great Cornard to be near my family.

PAMELA MARRINER (née Webber)

1936–1937

Memories recounted by Liz Olding (née Marriner) daughter of Pamela and mother of Philippa and Joanna Olding
Although my mother was only at New Hall for the last two years of her school life, she has happy memories of it all.

She remembers crawling through a hole in the wall of the Art Room (as many of us did in subsequent years), with her good friend Bridget O'Connor (later S.M.Christopher). They arrived over the nuns' Library where they must have found a gap in the ceiling, for they pushed a book off the shelf which landed on the floor – and on returning Bridget got a rusty nail in her foot.

S. Philomena slept at the end of the dormitory behind a curtain, and used to brush my mother's very beautiful long wavy hair 100 times.

My mother remembers the gorgeous pats of butter from the farm. And she says that when her sister Joan was a Prefect, S.M.Veronica (Housemistress) – who was quite fond of Joan – noticed a light under the door of her room in the Prefects' passage where she was reading by torchlight under the bedclothes. She was sent back to the dormitory no longer a Prefect.

Four generations of the Marriner family (Pamela, Liz, Joanna and Ben)

When my grandfather (her stepfather) used to go to London by train from Ipswich, he used to throw a food parcel out of the train window when passing the Avenue to New Hall. Sometimes it took quite a walk to retrieve it.

ANNE PONSONBY (née Maynard)

1937–1940

I had never been to school before arriving at New Hall. Having been brought up as a 'daughter of the Raj' and accompanying my parents to various army postings throughout India, I confess my education was virtually non-existent. Arriving at New Hall, I was nervous of being at the bottom of the class (which I was). The nuns and Lay teachers were sympathetic and helpful and I never felt a 'dunce'.

My homesickness was acute as my parents returned to India for two years. Fortunately I had a wonderful aunt who looked after me during the holidays so I survived. S.M.Veronica was the splendid Headmistress at the time, and I recall weeping on her shoulder during the first term. She gave me a lot of confidence without appearing to do so.

I think there were about 120 Fishes, all boarding, and we formed very close friendships which have survived to this day. New Hall was a 'home' while my parents were away. The nuns were a fascinating collection of splendid women most of whom had something special about them. S. Margaret Helen taught us English Literature and successfully introduced us to the Classics. I remember her reading *Pride and Prejudice* in a lovely well-modulated voice. Maths, however, was and remains a mystery. I never got beyond fractions and still struggle with numbers.

I was very overweight and ate the delicious home-cooked food with enthusiasm. Apart from tennis, which I loved, I was hopeless at lacrosse and gym terrified me. Watching my friends skim up and down various bars, ropes and horses increased a lack of confidence which lasted for years.

I left in early 1940 so was only there for a short time but the foundation of my faith was cherished there, my values were strengthened and that indefinable sense of what was right and wrong was instilled within me. For that reason I can honestly say that New Hall gave me a wonderful start in the world and the memories of that time have sustained me throughout my long life.

Tennis including Beatrice Coverdale (S.M.Benedict) in the 1930s

I joined the FANYs in 1943 and trained as a Wireless Operator. We worked in SOE and were responsible for sending and receiving messages to and from the French Resistance. I married Myles Ponsonby in 1950 and after he joined the Foreign Office we spent many years living in different places, including Beirut, Djakarta, Nairobi, Rome and Ulan Bator. Mongolia was our last posting. Both our daughters, Belinda and Emma, went to New Hall. I am grateful they had some security during our absence.

ANN HALES-TOOKE (née Petre)

1937–1943

I came to New Hall in September 1937 aged 11. My sister Mary followed me in 1939 and our younger sister Helen came later, after 1948. We were sent to New Hall partly because our father, William Petre, was the agent for the Community, and partly because it was a Petre-girl family tradition. My first cousin, Elizabeth Gough, was already there. Both Helen and I were very happy at school. Mary, who was severely dyslexic in the days when it was not understood very well, was less so.

However, I also had some unhappy times – I was bullied in my second year when Class 3 joined older girls who had been kept down and we made Class 4. I was bright and probably a know-all and some of the older girls really disliked this. I wrote about this in a memoir, *Journey into Solitude*. One night I was asked to go to the West Wing bathrooms with someone I regarded as a friend. All the lights were out. As we reached the swing doors I was grabbed by rough unseen hands, blindfolded and dragged to the bathrooms. Many hands hoisted me up and I was lowered into a cold bath.

I have a vivid memory of Queen Mary visiting in 1938 and all of us lined up in our best pink silk Sunday dresses along the lawn at the front of New Hall. I discovered recently that she also visited our cousin, Lord Petre at Ingatestone Hall, on the same day.

We were evacuated to Newnham Paddox in June 1940 and on our first night, before we had begun to unpack, Coventry, fifteen miles away, was bombed. The nuns hadn't time to look at the cellars so we were told to crouch under what would become the dining tables. The windows had no curtains and the eastern sky provided a fantastic firework display. I have no memory of being frightened. With every overhead 'crump' the cutlery laid for breakfast clattered.

On the nuns' side of the Victorian mansion there was a vast *faux* baronial hall. On summer evenings in 1940 the whole Community – Choir nuns, Lay sisters, gardeners and Miss Dolan – would assemble round a small radio set to listen to the news. Up on the first floor we older girls were allowed to creep along the corridor and crouch behind the banisters to listen to the radio below. We were thrilled to hear Churchill's speeches. 'We shall fight on the beaches . . . ' he boomed, and I remember thinking about making sandcastles at Waxham, swimming to the raft at Aldeburgh . . .

From that long hot summer I remember the dusty ballroom curtains that couldn't be touched or they might fall apart, the fungus and mould among the cherubs on the ornate plaster ceilings, the acute shortage of lavatories and the dwindling water supply. I still occasionally dream of a blocked lavatory behind a fine carved door.

Reading my mother's diary years later, I realised that many parents feared an invasion and dreaded never seeing their children again. Our mother used up precious petrol coupons driving over from Norfolk to see us several times during 1940 and 1941, bringing two-year-old Helen with her. Half the School left, as many parents sent their children to safety in America. The School became very small, and feeling quite depressed I asked my father if I could leave. Then a wonderful teacher arrived, a Miss O'Hara, who put a great deal of effort into preparing me for Oxford, where I went in 1944 to read Philosophy, Politics and Economics.

After a brief spell working in London I joined the Grail Secular Institute, leaving in 1953 to help nurse my father who was suffering from the results of a cerebral haemorrhage. After he died in 1955 I married John and we went to live in Cambridge where we raised three sons. Sadly my sister Helen died in California of leukaemia aged 43 in 1982, and my sister Mary died in 2007. I now live in a retirement block of flats in Cambridge. I have published a memoir and an historical novel and am working on a history of the Petre family.

The 1940s

What's going on in the world during the 1940s

Battle of Britain & the Blitz / Fall of the Third Reich / Street parties / London Olympics / Birth of NATO / Vera Lynn 'We'll Meet Again' / Royal Wedding

1940 The Dunkirk evacuation / Churchill's 'We shall fight on the beaches' speech / German occupation of the Channel Islands / Nylons for sale / Home Guard or 'Dad's Army' operational / Steinbeck *The Grapes of Wrath* / Charlie Chaplin *The Great Dictator* / Disney's *Fantasia* and *Pinocchio* / Michael Sadleir *Fanny by Gaslight* / Graham Greene *The Power and the Glory*

1941 U-boat captured with Enigma / Clothes rationed / Japanese attack Pearl Harbor / Nazi Rudolf Hess flies to Britain on peace mission / Siege of Leningrad / First Ronald Searle cartoon featuring St Trinian's / Glenn Miller 'Chattanooga Choo Choo' / Orson Welles in *Citizen Kane* / Humphrey Bogart in *The Maltese Falcon*

1942 RAF bombers attack Cologne / Anne Frank goes into hiding / Battle of Stalingrad / Battle of El Alamein / Nazis' 'Final Solution' fully implemented / *Desert Island Discs* first broadcast / Humphrey Bogart in *Casablanca* / Enid Blyton's first Famous Five novel, *Five on a Treasure Island* / C. S. Lewis *The Screwtape Letters*

1943 Warsaw Ghetto Uprising / Utility furniture / Operation Chastise (the Dambuster Raid) / Construction of Mark I Colossus computer to aid code-breaking at Bletchley Park / Elizabeth Taylor in *Lassie Come Home* / Laurel and Hardy *Air Raid Wardens* / Ministry of Information film *Desert Victory*

1944 PAYE introduced / 'Operation Overlord' code named D-Day / Hitler assassination attempt fails / Laurence Olivier's *Henry V* first work of Shakespeare filmed in colour / Abbott and Costello *Lost in a Harem*

Left: Conversation outside the gates of Newnham Paddox

1945 Germans surrender / Hitler commits suicide in Berlin / Microwave oven invented / United Nations founded / US drops Atomic Bombs on Hiroshima and Nagasaki / V.E. Day / Nuremberg Trials begin / Street parties / 'Demob' of troops begins /

Spitfires

David Lean directs *Brief Encounter* / Benjamin Britten's opera *Peter Grimes* first performed / George Orwell *Animal Farm* / BBC Light Programme begins broadcasting

1946 World sees the first bikinis / Winston Churchill gives 'Iron Curtain' speech / Coal mines nationalised / Television Licence introduced / Peter Scott opens Slimbridge Wetland Reserve / BBC Light Programme launches *Woman's Hour* and *Dick Barton – Special Agent* / Terence Rattigan's play *The Winslow Boy* premieres / Wilfred Pickles presents quiz show *Have a Go* / Birth of BBC's Third Programme

1947 One of the most severe winters on record in UK / Dead Sea Scrolls discovered / School Leaving Age in England and Wales raised to 15 / Polaroid Camera invented / Princess Elizabeth marries the Duke of Edinburgh / Compton Mackenzie *Whisky Galore* / Ealing Studios release the film *Hue and Cry* regarded as the first of the Ealing Comedies

1948 Berlin Airlift / State of Israel founded / Railways nationalised / Rowntree introduces the Polo Mint / Start of the NHS / London Olympics / *Mrs Dale's Diary* / *Any Questions* / *Hamlet* and *Oliver Twist* at cinema / Graham Greene *The Heart of the Matter*

1949 China becomes Communist / First non-stop flight around the world by US / NATO established / Siam renamed Thailand / Marquess of Bath opens Longleat House / First Badminton Horse Trials / Clothes rationing ends / Hollywood Oscars won by British films – *Hamlet, The Red Shoes* and *The Third Man* / George Orwell *Nineteen Eighty-Four* / *Billy Cotton Bandshow* / Enid Blyton introduces Little Noddy

What's going on at New Hall during the 1940s

New Hall could not but be swept up in the events of the outside world. The Community and School were evacuated to Newnham Paddox in May 1940, and for six years they and their beloved building parted company.

New Hall was used as an Old People's Home and suffered significant bomb damage in 1943. The repair work to the building heralded the start of a long collaborative relationship between the School and F. J. French Builders, who seemed to be permanently on site for restoration and extension work until the dawn of the new millennium. It was also the beginning of a close friendship between Thos Parsons of French's and the Community, which lasted until Thos's death in 2007.

The School and Community's time at Newnham Paddox is well recorded in the memories that follow. It was while there that they celebrated the 300th Anniversary of their Foundation in 1942.

From there they watched the bombing of Coventry, and there they celebrated V.E. Day in 1945.

The return to New Hall in 1946 marked the return to normality for Community and School, and thought was given to extension and expansion. The first three hard tennis-courts were laid at New Hall (the firm used was called 'En Tout Cas'). A Preparatory School was opened at Goodings in Berkshire in 1947 under S. Magdalen John (MMJ), whose leadership became legendary.

The front of New Hall before the bomb damage

S.M.CHRISTINA

Extract from document dating from early 1940s sent in by
Fr Stewart Foster, Diocese of Brentwood Archivist

In 1940 the situation had become so serious Parents urged us to evacuate, which we did on the 3 & 4 June to Newnham Paddox, Rugby, the seat of the Earl of Denbigh.

While we were there Regularity was well kept under very difficult circumstances, the Divine Office being resumed after a couple of days. We were there throughout the Coventry blitz and had the privilege of non-fasting Communion having had such disturbed nights. We gave shelter to Our Lord bombed out of one of the Coventry Churches.

Clothings and Professions took place as usual . . .

In April and May 1943 New Hall was blitzed and very badly damaged, especially the School, all dormitories being destroyed. New Hall had been rented to the Essex County Council; many people were injured and 12 killed.

In 1944, Lord Denbigh wished us to move. The Proc and I began house-hunting unsuccessfully until December 7th 1945 when we purchased Goodings, near Newbury.

We returned to New Hall July 9th and 10th 1946 . . .

The bomb damage in 1943

JENNIFER ROSKELL (S.M.Magdalene)

1941–1948

It was the uniform blazer which decided me to opt to join my cousins at New Hall. It was lightish maroon, with black chevron cuffs and black lapels with the school emblem on the breast pocket.

But when I started in 1941, the School and Community had been evacuated to Newnham Paddox in Warwickshire, a magnificent building but very run down. The rolling parkland was populated with sheep and some cattle but before we left a good bit had been ploughed up for crops. We had the run of most of it.

The dormitories were in the old library, the ballroom, and the drawing-room, and around the fireplace in the drawing-room many stories were told after lights-out. There was a huge chandelier in the ballroom which shed its prisms from time to time. These were eagerly sought after. In a square bow window was a piano where S.M.Peter used to practise when she was a novice, and occasionally we hid under a bed and listened to her playing – she was jolly good, and I particularly remember her rendering of *William Tell*. At bedtime S. Anthony used to sit in the ballroom dormitory, which was populated by us younger pupils, and we had to ask her permission to go through the drawing-room to empty our washing water. As she was concentrating on the priests' girdles she was making for the Sacristy, I often got a spurious permission to go to the library – which was in fact forbidden territory to us youngsters.

The classrooms were all at the top of the house in what had once been maids' bedrooms, exclusively heated by wood fires. S.M.Winifred taught us Maths. She was a large person and it took her a good five minutes to get her breath back on arrival. The attic became the 'Montessori classroom', and in it was a framed collection of butterflies, a great attraction.

Loos and their malfunction were a permanent topic of conversation and concern. There was an Elsan in the broom cupboard, which some-times was more efficient than the household loos as the water supply was often temperamental. This may have accounted for the episodes of 'runny tummy' which visited the school from time to time and were the subject of some poetry. There was a bathroom on the first floor called 'George the Fifth', and it had two loos which opened on to both adjoining rooms; they had no illumination and were known as the 'Black Holes of Calcutta'. You had to remember to lock both doors or hold on to both handles – quite a feat. It was in 'George the Fifth' that our hair was de-loused at the beginning of term. There was a loo outside the dormitories and one of the panels used to fall with a loud bang and clatter, which gave rise to that utility being christened 'Germany'.

The grounds of Newnham were wonderful, with many beautiful trees brought back from the wanderings of one of the Earls of Denbigh, and two magnificent artificial lakes which were home to two resident swans, Herbert and Mrs Herbert. Herbert was beautiful and good tempered until Mrs started a family, then, even if you were on the other side of the lake, he would hurtle across, hissing, looking three times his usual size; it was a brave person who stayed for his arrival.

Mr and Mrs Herbert – the resident swans at Newnham Paddox

There was always a mass of frog spawn in the due season, which one year all hatched into a carpet of pretty little yellow frogs from the lakes up to the house. There was a place for animal burial near the summerhouse, which was the resting place for several dogs. But the most evocative was the grave of a horse named Pilgrim, which became quite a meeting place.

In the rose garden, devoid of roses, there was a round pond and a defunct fountain, decorated with three stone herons, which we decided to clean. We also spent many wet and muddy hours housing leeches in jam jars and putting mud on the erstwhile rose beds, supervised by long suffering nuns who occasionally lent a hand with the leeches.

There were large expanses of grass, formerly lawns, and the Community were told that a condition of their stay was to keep the grass

Messing about on a Feast Day – pond dipping and jam jars

cut. There was no possibility of acquiring petrol for a lawnmower so S. Anthony Magdalen, aged 60 plus, learnt to use a scythe and spent hours cutting the grass. She always had a dog with her – was he called Rips? She must have left some areas uncut as we did our 'exam revision' hidden in the long grass – often with a good book, not necessarily to do with exams!

There was a farmyard, out of bounds I think. 'The Wilderness' had a Japanese Handkerchief tree which only flowered rarely; obligingly, it did while we were there.

The nuns' side was separated from the school by a large curtain which hung near the centre of the house where the Community gathered to listen to the nine o'clock news. It was past our bedtime but those interested could creep up to the curtain after shutdown and have a listen, watching out for a patrolling nun.

We were fed magnificently, sharing some of the nuns' rations. S. Mary and S. Anne did wonders with local rabbits (shot by Percy) and we had elderberries, nettles, Beetox (a Marmite-like spread), blackberries, lots of potatoes, Swiss breakfast (a forerunner of muesli) and chocolate tart as a treat, sweetened with honey provided by S.M.Paul's bees. Elevenses were a vital part of each day. We were given unlimited quantities of bread on which we put, separately or together, condensed milk, peanut butter (courtesy of the USA), sardines and jam (from our ration).

Patricia Owles discovered some discarded Community ration books in the rubbish bin and many happy hours were spent putting names to faces; the names were the Community's 'worldly' ones which were totally unknown to us Fishes in those days.

The library was where Ann Bamford (S.M.Thérèse) practised Beethoven by the hour, and where I got permission to go on to senior fiction having exhausted the junior section.

When wooding, we had no health and safety regulations, thank goodness. We sawed with 'man'-sized Bushmans and split logs with 'man'-sized axes. Thelma Beaumont cut her fingers badly greasing a saw with bacon fat.

Games were tennis, netball and rounders, occasionally enlivened by Cowboys and Indians in the local parkland, which happened on House Feasts and involved dressing as Cowboys and Indians and invading each other's space without being discovered. It was exhausting and often bloody bacause of brambles. We occasionally had a match against another school, petrol permitting.

Once a German plane landed in a neighbouring field, cutting our power lines so we were in total darkness for some time. We were not allowed to go and see the wreckage for several days, presumably while they sorted the crew, none of whom survived I think. I'm sure we prayed for them.

We heard the rumbles of the Coventry blitz and saw the flashes. The nuns explained it to us as a bad thunderstorm. I can't remember if we believed them; that sort of raid was beyond my imagination.

The chapel was special, even my artistic ignorance appreciated Pugin's style. Everything had to happen in daylight as the chapel did not have any 'black-out' and we couldn't show light. Italian prisoners of war from the local camp used to come to Mass, causing quite a 'frisson' among the seniors. The Italians sang beautifully.

Near the chapel there was a shortish avenue of trees, used by the nuns for meditation. The trees were also easily climbable, but it was bad luck for anyone up a tree when a nun started her meditation, because they were stuck there for half an hour or more.

There was a system of 'Sodalities' to each of which one aspired with varying degrees of success: the Child of Jesus was for the Montessori age group, then one moved progressively up the list to be an aspirant – 'Asp' – of each Sodality in turn. I made so bold as to ask the Head in my first term if I could be an Asp of the Aloysians, but was turned down in short order. I did become a Child of Mary in my last term.

THE ORDER OF SODALITIES
Child of Jesus
Asp (irant) of the Aloysians (Green Conduct Badge)
Aloysian
Asp of the Angels (Blue Conduct Badge)
Angel Protegée of the Children of Mary (White Conduct Badge)
Asp of the Children of Mary
Child of Mary

It was at Newnham that we took over the housework, and I can remember in the free days at end of term we had to 'spring clean' the house before the beginning of the holidays. The floors were polished

A group of Seniors, showing 'Child of Mary' medals.
Left to right, back row: Susan Bennett, Mimi Kenny, Jenny Sweeny,
Mary Elise Petre; Front: Moira Metcalf, Felicity Gilbey,
Diana Watson-Cook, P. Owles, Marcy Wood

with 'bumpers', blocks of wood with a sheet of lead on top and short bristles underneath. Heavy and effective.

At the end of the war there were great celebrations. The whole school had al fresco meals on trestle tables (what work for the sisters who arranged it all – I hope we were properly grateful). There was a huge bonfire in front of the house – the sort naturally not allowed during the war and all the houselights were turned on with no black-out.

In September 1946 some of us came back to school at New Hall early to help prepare for the term. A large part of the house was covered with tarpaulin, and brick dust was everywhere. It took several washes of each floor before they could be polished.

The classbooks had all been dumped in the Gym and had to be sorted and delivered to the relevant classrooms. As a bit of light relief, two of us decided to have a close look at the great bell on the roof. We got out of the Cockloft window and crept along the partly demolished roof to find that the bell bow was quite undamaged by enemy action. A member of the Community saying goodbye to a visiting relative in front of the house held us up for a while, but we returned unscathed.

While Newnham had been a dream place, New Hall was also beautiful but a measure of reality had to creep in. It was School Certificate year and there were several misspent years to make up for. Even so there was plenty of long grass at New Hall in those days for revision and whatever. Games came into their own with proper pitches and courts. Life became more disciplined, just in time to save an academic débâcle.

I've said very little about the nuns and their courage, humour and wisdom over what was a very difficult and uncertain time, but my memories are of their having amazing patience with us, good humour and real wisdom. This includes the non-School and mainly older members of the Community whom we saw at rare but memorable intervals.

I kept the second-hand blazer. It was several sizes too big when I got it and just about fitted when I left. It was a bit the worse for wear by then, especially as a pet bat had a home in it for a while.

When I left New Hall I was sent to be 'finished' in Switzerland. On returning to England I joined the WRNS and became an MT driver. At the age of 21 I joined the Community at New Hall and was subsequently, at various times, Linen Room nun, House Mother, Matron (untrained) and Cook (I spent nine months learning to cook in our house in Belgium). I was for a period at Denford, then did a nurse's training and back at New Hall became School Matron, Novice Mistress, Prioress, Infirmarian in the Community and finally Archivist. Seeing the Community's ability to pray, 'get stuck in' and enjoy whatever came taught me a lesson for life which has stood me in good stead.

VERONICA WEBBER (née Hitchcock)

1937–1940

In 1940 school life was continuing as normal in the peaceful surroundings of New Hall when we were suddenly told that we had to evacuate in twenty-four hours. There was a fear that this large building on the railway line was in danger of being mistaken for the vitally important Marconi Factory, just minutes flying time away for the German bombers, which were causing so much damage at the time.

For the Fishes this was an adventure, but not so for the Community. Some of the elderly nuns had entered in the days of horses and carriages, and had not ventured beyond the Avenue. They were absolutely terrified at the speed of the coaches they had to travel in. Apparently one of them was heard to cry out, 'Don't let the horses go so fast.'

When we eventually arrived at Newnham Paddox, it was quite an experience for everyone. Poor Fr Butler, our Chaplain, was particularly upset. He had refused to leave without his beloved bees. At New Hall we always had honey for tea. A special lorry was arranged to transport them, which he loaded with great care; but he forgot to close the hives so they all flew away.

Newnham Paddox had been abandoned years before by its owners, the Feildings, because of a family problem, and was something of a *Marie Celeste*, with Lady Feilding's hairbrushes still on her dressing table, and all sorts of personal things lying about. It was full of tiny frogs, inside and out. The once beautiful grounds were so overgrown that I sprained my ankle running down what appeared to be a grassy slope but what was actually a terrace with a flight of steps.

On our arrival we had to go to bed in the dark, or by torchlight, because we had no black-out curtains which were then compulsory, understandably so because that night there was a tremendous air raid. We thought it was on the next village, but it might have been the terrible raid on nearby Coventry.

The nuns made it a priority to restore the abandoned chapel to its former glory, and we all settled down. My class was due to take the School Certificate in a few weeks, which for us was the culmination of our school careers; the Higher School Certificate, to my regret, was not an option at New Hall then. In the weeks before the exam we had no textbooks, and some of the Lay staff had not come with us, so it was not ideal, but an attic room was set aside in which we sat the exam, and somehow we all survived it.

One of my worst memories is of having been asked to go over in the holidays to collect certain books as my home was not very far from New Hall. To my horror, the beautiful building was being used to house patients from what was then known as a lunatic asylum, and the wonderful calm and serenity of the Community side was full of screaming, shouting and banging, which I found both distressing, and shocking. If it was dangerous for us to stay at school there, why was it being used for these unfortunate people, two of whom were killed in a subsequent air raid which damaged the building severely? It was later repaired using bricks from Hampton Court.

It made me realise how difficult it must have been for the brave Community to leave New Hall. Its atmosphere and beauty made a huge impression on me.

PRISCILLA MARY CLARE NOBLE-MATHEWS

1937–1944

I remember so well arriving on the first day and being so nervous and shy. An older girl called Jean Bennett looked after me until the Pack Train arrived. They all seemed to know each other and I felt friendless and fearful, especially when one girl, Prue Wellman, said, 'Who is this queer looking owl?' The dragon at New Hall, just outside the main entrance, bore the motto: 'I watch who comes, I see who goes.'

When it was cold we'd sit on the large radiator in the Ambulacrum, and once we swept the whole room with damp used tea leaves – amazingly effective at cleaning.

We took our work each week to Mother Margaret Helen during prep to get a mark which went towards the House Shield. We'd get ticked off by the House Prefect if our marks were too low. At that time there were only Mores and Poles. I was a Pole, Fishers House was added not all that long after.

Mother Mary Veronica, our Housemistress, was very strict; a smile from her was fantastic! I remember S.M.John had a slight American accent. S.M.Benedict taught needlework – I think it took me two years to make a nightdress for my mother. S.M.Paul taught Botany, and we never got on as I could never draw the plants properly. However, when we returned to New Hall after Newnham, she began teaching Religious Knowledge and we got on famously.

Winifred Dolan, who taught us elocution, was tremendously strict and girls would come out from her lessons crying. She was a former Shakespearian actress, now old and very lame, and she used a stick which also lent emphasis to her teaching! But how pleased she was when I received the prize for elocution. I can still recite the whole of Portia's speech from *The Merchant of Venice*. Miss Oram who taught Geography used to recite, 'And the fleas that tease in the High Pyrenees . . .'

There was a Lay teacher who died quite suddenly – I think someone found her in the bathroom. I remember Fr Butler SJ and his poor fingers! (In the light of medical hindsight, I am pretty sure he had Raynaud's Syndrome and also Sjogren's Syndrome and had been sent home from India.) Matron was very strict and nit-combed then treated my hair with some terrible disinfectant, burning the side of my face. I got extra marks for good conduct for not complaining.

I remember all the ghost stories and the strange feel of one or two of the rooms. The nuns were reported to have seen ghosts in the nuns' Library at the top of the house on 'their' side. We were not supposed to talk about such things! I also remember the bullying. One girl took my head and crashed it down on the Refectory table. I do not think that much was done about this; it was part of school life.

The evacuation to Newnham Paddox we all found very exciting. In particular we loved playing at being part of the Feilding family in

81

Left to right: Joan Welch, Tessa Fenton, Jennifer Roskell,
Mary-Rose Henderson, Marcy Wood, Gillian Grindon-Welch
Front: Melissa Metcalf. New Hall, circa 1946–7

ancient days and galloping up and down the lime walk on pretend horses. The gorgeous display of daffodils between the two lakes and all around the grounds and the beauty of the chapel were sublime. The ghastly tummy upsets we had every term I suspect originated from the water, as we had seen strange red insects coming out of the taps!

It was the first year that the office of Head Girl was instituted. Moira Russell served for a term but I was elected Head Girl after that and also President of the Children of Mary. You wore two chains, one with the medal of Mary and one with the cross of the Holy Sepulchre and they clanked when you processed into chapel.

I remember so well my mother, my brother and Uncle Frank (a secular priest whom my father had appointed as a guardian to my brother and me), all coming up to Newham Paddox during the summer holidays of 1944. Mummy and Uncle Frank made an apple-pie bed for S.M.Veronica – it makes me blush to think of it! She took it in surprisingly good part.

MELISSA METCALF

1938–1949

My sister Moira and I arrived at New Hall for a visit in the summer term of 1938 to see a production of *Toad of Toad Hall*, with Bridget O'Connor (S.M.Christopher) playing a splendid Toad.

When I started I was the youngest in the school and I was thoroughly spoilt. The first production I recall once I was there was *The Bishop's Candlesticks* (an incident from *Les Misérables*) in which S.M.Christopher played the convict. I call still remember the scenes vividly. This long tradition of putting on really good productions under the direction of Miss Dolan continued throughout my eleven years. In the Nativity Plays, I started as a little angel, kneeling by the crib beside a lovely fair-haired Gabriel Plowden as Mary, who helped me to hang on in spite of terrible cramp in my leg. I progressed until in the Sixth Form I was one of the Kings. I remember catching up a piece of the scenery and dragging it off with me, to S.M.Benedict's despair. (S.M.Benedict was in charge of the Green Room for a long time and the costumes were wonderful.)

One of Miss Dolan's drama productions at Newnham Paddox

S.M.Paul and her bees

The evacuation to Newnham Paddox in 1940 remains the memory of a great adventure. The mattresses sliding down the stairs at New Hall and the journey by coach with the nuns. We experienced the raids over Rugby and Coventry a few weeks later, so it was down to the cellars again and the wonder of seeing the nuns in their night attire, the enjoyment of sing-songs, rosaries and hot chocolate.

At Newnham we learnt to gather and saw wood for all the little fires in the classrooms and the bigger ones in the ballroom and the library, under the kindly direction of Fr Butler. I loved the candles and night-lights we were allowed to have on little private altars during our three-day retreats. I shall not forget S.M.Veronica's dismay at seeing the great black hole that had burnt in my table, and her relief that the fire had stopped there and the house was not ablaze.

My memories of Newnham are of the long walks across the fields, the sheep and lambs, picking daffodils that grew in abundance, weeding the terraces for the Corpus Christi processions, housework in beige smocks and netball on the gravel in front of the house. There were the Italian prisoners raising the roof in the lovely Pugin chapel, and the poor Polish airmen who died in a plane crash.

I remember S.M.Paul helping Fr Butler with the bees in a wonderful veiled straw hat, and S. Anthony Magdalen scything the grass. The arrival of S. Catherine (S.M.Ignatius) heralded wonderful Geography, Latin and French lessons. S.M.Martha, who taught Science, had a favourite phrase – 'I'm not as green as I'm cabbage looking.' One day I finished it for her, but, though taken aback, she appreciated my look of stricken realisation and no more was said.

I was eleven years as a Fish at New Hall – Head Girl, Games Captain, President of the Children of Mary and More's House Captain. My Jubilee (10 years) remains a great memory. The song composed by S.M.Ignatius will be my contribution to the Archives. The Jubilee of Marcy Wood (S.M.Francis) the year before was also memorable, when Joan Welsh played Pooh and I was Piglet and the names stuck for quite a while.

There were only three of us who went to Newnham and came back. Patricia Owles, Marcy Wood and myself. The return was a great joy in spite of the results of the bombing. To be in the Ambulacrum, to have Mass in the Chapel, big classrooms in the Wings, the Six Acres to play lacrosse in again and the new tennis-courts, and to see the rebuilding

Feast Day at Newnham 1941 (showing the whole School at the time)

of the Library and the Refectory was all wonderful. But the life we had at Newnham, in very close contact with all the nuns, was something that brought us into a relationship with the Community that was quite exceptional.

I am 80 years old now and living in France.

MOIRA METCALF

1938–1946

The end of term fear of only producing 23 handkerchiefs, instead of the required 24, is hard to imagine now. The wrath (and I use that word advisedly) of Matron Stafford over such matters was formidable. I was an untidy child and a great loser of things, so often in trouble.

In those pre-war days we sat down to table with each place setting complete with numbered cutlery, including fish and fruit knives and forks. I have some similar cutlery in my kitchen drawer, which reminds me of the dedicated way S. Teresa and S. Philomena looked after the Refectory at that time.

Community Refectory New Hall until 1965

Feast Days were often occasions of great fun or unusual activities. St Stanislaus was the occasion when new pupils were allowed into the Enclosure, and particularly into the Noviciate, where we solemnly jumped on a particular board – a squeak indicating a possible vocation.

The Great Feast was also known as the 'Nun's Feast'- the 'Nun' being shorthand for the Headmistress of the time. Activities included a paperchase (really adventurous at Newnham where the woodland paths provided plenty of red herrings) and the presentation of Tableaux on a given theme.

The Feast of the Immaculate Conception in 1938 was very special as there were five First Communicants, including my sister Melissa who at seven years old was the youngest in the school. It was also a family occasion which in those days was rare. After Mass and breakfast we all processed to the classroom in the East Wing where five desks had been draped in white and decorated with flowers and presents, which were mainly Holy pictures. Melissa thinks her tally that day was nearly 100 and some survive to this day.

In 1938, just before the war, we learnt Greek dancing and wore specially designed pink tunics (very similar to those seen in the fashion photos of the time). But during one of the war years I was the only pupil who took Dancing, and the task of teaching me was given to the PE teacher, who specialised in Irish jigs rather than ballroom dancing. However, in later years more of us learned, and we left as proficient rumba and tango dancers.

The strictures of wartime living were particularly evident in our diet. During the summer we picked young nettles for soups and vegetables and dandelion leaves for salads. In autumn the elderberries appeared in every shape and form – jams, mousse, puddings, even replacing currants in our buns. S. Mary (savoury) and S. Anne (cakes/sweets) still managed to give us some delicious treats from time to time. Margarine with sugar became a tea-time favoutite.

On 30th November 1942 we were plunged into darkness. We were told that a plane had crashed into the cables near the lakes. Later we learned that Fr Butler SJ and Percy Sygrove had struggled into the lake and Percy at great personal risk had retrieved the bodies of three Polish airmen. To children who had been told that the reason we were at war was the invasion of Poland, this suddenly provided a link with that unknown country.

PATRICIA ('P') DE WATTEVILLE (née Owles)

1939–1947

I was one of only three, Melissa Metcalf, Marcy Wood and myself, who completed time at New Hall, the whole period at Newnham and then years back at New Hall. I was known then simply as 'P'.

Almost every month we used to put on a Fundraising Revue for the Red Cross, using the bay windows of the ballroom at Newnham as our stage. I don't think the standard was very high, but the enthusiasm made up for that. I sang, 'I'm a little airy fairy, every day I grow more hairy, No one wants to cultivate me, so I'm as hairy as hairy can be!' We were allowed to go down to the village to sell tickets. Lots of people came and we served tea and had official Red Cross collecting tins.

There was no central heating at Newnham and we spent nearly all our weekends with several nuns collecting huge branches to make into logs. We loved doing it and had such fun. On Sunday mornings we had supervised darning of socks in class. My mother made my socks so

The Community wooding
Left to right: S.M.Martha, S. Magdalen John, S.M.Christopher,
Priscilla Noble-Mathews (S.M.Clare), S.M.Peter

they never had holes and I remember thinking it was rotten having to mend someone else's!

We all enjoyed the Great Feast, a secret day that was not announced till the evening before, and a day off with special food and the 'Tableau' which we made to a given theme with a prize to the winning team. Once we brought a horse into the West Wing at the last minute.

Although I was notoriously naughty I reformed when shown the advantages, and eventually became Head of School.

I got a BSc in Maths, Physics and Chemistry and became a Research Chemist. I married into the army and we lived in Newbury and then here in Chichester. I have five children and 17 grandchildren. I did eight years of political work and became Deputy Mayor. Now I am disabled with an undiagnosed balance problem, which means I use a scooter a lot. I play Scrabble once or twice a week to keep the old brain ticking! And have a trainer to keep me mobile. I used to breed Westies but now only have one.

BRIGID UTLEY (née Morrah)

1939–1944

The arrival at Newnham Paddox and the excitement at finding that everyone was to sleep in a dormitory that had been the ballroom! No one minded the fungus on the walls.

The two siblings (S. Ann Francis and, I think, S. Margaret Francis) playing 'rush in the workroom' with the children on the Feast of the Presentation. For the game, they were called Sister Spitfire and Sister Hurricane.

ANN BAMFORD (S.M. Thérèse)

1941–1945

My first dormitory bed was in the library at Newnham Paddox and when a book fell out on me I was told there were rats running about on the shelves.

Dormitory memories are many: S. Antony trying to keep us in order from her 'bedroom' in one of the bay-window areas. 'Oos that a-talking?' she would ask and momentarily we would stop. Huge log fires burning in the open fireplaces when the cold was acute. Bitterly cold water in our upright washbasins which we had collected the night before and in which we 'strip-washed' each morning. We were allowed one bath a week and friends would queue to use the water of the lucky one whose day it was, which made bathing a noisy and sociable time incurring supervisory wrath.

Food parcels were major features of life especially when they arrived for someone in the bed opposite. Would she, wouldn't she share? Food was important. We were accustomed to shortages at home, and at school we had our ration of jam and butter to last a month, but I never remember going hungry. We had elderberry trees in the grounds and the fruit arrived in various guises: jam, sauce, pudding filler, flans, pastry turnovers called 'Grandmother's Toenails', and imaginatively we had nettles instead of spinach. I think some of the Community gave up their sweet coupons for us on Festive occasions. S.Mary, S.Anne and other sisters in the kitchen were amazing the way they fed us. S.Anne's speciality of 'dog biscuits' were delicious and memorable.

S. Margaret Helen with whom I was friendly ran the Tuck Shop. I loved to help her and that began an involvement in the Shop which was to continue long after I became a member of the Community, and led to a friendship with S. Margaret Helen which continued to the end of her life.

The freedom was an element that greatly appealed to me. The grounds, fields, woods and lakes around the house were there for us: don't disturb Herbert the Swan for he is dangerous; in the spring you may not care for the heaving mass of baby frogs on the paths round the lakes; the Japanese Handkerchief tree is rare and has valuable 'flowers'; there are plenty of trees to climb; there is long grass where we can lie unseen and glory in finger-licking the contents of someone's condensed-milk tin from their food parcel.

We lived close to the Community and shared work with them, logging and collecting berries, playing wild games with them, particularly with a group of young 'White Veils'. We did most of the housework, wearing our blue housework overalls and with our hair wrapped in scarves: sweeping and cleaning; shaking the bedding at end of term; polishing the wooden floors using lead-weighted bumpers. It wasn't work, it was fun even though really tiring.

We were of the generation that didn't question much and trotted into chapel with white veils on our heads every day, and twice on Sundays for Mass. We had processions and Feast Days with as much ceremony as we could muster. There were Retreat Days and aged 11 I remember feeling fearfully holy when I made a little altar in one of the bow windows and prayed there. This was an introduction to prayer and laid a basis for my way of life in later years.

The classrooms were mostly on the top floor in the maids' quarters. I remember P. Owles carrying up all those stairs some largish part of a motorbike to hang in her classroom. Why? I don't know and it didn't stay long but it was memorable.

The classes were so small it was easy to learn. There was History and Latin with S. Margaret Helen. There were Sciences of all sorts but with little or no apparatus with S.M.Martha, and Religious Knowledge with S.M.Paul, whose worth I appreciated much later in life. We had an inspired Music teacher and we sang many songs which I half remember now. I remember going to an external piano exam, in the one and only

Fishes using 'bumpers' to polish the floor in the Pink Room

school car, clutching a hot potato to keep my hands warm. Games were limited but huge fun, and here also was S.M.Martha with her habit well tucked up: lacrosse and rounders on a steeply sloping field, tennis on some quite civilised courts though a bit bumpy, gym with the odd bench and 'horse' and not much else. We actually played 'away' matches with some other evacuated schools although I don't remember ever winning.

Then, as now, friendships flourished between ourselves and with the Community, whom we got to know really well. There was a cry 'Twos, Twos' heard by those recreating on walks which we seemed to have inherited from New Hall days. It meant 'don't walk in twos' and had something to do with 'particular friendships' and discouraging of favouritism, which really did not apply to us or our ways! There was a certain amount of competition to get hold of a corner of the apron worn by the nun who was taking the Recreation Walk up the Avenue. In free time we sometimes gathered in the evening with our rugs and lay on the floor listening to '78' records.

Our ways were simple, and we made our own entertainment. I have good memories of Newnham Paddox and am very grateful for the care the Community took of us all at a time which I now realise was as strange and new for them as it was for us.

At 18 I wanted to join the Community, but my parents were set against it. Three times I turned down an opportunity to go to university and instead I studied at the LREM. I joined the Community on the day I was 21 (1949). There were quite a few of us noviciates at that time, Mary Rose, Joy, Catherine, Jean Henderson – eight of us in all, and the division between the white and black veils was considerable. Sister Margaret Helen was my stalwart friend then and for the remainder of her life.

*The Chapel circa 1945, showing no paintings but the
High Altar pre-Vatican II*

MARIANNE WATT (née Cardis)

1942–1947

My earliest memory is of being on Rugby Station waiting for the Pack
Train to arrive, when Mother suddenly said, 'Oh, there's a nun over
there with some girls, I wonder if they're from New Hall.' I looked
across and saw a tall nun laughing heartily as a bunch of girls bounced
round her, all trying to tell her about their summer holidays. I thought
to myself, 'Oh, no, I'm sure they're not, the nun looks far too much
fun.'

But, indeed, my years at New Hall were very happy and great fun. I
want to write here of my debt to several hard-working, inspirational
teachers. Maths was one of the five obligatory subjects for School
Certificate, all of which had to be passed at one attempt. S.M.Ignatius
made later study possible for me by towing me, against the odds, to a
pass in it. S. Margaret Helen, at various times, taught me History,
English (Literature and Language) and Latin. S. Magdalen Dolores
taught me French and started me off on Spanish which I was to read
for my degree.

S.M.Paul taught Scripture and Religious Knowledge. In the Lower

School, R.K. was based on *Hart's Christian Doctrine* – 'Take out your red *Hart*.' She dictated long notes, more like essays, and had us counting the repetitions of her catchphrase, 'Isn't it, isn't it?' In Class 6, however, the subject took off. For me, it became a great adventure. For the Higher Certificate in Religious Studies, the syllabus alternated between the Existence of God in one year and Christian Marriage in the other.

Perhaps my greatest debt was to S. Margaret Helen for the coaching she gave me in Class 6. She made me aware of the need to analyse one's own rhythms of study as well as understanding the demands of the subject and the questions it posed. In addition, she stressed the need to budget the time available for private study, assessing the distribution of time for each of the four principal and one subsidiary subjects I was studying. In practice, that meant I should study those parts I enjoyed least, in which I was weak, in the mornings, my best time for working. I was being shown how to take personal responsibility for intellectual progress; an admirable preparation for university study.

Looking back, I am conscious of the dedication to the Lord of each one of these very different women. Faith is both taught and caught. The New Hall Community of that time still consisted of Choir nuns, who sang the whole of the Divine Office daily, and Lay sisters, those without Latin, who took care of almost all the housekeeping work in both Convent and School. It was heavy work in the 1940s, carried out around a considerable amount of daily prayer. They worked incredibly hard, with remarkable cheerfulness and devotion. I'm privileged and grateful to have known and been so influenced by the entire Community.

I was born in Leeds in 1929 and am the eldest sister of S. Catherine, S. Stephanie and Winefride-Mary Piasecki. At the University of Leeds, I read Spanish, graduating with First Class Honours, and went on to postgraduate study in Portuguese in Lisbon. In 1954 I married fellow student John Anthony Watt (later Professor of Medieval History at Newcastle). I taught Spanish at the Marist College, Hull, and later became Tutor in the School of Education at Newcastle University. I have five children, 21 grand-children and a great-grandchild.

DIANA SPALTON (née Watson-Cook)

1943–1947

Most of all I remember the grounds at Newnham Paddox, the three lakes and impressive arboretum. It was huge. I dug up a very small sapling tree from there, packed it in the bottom of my trunk and brought it home. It grows today in my mother's garden. It is an Eastern Balsam Poplar.

Of course it was freezing cold in the winter. But I was in my seventh heaven because it was deep countryside. We never went off the premises, we had no need. We had much freedom to wander. Particularly when we had a Retreat, which lasted two to three days, when we wandered the expansive grounds. We were in silence until supper time. We had no lessons and instead there were talks by visiting priests. So we wandered, in complete freedom, in contemplative mode, the wonderful grounds. (I was disappointed when I arrived at New Hall because I missed the huge wide spaces.)

I remember one Easter going up to my dormitory – in those days you slept in one large room with all your class – and my bed just wasn't

Lake at Newnham Paddox

there. All of it gone. It may have been Easter but it was also April 1st, and the class had dismantled and moved the entire bed to another place, some way away, up another flight of stairs. S.M.Christopher was in on it.

The scent of mock orange blossom – and I'm straight back to Newnham Paddox. For Corpus Christi we had a procession in which girls would strew orange blossom flowers along the way. I have one in my garden, planted purposely. I'm straight back.

In 1976 my family home had to be sold. While emptying it of furniture, my husband discovered a secret drawer in an old chest. In this was a bundle of letters tied with blue ribbon from my grandmother to her then fiancé. Imagine my astonishment when I saw that the address was Newnham Paddox near Rugby! They were all dated 1903 and were not what we would call love letters. It transpired that my grandmother was governess to the children of the then Earl of Denbigh. She writes amusingly about her charges and obviously enjoyed her time there. I wish I had known about this when I was at Newnham Paddox.

STEPHANIE CARDIS (S. Stephanie)

1942–1951

When the Community was preparing for the transition from New Hall to our new home in Colchester, we were each invited to name one object which held special significance for us. A silver Liège goblet was my item. One has, in fact, been kept in the Archives. We used these goblets in the School Refectory. As a bemused and very homesick new Fish of eight years old, I remember the comforting pleasure of the tulip shape, and the cool feel and fresh taste of the water. They were taken out with the rugs, baskets of food and bottles of squash to picnics in the grounds.

Meals were supervised by the First Mistress or Housemistress when the roles of Head and House were separated. S.Teresa and S.Philomena served the dishes and then stood ready to respond to the Table Prefects' 'holding up' of a dish or plate to request that it might be

Newnham Paddox in the 1940s – south and east fronts

filled with more. The sisters were like team players in a competition when chocolate tart or beans in pastry were on the menu! Occasionally S.Mary and S.Anne would be asked to come through from the kitchen and Pastry Hole so that the School could applaud their thanks for some special treat.

In the Denbigh library at Newham Paddox, we formed the Class Ranks which were nodded to in turn by the Head as the signal to climb the flights of stairs from the ground floor to the attic rooms which were the classrooms. There was a weekly rota: cleaning the board and banging the board rubber, and squinting along the desks to get them perfectly aligned, were the tasks and skills, but the pleasure was tending the wood fire in the small grate, smelling the burning logs, stirring up and gazing into the fiery pictures. Even better were the huge log fires in the ballroom and drawing-room dormitories round which we washed at our wash-stands with their tin basins. We were meant to keep silence in the dormitories; there were, of course, many fireside stories, but best of all was the companionship of the flickering light and sounds from the fire.

It was great to be in the Nativity Play, whether as a wondering bystander or as one of the choral angels and, if the latter, being given throat-cure Nippets of fierce strength by S. Margaret Helen to keep our voices clear as we waited on the stairs to descend to amazed shepherds on earth. Percy Sygrove perilously climbed a high ladder to cover the crucifix and statues in purple as Lent advanced. In the Summer Term there were flaming red peonies for Pentecost, and then the golden canopy, with its tinkling bells, and smells of syringa and incense at Corpus Christie.

On a beautiful summer's evening when we were having a needlework lesson outside, I made a discovery. Our teacher was a Lay matron, an over-pious woman who decided that we, the smallest children, were not being trained properly to be the strewers of flower petals in front of the Blessed Sacrament during the Corpus Christi procession. In the needlework lesson she had us practising up and down the little path to the lakes: three steps forward, take a few petals from our basket, kiss them, a little prayer, then strew them with a half-turn bow. Suddenly, pursuing us along the path, came S. Margaret Helen in doomsday fury. A stop was put to the 'Nonsense'. I took in that adults can get into trouble too . . .

Chapel brought useful tips as well as learning. Being very small, I was placed in the front bench next to Ann Petre who was Bench Prefect. Ann being Head Girl wore a silver New Hall cross on a chain together with her Child of Mary medal, with her White Badge for Good Conduct, on Sundays. She helped me find my way around my Sunday Missal (a brand-new copy with which to come to School) and explained that it was not intended I should make a Sign of the Cross each time there was a small black cross in the text that indicated the priest's hand movement. My efforts had become a race against time.

Annual epidemics were prime opportunities for social networking across the classes. Going to the Infirmary with those variously stricken with mumps, measles, whooping cough or German measles, was part of our social history. Once, when our temperatures obstinately remained high, it was decreed that we must stay in bed and keep silence all day. Rummy was the craze of the moment, so we set up a postal service, throwing round in a pillowcase every card and move to be delivered, and literally stifled the added hilarity with gags.

Newnham, with fields, lakes and neglected formal gardens, gave endless possibilities. Lying on our stomachs, hanging over the edge of the fishpond, Awly Capel Dunn and I used to float 'boats' and invent for them a narrative of exploits involving various relations and fictitious characters who were in the Forces. Tragic reality intruded when Awly

*Newnham Community: S.M. Martha, S.Magdalen John, S.M. John,
S.Margaret Helen, S.M. Christopher*

and her sister were told that the plane on which their father had been travelling to the San Francisco Conference had been shot down.

Sudden darkness shocked us one evening. A plane had flown into the power lines. Later we knew Fr Butler had gone over to the crash-site. There were exceptional evenings, when the school was allowed to listen to Churchill making a speech to the nation. Then came V.E. Day and a mighty celebration bonfire, which S.M.Benedict and S.M.Ignatius stoked wearing their gas masks and ARP tin helmets.

So 'After the War' had come, and that's another time, another story. But for now, I'm glad the Archives hold silver Liège goblets.

After leaving school I completed a university degree at Leeds and did some teaching before entering the Community at New Hall (1961). I've had various jobs in the Community and School, and three valuable years in Belfast. An Ignatian Spirituality training gave versatile preparation and has transferred well to life now in Colchester.

GILLIAN GRINDON-WELCH (S.M.Stephen)

1942–1949

My memories of my first years are of Newnham Paddox, and of a wonderful freedom. There were no roads for miles and we were allowed to roam the fields near and far. As long as we turned up for meals and any other commitments and were not alone, there seemed to be no limit. I spent much of my time up trees (not officially allowed) or sitting and playing around the beautiful lakes. I have many memories of how in winter we collected firewood and split with an axe the daily ration of logs for fires in the classrooms and dormitories; we had no central heating and only rare baths. We were given salt to gargle with to fend off sore throats, but after lights-out we would put it on the dormitory fire and create wonderful green flames.

On V.E. Day we had a festive meal out on the terrace and in the evening a magnificent bonfire in front of the house.

When we returned to New Hall after the war I was very doubtful of how I would survive with all that freedom gone. But by that time I was in the last year of School Certificate and so was well focused in the direction of work.

No one had been able to go home for half-terms during wartime but now they went as before, and only a few of us stayed. We enjoyed the time so much that we resented the return of everyone else! School – including all the Community members we knew – had become more family than home for me, and I was desperately sad to leave and go on to university.

When I joined the Community, Drama was growing in importance – at first with the annual Nativity Plays and later with a broader spectrum. One of my first jobs as a novice was painting stage scenery and it was a really creative way to be involved in what became such an important part of the School.

After school I studied Fine Art at Reading University, before joining the Community in 1951. I studied Art in Turnhout in Belgium, before teaching full-time from 1957 to 1991, with a course in Swansea in between. In 1991 I was involved with work in the Barn. Painting is my primary job now, being published by McCrimmon worldwide and with exhibitions in various places including New Hall; Glasgow; Chelmsford Cathedral; Brentwood Cathedral; Castle Methodist Hall, Colchester; Ascension Church Hall, East London; St John Payne School, Chelmsford; St Joseph Hospice, London; New Hall Prep School; and Blessed Sacrament Church, Chelmsford.

An early drawing by Gillian Grindon-Welch, aged 15, while evacuated to Newnham Paddox

CATHERINE CARDIS (S. Catherine)

1942–1948

From a transcript of the CD Voices of New Hall*

At Newnham Paddox there were two nuns in the kitchen, S. Mary and S. Anne, the pastrycook. The nuns were allowed to listen to the news on the wireless to know what was going on, and with special permission S. Mary and S. Anne listened to the programme that helped people to

---

* A series of interviews made by Stella Beer in the mid 1990s and recorded by Bob Smith, Matthew Tunstill, Warren Songhurst and John O'Keefe.

adapt a good diet from very little. My mother commented that she didn't know how we were so well fed! We came from a city where there weren't such ready resources, like nettles, for the taking.

Breakfast was porridge and wartime bread, the nearest thing to grey in colour. We had a portion of butter which was very slightly larger than a postage stamp in surface area, and half an inch thick. Some of us used to cut it in half, use half for breakfast and, securely identified with initials, we used the second half at tea-time. We could have extra milk, a mug each day, that our parents paid for; my mother managed to pay for our extra milk, although life wasn't easy for her.

Tins of condensed milk were a delight. One of the joys of end of term was when the tins were all put out and there was a free for all; you ate up anybody's. Once somebody put condensed milk on top of sardines which was quite fun!

Lunch was stews, fishcakes, or a favourite, baked beans with tomato sauce between two layers of pastry. Spam turned up quite often, which I didn't like. We had lots of vegetables, especially swedes and turnips, which we'd see in mounds in the fields as we went for our walks. Nettles, when cooked, were like spinach, but a bit rougher.

We had quite a lot of apple-based puddings like crab apples spread on pastry. Most memorable were the elderberries; these were used in between pastry or as currants in buns or puddings; they looked good, but tasted mediocre.

At tea-time we had bread, with the butter you'd left in the morning, and jam. The favourites were apricot and strawberry, but I chose the less popular plum because there was less competition for it! The bit of butter you had left in the morning came back safely – I don't think anyone would've thought of changing the initials; there were only 45 of us, and you didn't do that sort of thing. Sometimes people would ask for some of yours, but I was mean and used to say, 'No, you've had yours and you've finished it,' because I was the sort of person who would've made it last to the last day by cutting down and down, so I could have a taste on the last day!

Supper was often soup, sensibly made from lunchtime leftovers with croutons. This was followed by stewed fruit, milk puddings and 'dog biscuits' – the Community loved them! They were thin and crisp with a brown edge, made with golden raising powder. Delicious! This went on well into the 1950s.

It was very cold in Newnham and we had terrible chilblains. Shortage of water meant few baths, one bath a term generally, and when we had a party, six of us were put in one bath; we would stand up and be scrubbed down.

One memory above all is the frogs. In the spring you couldn't put one foot in front of the other as everywhere was a carpet of frogs. It was almost impossible to miss every one, even if you shuffled. Additionally, there were two leech ponds, with leeches by the million.

Down beyond the rose garden was a hedge and through it was a wild bit in which we had our dens, shared with the newts. Over in the fields, there were hundreds of sheep, and

Fishes up a tree with S.M.Christopher

between the fields were streams and beautiful little wooden bridges. At half-term S.M.Christopher used to take us there in our Science overalls, so we could play in the streams with jam jars and Pooh Sticks.

On Saturday afternoons S.M.Martha organised wooding – collecting wood for the fires. Once collected, the wood was stacked in the back yard and S.M.Martha would cut it. Then we children would line up and pass logs down the line to her in the cellar where it was stacked to dry. Every day, our job was to bring up dry logs – we were very fit and it was great fun!

Often we collected round one of the fires in the upstairs drawing-room, sitting about on the floor; then S.M.Christopher and S. Margaret Helen would come in and we'd have a sing-song, or we'd put on a record. Many a time some of those who did Dancing would entertain us with impromptu dances. It was real recreation, enjoyed by all.

JENNIFER (Jinks) BARR (née Hickey)

1943–1951

The vast grounds at Newnham Paddox were protected by huge, never used wrought-iron gates which had somehow escaped the greedy war machine. There was a hazel wood, a wilderness, a spacious Arrival Area which became our netball court, room for two or three tennis-courts, and a rose garden with a fountain in the centre where we nurtured little black tadpoles. On the field side of the house were the Ha-Ha walls. Best of all were the two big lakes with high rhododendron bushes grouped closely along the shore and only a winding footpath through them.

The ballroom and drawing-room, which became our dormitories, were hung with oil paintings of past Denbighs, mostly women with bosoms spilling out of tiny tight bodices. They watched over us as we shuffled through the rooms with our enamel bowls full of tepid water for washing. Poor S. Anthony had to sleep in the alcove originally built for the orchestra and try to keep us from chattering. Useless as a rule enforcer, she would say, 'Ooo's that talking?' and tell us to report to Mother Mary Veronica. Once when I mistakenly took a swig of eucalyptus oil to cure a cold and felt on fire inside, what did S. Anthony say as I was writhing on my death-bed but, 'Ooo's talking? Report to Mother Mary Veronica in the mornin'.' Finally they put S.M.Joseph outside the slightly open door, where she read till we were all asleep, and being fully dressed could come flying in at any time!

My friend Angie (Morris) was very conscientious about curling her hair, which may have given Merilyn Reynolds the idea of trying to curl her own red but straight hair. The trouble was, unlike Angie, she had no rags to do this with. Undaunted, Merilyn used plasticine. What a mess! S.M.Christopher and two older girls spent hours until after we were asleep combing her hair clean!

We little girls used a huge bathroom with taps marked 'C' for hot (*chaud*) and 'F' for cold (*froid*). This was our introduction to French as a living language. In total, as far as I recall, there were only three proper lavs in the whole building: one downstairs and two upstairs, called the Black Holes of Calcutta.

104

In the room where Miss O'Calaghan taught us, there was a picture of St Francis and the birds, and as our punishment for any wrongdoing was to stand in the corner near it, I grew quite familiar with those birds. Later we had Miss Quigley who wrote her Qs like the letter 2. Miss Unsworth wore a flowing gown and had a gold pencil on a cord or chain. At Newnham we had no Science teacher, so Botany – or Nature Study, as we called it – had to do until the Science teachers who survived came back from the war.

The Cockloft was out of bounds but Angie's suitcase was up there so we'd sneak up to look at it and anything else we fancied. It was a small room way up at the top of everywhere. Best of all was a glass-sided wall screen, in which were impaled dozens of wonderful butterflies, from huge foreign-looking ones down to tiny blue stonecrops. Now it seems a callous thing to do, but then I just saw the sacrificed beauty.

On V.E. Day we spent all day collecting twigs and branches and anything that would burn. Then in the dark, with as many of us as possible wearing some blue (with our red uniform and white shirts, making patriotic colours), we watched as Percy Sygrove set our huge bonfire alight. A small plane put the jewel in the crown as it flew overhead and dipped it's wings. We jumped up and down waving. 'Thank you! Thank you!' we yelled as it flew off into a night filled with lights and hope.

After our return to New Hall, another of Henry VIII's martyrs joined us, in that our Houses increased from More and Pole to include Fisher. Fishers won almost everything in that first year.

As well as the nuns we also had Lay teachers: Miss Engel took us for English in the lower classes. She was from Austria and had a short temper. If she were not pleased with our work she'd hurl our exercise books back to us while her face went an interesting purple colour. This sort of teaching was quite new to us and we loved it. 'Let's see who can make her throw things today,' was our attitude. At the beginning of one term Miss Engel told us we could choose between the two books for the term. I forget the other, but the one we chose was called 'Donkey Hottie'. This conjured up visions of the life of a donkey. Imagine our dismay when we discovered it was really *Don Quixote*!

Imagine our surprise when we came back from our holidays to find Miss Engel walking demurely about dressed as a novice. She eventually did become a nun. After her death her obituary described her as a model of patience and perfection. Much later Angie told me that Miss Engel's family was Jewish and had escaped from Nazi Germany. We might have been more understanding had we known that, but in those days any details of a grown-up's life seemed to be taboo.

Further up the school, Miss Jackson taught English. Chaucer and his ancient English held no mysteries for Miss Jackson. She read it as easily and clearly with as much understanding as if she were reading Dickens. She it was who instilled a love of words and poetry in me.

Every day we had gym during lesson time and then we had Games after lunch: lacrosse and netball in the winter, tennis and cricket (and for 'fun' we played rounders) in the summer. I missed the long walks we had taken around the grounds at Newnham. During lacrosse practice Angie and I would toss a ball to each other at the edge of the Six Acres field near the chickens, which had a huge area under apple trees, and discuss the 'Facts of Life' as we knew them. Nothing very accurate! After Games we had to wash 'all over' at a washbasin. At least we didn't have to fetch the water in enamel bowls and try not to slop it on the floors on which the privileged had once danced the minuet and the gavotte.

On Sundays, we went to church twice, once for Communion and later for Fr Butler's rather dull sermon, and sometime on Sunday we had an hour set aside to write home to our parents, but to no one else.

Two girls celebrated their Jubilee – 10 years at New Hall. Marcy Wood had been there since she was a very young child of five or six. She left aged 17 in July then returned as a novice that September. Her Jubilee song was based on a Gilbert and Sullivan tune: 'We are here to sing a song of Marcy Wood, Marcy Wood, Telling tales of all she's done, as we should, as we should . . . ' The second Jubilee was for Melissa Metcalf, whose song was also set to Gilbert and Sullivan by S.M.Ignatius: 'Here's a golden opportunity, for reminiscence with impunity . . . '

I did some rotten things at school, and while they are shaming now to remember, at the time they seemed all right. A new girl arrived, named Gertrude. As if this name wasn't ugly enough the portable toilet had long been affectionately known as Bertie. So in a normal association of ideas the poem was 'Dirty Gertie sat on Bertie . . .' It wasn't said to her face but she must have known. I was walking with Fr Butler, who was

V.E. Day celebrations at Newnham Paddox

OK when he wasn't giving sermons, and saying how I disliked her. Well I told Fr Butler, it was all right to hate her because she was Jewish. 'But Jesus was a Jew,' he answered. That really shook me. Of course I knew that in my mind but not in my heart. That meant she probably had a stronger connection to Jesus than we had . . . Poor old Gertie left after a short stay and when we found out she'd moved to a notorious convent, my mother and I went to see her there and take her out to tea. No one deserved *that* school.

Gill Fotheringham had an exercise book in which she wrote love stories about desperate damsels swooning and pining for always-handsome men and asking questions like, 'Did you take advantage of me while I was unconscious . . . am I your mistress?' (Whatever that meant!) Of course she was discovered and those of us who had secretly read the book, in eagerly awaited instalments, were given a long talk about suitable behaviour for young Catholic girls. I was surprised to hear years later that she was an artist. I'd have thought she'd be an author!

My final report did not impress my mother. It said: 'Has lost interest in and outgrown school life.' (But my health was still: 'Very good'.) It seems to me that is the whole point of school, to prepare one for leaving. Anyway Ireland was waiting.

I did a year's Household Management at Colaiste Muire le Tigeas in Dublin, before completing Nursery Nurse's Training and working as a staff nurse. In 1956 I went to Canada and had various jobs in private houses while I worked my way across to British Columbia. I married Larry in 1960 and we have four children (Laurinda, Conall, Kevin and Moira) and eight grandchildren. We have been running a Bed & Breakfast since 1984.

TESS (Tigger) ROSSITER (née Morris)

1944–1952

Mum, Granny, Michael, Angie, Zelie and I came to Newnham Paddox because my mother took up a post as Teaching Assistant to Mother Magdalen John in Domestic Science.

We lived in a little cottage just a few yards from the main house and it was a very happy time both during term-time and in the holidays. The Avenue leading up to the lakes was particularly fine, lined with lime trees. I have a vivid recollection of meeting both S.M.Peter and a peacock butterfly. Yes, there were two lakes, one beyond the other; on one side was parkland and on the other farmland where cows grazed in the summer months. One winter – '44 or '45 – it was very cold; the upper lake froze over so solidly it was safe to skate, and I recall a man skating in great style.

Newnham Paddox was a grand building, fronted with the most magnificent wrought-iron gates. Upstairs the rooms were large with massive fireplaces. When I joined the School this was where us little 'uns slept, lovingly looked after by dear S. Teresa Magdalen. On V.E. Day a huge bonfire was lit in front of the grand gates, which we had to watch out of the dormitory window. Every time an aeroplane flew over a great roar of joy broke out among the Fishes gathered round the fire.

We were playing on a long, low branch of a horse-chestnut tree, pretending that we were riding on horseback, and S.M.Paul told us to get off. I didn't, but fell off and broke my arm. Just for good measure I broke it again playing leapfrog nearer the house where there was a large pond, which I think was empty.

Tennis
Left to right back: Jean Henderson, Ann Bamford, Mary Elise Petre
Front: Mary-Rose Henderson, Judy Roberts, Ruth Bennett

The chapel, which was attached to the house, was rather dark and gloomy. It was there that I and others were confirmed and also there that I witnessed a Requiem Mass for one of the nuns.

Back at New Hall we had the Great Feast – announced out of the blue and greeted with great excitement. We were divided into four teams, ours led by the very artistic S.M.Joseph, and were given the title of a well-known painting *And When Did You Last See Your Father?* to act out. The slim, fair-haired Elizabeth Waring was the ideal person for the central character, a little Royalist boy being quizzed by the Roundhead 'police'. We won!

Carolyn Luck (née Flewitt) and I shared a Jubilee day as we had both been at Newnham Paddox and New Hall for 10 great years. Happy days!

I trained in Domestic Science in London then worked for the London Electricity Board before getting married in 1958. I had four children – Harry, Annabel, Beatrice and James (who came a little later in 1966). Very sadly, Annabel died of a brain tumour in 2002 and is buried in the cemetery at New Hall. I now live with my second husband, Richard, in Suffolk.

109

ANGELA MORRIS (S. Angela)

1944–1953

Newnham Paddox was a rambling and rather decayed Victorian mansion – and very cold. The ballroom was turned into a dormitory with the beds head to head, inviting conversations, and S. Anthony in the orchestra pit, who would ask in the most lovely Lancashire accent, 'Was you talkin'?'

The grounds at Newnham Paddox were neglected and that was wonderful because we could roam freely. 'Paddox' means wet meadow and there were masses of frogs and in season when the females were going down to water you couldn't walk anywhere without treading on copulating creatures.

On V.E. Day we had a huge bonfire in front of the house. The young nuns – S.M.Christopher, S.M.Peter, S.M.Martha and S.M.Benedict – and probably also S.Magdalen John, helped to build it. It was at night, and amazingly exciting – all the more so when an aeroplane flying over dipped its wings.

We moved back to New Hall in 1946. It was recovering from serious bomb damage, the front two bays got a direct hit, and huge baulks of timber were pinned as temporary cladding protecting against water penetration. Workmen were around constantly, along with stonemasons restoring the stonework and doing carvings.

Fr Butler, a lovely, gentle, retired missionary Jesuit, was very interested in the history of the house and when the stonemasons asked him what images should they create, he said, 'Why don't you do fishes?' So if you look at one of the decorations at the top of the bow on what was the Convent side, you can see two little fishes. There's also a brick on the left-hand side of what is now Priory House with the letters 'TSF'. They stand for Thomas Earl of Sussex (*c*.1525–83) and Frances. Frances was his wife, who founded Sidney Sussex College at Cambridge.

I felt a huge freedom when I was at the School. There were only about 60 pupils. Our clothes were all numbered, and I was number 61 and my sister, Tess, was 62. When I left in 1953 the numbers had only increased to about 100. There were only five of us in the Sixth Form, and three of us went to university. The general expectation was that

S.M.Christopher and S.M.Martha as novices

boarding-school girls would be secretaries or go to finishing school and do the Season afterwards, but my parents had different ideas. I read Geography and English at Queen Mary College, London – a real culture shock after New Hall!

After I graduated from Queen Mary College, London, I did the obligatory secretarial course, and then worked for a literary agency for a short time. During that period I decided I would join the Community, which I did in October 1958 – and I've been with them ever since. I'm involved with Bible Study Courses in three parishes, Spiritual Direction, leading days of prayer (particularly on poets – Gerard Manley Hopkins, T. S. Eliot, Wordsworth, George Herbert, etc.) and being a team member for Individually Guided Retreats.

PADDY BERNARD (née Moyes)

1947–1952

My sister Mary had started at New Hall the term before me. She was much braver than I, but after six weeks and doctors, priests and pleadings she was taken away. One can imagine how scared I was! My parents did not have a car so I arrived, aged 11, on the bus at Chelmsford Station. Most of the girls had come from London in the 'Pack Train' and were sitting on the coach waiting for me. I wanted to disappear under a seat I was so shy and embarrassed. However, a girl called Jane Foley gave me a barley sugar and after that I felt much better.

We arrived down a very long straight drive and stopped in front of a very large, very strange building. The two front bays were in gaping ruins, having been bombed during the war.

The first night I felt homesick and scared but I was much too shy to make a fuss. Our Home Mother was a beautiful nun, S.M.Clare, who looked after me and that was the end of my homesickness.

The whole School went to Mass on Sundays, Mondays, Wednesdays and Fridays. We were woken with a prayer before seven, put our veils on and went to the Chapel. We had to be very quiet entering, as the nuns were singing their Office. There were about forty nuns in the Community at this time, including the Choir nuns, the Lay sisters, the white-veiled novices and the 'Tadpoles' – the postulants trying their vocation, who were in the Choir loft.

Breakfast was very good. We had lots of cream and butter, as the school had a farm. After breakfast we had the 'Run Round' the Plot – rain or shine. This had to be done twice a day and there was a notice we had to tick to prove it. As soon as we got back we all went up to the broom cupboard at the very top of the house where we were presented with the cleaning materials for our designated housework task. We learnt how to clean a house and how to behave at the table. With our own silver goblets and cutlery and the plates on beautiful green linen mats we could hardly do otherwise.

The weekends were fun. On Sunday afternoons we all walked down the Avenue as far as the level-crossing, accompanied by a nun. The first two girls to get to her were able to hold the corners of her apron. We talked and laughed and she told us stories of her schooldays, as many of the nuns had been Fishes themselves.

We played horses and made stables and ate sorrel. The grounds were wild and we ran freely through them. We climbed trees and had dens in the moat, by the Six Acres. At the far end of the Plot there was an enormous heap of wood from the war damage, with which we made wonderful seesaws.

The school was so small – 75 girls in all. Our class took O Levels but very few girls stayed on to the Sixth Form to take A Levels. Fewer still went to university. The fees per term in 1947 were £45.

The school year followed the year of the Church. There were Corpus Christi processions, when six children dressed in white dresses cast flowers in front of the priest carrying the Blessed Sacrament. He led the School, singing hymns, all round the grounds in a progress which culminated at the altar. The altar was a little chapel, in memory of a Fish who had died as a child, in a building called the Pavilion, which stood where Beaulieu stands today. The most important feast was called the Great Feast. This was a surprise and no one knew when it was coming. At supper S.M.Christopher would start by telling us how badly we sat or some such thing and then in a quiet voice would say,

Primrose – the Pack Coach

'And by the way, it's the Great Feast tomorrow.' We would all go quite wild with excitement. For my first one in 1947 it was still traditional to have a 'Tableau Vivant'. We were divided into groups and given the name of a picture to copy – nothing was too much trouble. Our picture was Constable's *Haywain*. We were dressed by S.M.Benedict in suitable clothes. Straw was brought in from the farm – and so was the horse and cart.

Every fourth year the whole School stayed for the Celebration of Easter. We had lots of fun and

Fishes up a tree

games, except on Good Friday when we all had to be rather solemn. Holy Saturday afternoon was a treat as the priest blessed the School and 'the Other Side' – the nuns' quarters, which were out of bounds. Nuns were of great interest to us girls. They intrigued us. The Choir nuns wore veils that they pinned back if they were busy. S.M.Martha would pin up her habit and tear down the lacrosse field during games. We all loved seeing the blue stockings!

My five years at New Hall went very quickly and I cried for a week when I left. The man at the level-crossing was reported to have said, 'They cry when they come but they cry much more when they go.'

After qualifying as a primary-school teacher, I ran a nursery school for the parish. I am married with four children and seven grandchildren.

ELISABETH (Buff) SCOTT TOWNSEND
(née Scott Stokes) S.M.Bernadette

1948–1955

I was about 10 when I started at New Hall, and I loved it although I was shy and talked little.

S.M.Peter taught us to begin with and I thought she was a wonderful teacher. I slept in St Joseph's dormitory on an iron bedstead with a horse-hair mattress. On our way to bed we had to fill the metal basin in our washstand, which stood beside our own bed. There was no central heating and in the winter after a cold night we had to break the ice to wash in the morning.

Miss Westlake taught me Elocution. Miss Kerslake taught Music and this was the only time in my life that I consider myself to have been in any way musical. Mrs Ashcroft taught Dancing, wonderfully. I became a ballet dancer, stood on my points and ruined my toes, but I loved it, and wouldn't have missed it for the world.

S.M.Martha taught me General Science, S.M.Ignatius Geography,

Nativity

115

S. Margaret Helen English Language and English Literature and S.M.Paul Religious Knowledge. These subjects have remained main–stays for my entire life.

In 1953 and 1954 I was the Madonna in the Christmas Nativity Play and the statue that stands in the Ambulacrum is based on me! I have a card that was made at the time with a lovely quote.

One of my very special memories was going into the Chapel in the dark evenings to listen to the nuns singing Compline, and staying in the Chapel when it was over in silence and in darkness, with only the Sanctuary lamp. Gregorian Chant has been my favourite music ever since, meditation and contemplation the same.

I was a Child of Mary and I was Head of the School. I left school after my O Levels to enter the Noviciate at the age of seventeen.

GILL (Fothy) FOTHERINGHAM-OLIVER
(née Fotheringham)

1946–1950

Newnham Paddox, the seat of the Earls of Denbigh, was landscaped by Lancelot Capability Brown between 1745 and 1753. In 1952 the three great houses, beyond repair, were demolished, enabling the preservation of the farms and the creation of a Sculpture Garden which opened in 2003. Gill's memories are of a visit to Newnham Paddox before it was demolished.

The pink candelabra blossoms were on the horse-chestnut trees as we drove gingerly up the secondary drive towards the main house. Every-thing looked in a state of dilapidation but it was good to see that the beautiful wrought-iron main gates still looked challengingly out towards the lost Avenue which had once cut a swathe through the now chest-high grasses.

We entered the garden looking sadly at the overgrown fountain and small formal garden which lay to the side of the great house. I turned the handle of one of the French windows which used to lead to a common room during our schooldays. We wondered if we dare try to get in. It groaned but turned easily enough to allow us entry, and although accompanied by the guilt of trespass, my curiosity over-came me.

On the peeling walls of the hall there still hung various heads of stags and sets of antlers. The stairs looked reasonably safe, and I was eager to look again into the ballroom with its long windows and semi-circular bandstand, and the golden cane chairs – remembering how, when I was in my dormitory, I would lie in bed on summer nights imagining the music and the swirling dresses of the dancers. A warning hand on my arm stopped me halfway up the stairs – I had not noticed that the upper corridor floor had fallen into the passage below. It was dangerous to explore further, so, stepping carefully, I regained the safety of the ground floor.

Longing to see more, we crossed over to what had been the nuns' side. Vast, damp and neglected, the floors were strewn with leaves and from the walls, running with water, large oil portraits of unknown dignitaries stared at us with surprise.

Our steps turned through the labyrinth of rooms, coming finally to the chapel. The light streamed from above and even with the over-whelming cloak of sadness and decay which seemed to fill the house, the chapel still held its aura of sanctity and peace. The jewel-encrusted doors of the altar tabernacle were still intact and I felt that it was by some miracle that no one had stolen them.

On leaving the house we walked through the grounds to look at the specialist woods which in my schooldays were filled with many varied trees and bushes brought from all over the world, like the Handkerchief and Tulip trees. Most of the magnificent beeches and oaks had been logged and much of the land cleared, but the ornamental lakes remained, albeit overgrown with rushes which were home to a few moorhens.

My return to this once splendid English country house, now an empty ruin, brought memories of my happy schooldays tumbling back.

After a First Class Honours Degree in Art at Edinburgh Art College, I painted – mainly seascapes – in my Cornish studio for nearly 30 years. I am married with three sons and currently live in Mallorca where I continue to paint.

Photographs indicating the growth of the School in the 1940s

The 1950s

What's going on in the world during the 1950s

Queen Elizabeth II / New roads / New comics / New gadgets / Skiffle / Rock and Roll / Rise of television / Sci Fi / Wide skirts / High heels / Spies / Atom Bombs

1950 Credit Card introduced / First organ transplant / Sainsbury's opens first self-service supermarket / Festival Ballet founded / Andy Pandy makes his television debut / *Annie Get Your Gun* at cinemas / *The Eagle* comic first appears

1951 George VI opens the Festival of Britain, featuring the Skylon, in London / Guy Burgess and Donald MacLean defect to the USSR / Peak District becomes first national park / Zebra Crossings introduced / *The Archers* and *The Goon Show* are first aired / Dennis the Menace appears in the *Beano* comic / *The African Queen* and *A Streetcar Named Desire* are released / John Wyndham *The Day of the Triffids* / C. S. Lewis *Prince Caspian*

1952 Car seat belts introduced / Polio vaccine available / King George VI dies, Princess Elizabeth becomes Queen / Churchill announces UK has an Atomic Bomb / De Havilland Comet – world's first jet airliner / 'Great Smog' hits London / Agatha Christie's play *The Mousetrap* begins its London run / The Flower Pot Men / *High Noon* at the cinema / Mary Norton's children's novel *The Borrowers* is published

1953 Crick and Watson present the DNA double helix / Edmund Hillary and Tenzing Norgay climb Everest / The 10 Rillington Place murders / Samaritan helpline launched / *Good Old Days* appear on television / Ian Fleming publishes first James Bond novel, *Casino Royale*

1954 First Atomic submarine launched / Roger Bannister runs four-minute mile / Segregation ruled illegal in US / Food rationing ends / First weatherman is televised / David Attenborough's *Zoo*

Quest on television / First broadcast of Dylan Thomas's radio play *Under Milk Wood* / Radio comedy *Hancock's Half Hour* / *Seven Brides for Seven Brothers* at the cinema / J. R. R. Tolkien publishes first volume of *Lord of the Rings*

1955 Disneyland opens / Warsaw Pact signed / Donald Campbell breaks water-speed record / Aircraft carrier HMS *Ark Royal* completed / Ruth Ellis last woman to be hanged in Britain / *Guinness Book of Records* first published / *Pick of the Pops* and *Educating Archie* (with ventriloquist Peter Brough!) on radio / *This is Your Life* and *Crackerjack* on television / *Oklahoma!* and *Lady and the Tramp* in the cinema / Wainwright's first hand-drawn volume of *A Pictorial Guide to the Lakeland Fells*

1956 Grace Kelly marries Prince Rainier III of Monaco / Velcro appears / Double yellow lines first used in Slough / Corgi toy cars in shops / Queen opens world's first commercial nuclear power station at Calder Hall / British troops withdraw from Suez / Humphrey Lyttelton records 'Bad Penny Blues' / Gerald Durrell *My Family and Other Animals*

1957 European Economic Community established / Soviet satellite Sputnik launched / The 'Cavern' club opens in Liverpool / Britain tests its first Hydrogen Bomb / ERNIE picks the winning Premium Bonds / Patrick Moore presents *The Sky at Night* / David Lean *The Bridge on the River Kwai* / Ted Hughes *The Hawk in the Rain*

1958 Lego toy bricks available / NASA founded / Sir Edmund Hillary reaches the South Pole / London Planetarium opens / Parking Meters / Preston By-Bass, first motorway / BBC Radiophonic Workshop created / *My Fair Lady* opens in Drury Lane Theatre / First Carry On film, *Carry On Sergeant* / Launch of *Blue Peter* / Michael Bond *A Bear Called Paddington* / John Betjeman *Collected Poems*

1959 Castro becomes dictator of Cuba / 'Barbie' appears in toyshops / Dalai Lama escapes to India / Mermaid Theatre opens at Puddle Dock / UK postcodes introduced / Dounreay Fast Nuclear Reactor comes on line / Ronnie Scott's Jazz Club opens / Children's television series *Ivor the Engine* / Radio comedy *The Navy Lark* begins on the Light Programme

What's going on at New Hall during the 1950s

During the 1950s, New Hall continued to expand and respond to the changing demands of the educational world. More Lay staff joined the School, including two young women who were to be an integral part of New Hall life for several decades, namely Murielle Ashcroft who came as a Dance teacher in 1954, and Ruth Raven who arrived in 1955 to teach Games.

The School remained under the leadership of members of the Community, as Heads, teachers and as Pastoral staff.

S.M.Emmanuel, S.M.Veronica, S.M.Christopher and S. Margaret Helen had particular leadership roles during this decade and are remembered in the pages that follow.

More renovation and extension work was done to the building, and two of the major projects were the redecoration of the Chapel and the building of the outdoor swimming-pool.

In 1953 the Preparatory School moved from Goodings to Denford Park, a gift to the Community from Sir Harrison-Hughes.

Changes in society impacted on life in the School with the advent of television and the growth and accessibility of pop culture.

Convent of the Holy Sepulchre, New Hall.

SCHOOL UNIFORM

Everything on this list is obtainable at the School Outfitters, DICKINS & JONES, REGENT STREET, LONDON, W.1.
All items, except underwear, linen, cutlery, etc., must be obtained from this firm.

1 Camel-hair Overcoat.   1 Beige Felt Hat.
1 pr. Beige Gloves.   1 Red Scarf (if required).
1 School Blazer.   1 Red Jersey.
1 Red Skirt—Winter style in serge.
1 Red Divided Skirt—Summer style in rayon.
6 White Aertex Shirts—short sleeves.
1 pr. Red Shorts for Gym (regulation length).
1 or 2 prs. White Shorts for Tennis (regulation length).
1 White Games Sweater.
2 prs. Red Knickers for Gym.
6 prs. White Ankle Socks (worn all the year round, for preference) otherwise for WINTER TERMS ONLY Beige ¾ length Socks OR Beige Stockings.
1 or 2 prs. BROWN Sandals or House Shoes.
1 pr. BROWN Outdoor Shoes.
1 pr. Wellington Boots.
1 pr. BROWN Lacrosse Boots.
1 pr. BROWN Gym Shoes.
1 pr. White Tennis Shoes.
1 pr. Bedroom Slippers.

6 White Vests (preferably Aertex).
6 prs. White Knickers (preferably Aertex).
3 prs. Pyjamas or Nightdresses.
1 Dressing Gown.   2 doz. Handkerchiefs.
2 prs. Sheets and Pillowcases.
1 Eiderdown or Rug.
2 Bath Towels.   3 Face Towels.
3 Table-napkins.   1 Napkin Ring.
1 Goblet (silver if possible).
2 Stainless Knives (1 small, 1 large).
2 Stainless Forks   ,,   ,,
1 Dessert Spoon.   1 Teaspoon.
Needlework Requisites.   Toilet Requisites.
Lacrosse Stick.   Tennis Racquet.

FOR THOSE WHO LEARN DANCING:
1 Silk or Cotton Frock—full skirt, floral design in pastel shades.
1 pr. Dancing Shoes or Sandals (NOT crepe soles) either white, red, silver, gold or bronze.
1 pr. Ballet Shoes (if required).

EVERYTHING TO BE MARKED WITH FULL NAME IN CASH'S NAME TAPES.

List of School uniform available from Dickins & Jones

GABRIELLE HORTON (S. Margaret Mary)
*The 1950s – Beginning the Cycle (Part 1 of 3)**

September 1954   One of the first things I saw when, aged 11, I arrived at New Hall was the stone mounting block outside the front door – familiar only because I had seen a photo of my grandmother, whom I never knew, sitting on it with my mother, a young First Communicant, back in the late 1920s. Having feasted on Enid Blyton's *Malory Towers* for weeks beforehand I was excited and ready to be up to all the pranks! It didn't work out quite like that, but I loved it all the same.

What do I remember of those years? Buying and naming black babies – there was Damian and Sebastian and countless others and as far as I remember there were never any girls. There was food: break-boxes, mine contained mainly raw jelly, condensed milk and Marmite, which were consumed mid-morning at breakneck speed. Puddings: 'Reverend Mother's Leg' – jam roly-poly; 'Father Butler's Hat' – suet pudding with apple inside (Père B, as we called him, was the Chaplain, who took us for walks when we were in quarantine for measles or the like); 'Toenails' – half-moon shaped pastries with jam or marmalade. Tea-time was memorable for fresh homemade bread, slice after slice of it with thick butter and jam which I just kept eating until the bell, a hand-rung one (the Head Girl's privilege), sounded and we had to stop and run.

And people: really good friends all had nicknames – POF, Lal, Peeler, Gis, Rowie, Ci, Mon, Mouse . . . There weren't many Lay staff, but Madame, a French woman, remains vivid in my mind. She put us through our Whitmarsh paces and there were compulsory French 'Walks with Madame' at weekends. What lengths we went to to avoid our turns! Miss Westlake, or Westy as we called her, taught us Elocution and Drama. 'Slowly silently, now the moon . . . ' is with me to this day, as is 'Round the rugged rock, the ragged rascal ran . . . '

The annual Nativity Play was a massively important event in the School's calendar. I was never chosen to be an angel but progressed through boy shepherd to older boy shepherd to page. Classes seemed

* See page 196 for Part 2 and page 269 for Part 3.

to stop in the week leading up to it, and nothing else mattered. Two other teachers who have travelled with me over the years were Ruth Raven and Murielle Ashcroft. Ruth arrived a year later than I did, and taught PE. She was young and we thought her summer skirts were very trendy. I loved PE, and lacrosse matches were important weekend events. Murielle, the inimitable Murielle, arrived to teach Dancing the year I began at New Hall. She held classes in Colchester and rumour had it that the father of Ci Madden who attended these classes struck a bargain with the nuns – if Ci came to New Hall then her dancing teacher did too! Murielle and her pianist, Brownie, came every Wednesday afternoon and as well as ballet we learnt jive, cha-cha-cha and all the ballroom dances. (Murielle taught Dance at New Hall into her nineties and died aged 101 in 2011).

There were so many things that made these years happy: picnics in the fields; Great Feast celebrations and the amazing 'Tableaux'; Saturday-night dancing – the Eightsomes, the Gay Gordons; Sunday-night records under our eiderdowns in the Ambulacrum. 'Being Made' was all to do with the Children of Mary – a very complicated ladder you aspired to climb which was semi-behaviour, semi-religious – I never really 'got it' but I struggled up the ladder with everyone else nevertheless. Celebrating Jubilees – I remember the whole School going

Nativity Shepherds

Dance with Mrs Ashcroft

on an outing to Epping Forest to celebrate once. Then there were half-terms: some people who lived at a great distance stayed for half-term, and some of us who lived closer contrived to be allowed to stay as well – odd as I had such a happy home and family – as we had a ball. We seemed to spend a lot of time with a record player in the Cockloft and to be very unwelcoming to the rest of the School when they returned. One not so happy memory was spending some nights in a bed moved to outside the Housemistress's room – a punishment for bad behaviour in the dormitory.

There were sad memories too, and one is of Flindy. Flindy lived in Germany, her father was a Colonel. She was a weighty girl (so was I) who ate a lot of sweets, and we even called her 'Scoff'. But one term she returned having lost a lot of weight. As time went by she became ill and had to be sent home. I remember a few weeks later the School being assembled to be told that Flindy had died. She had had leukaemia. The death of a contemporary is overwhelming for a 12-year-old. It was my first funeral – Flindy was buried in the New Hall cemetery. We all attended. I don't remember much detail except that it was a huge experience and I felt terrible guilt because we had nicknamed her 'Scoff'. Her disease gave her a yearning for all things sweet.

The significant feeling that came out of these years was a desire to join the Community. I loved the nuns. There seemed to be lots of them and we had great fun with them. The 'young nuns' seemed omnipresent as Home Mothers, teachers, housework supervisors, putting-to-bed nuns, Tuck Shop keepers – whatever they were, they took good care of us, laughed a lot with us, comforted us at bad moments and called us to order when needed: S.M.Thérèse was a great part of this; S.M.Francis was always someone you could talk to; S.M.Stephen was infinitely patient with me as a complete non artist; S.M.Magdalene as Home Mother and in the Linen Room was the same gentle and unfailingly kind person that she is today; Catherine (then S.M.Thomas) took my needlework (pale blue baby clothes!) and finished them off for me; S.M.Dismas, S.M.David, S.M.Paul (with her 'Get it?' our 'Got it', her 'Good') – the relationships between them, and their example of a life well lived for others, set the seeds of what led me into religious life and the recycling process.

To be continued . . .

PAT ALGAR-JONES

Teacher 1950s

In 1948 a personal friend, Fr George Barret SJ, invited me to New Hall one weekend. Everyone was so friendly, everything so good, so peaceful, that I was sorry when it was time to return home. When the opportunity came to teach at New Hall, I accepted willingly, and how I enjoyed the years I spent there.

It was during that time that New Hall was persuaded to take in a real Cockney girl. S.M.Francis did her utmost to ease her in, without letting the girl get stressed by it all. In those days there was still the

Enclosure, separated off for the Community and strictly out of bounds. The girl was walking along with S.M.Francis approaching the Enclosure.

'I'm going through that door. What are you going to do?' said S.M.Francis, hoping for the reply, 'Open it for you.'

'I'm a-comin wiv yer,' came the reply.

The Community always worked so hard to give us a perfect Easter. One Easter Sunday in the middle of our meal one of the sisters came to tell me that my aunt had died. I'll never forget the kindness of S.M.Magdalene, who took me to her office so that I could phone the hospital, and went and got me a drink. No one could have been kinder or more helpful.

For the past 63 years the Community have always been my dearest friends, although it is not possible to see them often now. I thank God for my lovely memories, which include S. Margaret Mary as a schoolgirl, and S. Anne's words when I took her an early cuppa on Easter Sunday, 'This is the last one you can bring me. I'm entering.'

VICTORIA FRIIS (née Gordon)

1948–1958

New Hall was still partially under tarpaulins in 1948 when I arrived. There were about 65 pupils and we wore a variety of red garments, which tried to resemble a uniform as the correct clothes weren't available. I think I wore my brother's cast-off pyjamas. Later on we younger girls wore red skirts with lovely deep pockets, and the older girls wore red panelled skirts.

Even if one wasn't a Roman Catholic there was obligatory attendance at Mass on Mondays, Wednesdays, Fridays and Sundays. The nuns were out of sight up in the gallery – but we could enjoy their beautiful singing. Fr Butler was the gentle, elderly resident Jesuit priest, after whom we named a pudding.

We each had to have a silver mug from home, as well as our own set of cutlery to use at mealtimes. Those without their own mug could borrow one of the small characterful silver beakers belonging to the School. We each had our allotted place in the Refectory, and sure enough, one's own mug was laid there each time by whoever laid the tables.

I slept first in St Joseph's dormitory on a cream-coloured iron bedstead with a white bedspread and a chair beside the bed. Wooden lockers for our clothes were against the walls and in the bay area were cream-painted washstands for the enamel bowls in which we washed. Water was collected from the nearby bathroom, and it must have been a splashy business taking the bowls of used water back to the bathroom to empty them. By the door, behind a folding screen, S. Agnes or S. Anne or S. Teresa slept, using a torch or possibly a candle for light when finally coming to bed.

We were aroused each day by the shrill tones of the little brass bell with squirrel handle which the House Mistress, S.M.Christopher, rang as she walked briskly around. Then came housework, when the older girls swept and the smaller girls dusted.

We had small 'allotments' in the area beside the courts.

For the weekly (optional) Dancing lessons we had to have a pretty dress and dancing pumps. We danced girl with girl; Georgia and I danced together but I don't think that either of us was at all good at it! There were others who chose ballet.

Much attention was paid to Drama and most of us had the

Refectory showing 'Liège goblets'

Housework team in the 1950s (one a Critchley-Salmonson)

opportunity to take part in some way. Many girls left an indelible impression, the redheads being memorable for their hair: Angie Morris's was wavy, Marguerite Braun's auburn, Merylyn Reynolds and the Reid twins, Margy and Francy, all had identical pale and straight hair.

I still recall the familiar movement of the nuns' black garments of finest black cloth, their 'swishing' skirts, their veils drawn forward covering the face or thrown back revealing the purest white starched 'cap' and the 'bib'. Sometimes they wore long cotton aprons of blue and white small-checked gingham which were pinned up on to the bosom, but not to cover the red New Hall cross they all wore on their robe.

JENNY HOLFORD (née Wolff)

1949–1954

My parents were desperate and did not know what to do with me. Inspired by a friend of theirs, whose daughter (Angela Peel) was going, arrangements were made for New Hall. Angela and I set off by train from Liverpool Street Station aged 11. We were both in our uniform – camel-hair coat, red skirt, Aertex polo shirt and a red twin-set. This was the last I saw of my parents for quite a long time.

In my first year, I was in St Joseph's dormitory, an open room with rows of beds and a washing bowl beside each one. This was a bit public for me as I was an early developer! We moved to cubicles as time went by but we only had two baths a week on a rota system, however I recall much washing was done.

We had to line up for everything and had a place to sit or stand in every situation – in the Dining-Room, the Chapel, and even standing in the corridor, we had to be in our right place.

Each day we had to run a quarter of a mile twice over, once after breakfast and once when we could fit it in. I soon learned how to escape this! This led to perhaps my first lie, for we had to tick a noticeboard when we had done it.

There was a door beyond the Chapel through which we were not allowed to go; leading to the 'other side', it was for the nuns only.

S.M.Christopher was the Housemistress assisted by S.M.Dismas. SMC, as she always signed herself, gave most of us nicknames and she called me Pooh Bear because I looked like the picture in the Infirmary bathroom (some things don't change). S. Margaret Helen was the Headmistress.

All the nuns were kind to us. S.M.Thérèse, who ran the Tuck Shop, was always good fun. S. Anne Joseph looked after our health problems and gave us ginger wine when we had menstrual pains! I only had four days off sick during all my time at New Hall; when we had an epidemic of German measles, we continued going to classes.

MARGARET BURN (née Reid)

1951–1957

After a glorious time in the New Hall Prep School of Goodings, I came to New Hall – Big Scary School – in September l951. We arrived a week late because my mother was ill and away so nobody had noticed that term had begun until the School rang, when we were seized and delivered. We were the first twins at New Hall. Everybody stared at us in the class line-up, especially as gym was the first lesson, perhaps because we had no uniform except red knickers sent on from Goodings!

But New Hall grew on us. It was such a happy caring place, in deeper ways than I imagined then. The cedar trees, the beautiful building and grounds, Gregorian Chant, wonderful sung Masses with the smell of incense.

New Hall offered us standards and ideals that we had not met with elsewhere. Someone once asked me what I'd got from my school, and I said, 'That we are here for others, not just for ourselves – and knee caps that were never able to get sunburnt as they'd been knelt on for so many years that the skin had thickened.'

I first met S.M.Magdalene when I was sent up to the Infirmary with concussion. She was so incredibly kind to me and told me she was about to 'enter'. When she left for the Noviciate, she gave me a medal of St Christopher 'to carry me over the water', which I have treasured all my life.

I am so glad that we were both sent to New Hall, instead of to Benenden!

Rosary dormitory

ANNE BROWN (née Savage)

1951–1956

There were 120 in the School, 12 in each class, and all were boarders except for one day girl, Elizabeth Waring.

Housework every morning was followed by the 'Running Round'.

We all wore veils for Chapel.

When Bishop Beck visited the School, we all lined up in the Ambulacrum and each then had to genuflect and kiss his ring.

In my first summer term, I remember Class I being taken down the Avenue by S.M.Christopher, with her reading us stories as we went about Mary Plain and the Bear Pit in Berne.

I remember the dogs – Jasper, a beautiful, slobbery Gordon setter, and Mankin, a terrier. S.M.Martha used to wash Jasper in the children's baths, which horrified my mother.

Group with S.M.Christopher

Here are some of my other memories:

– S.M.Martha hitching up her habit as she ran along Six Acres during lacrosse games, urging us to further action.

– Fr Butler and S.M.Paul with the bees – S.M.Paul looking splendid in her protective beekeeper's clothing over her habit.

– The Great Feast when we all had to do Tableaux – encouraged by S.M.Joseph.

– Amazing drama with Virginia Maskell as the star and S.M.Benedict working wonders in the Green Room.

– Sitting at benches in the Refectory with a nun digging you in the back if you did not sit up straight.

– Gardening in our own little plots under the eagle eye of S.M.Ignatius. Once I lost a trowel which was found months later in the compost heap.

– My classmates who stayed on in the Sixth Form – Eve Gallwey was the first New Hall girl to get to Oxford and Ann Feighan went to London University.

– Percy Sygrove who looked after the maintenance.

– S.M.Bernadette's clothing ceremony.

– Watching the film of *Henry V*, starring Laurence Olivier.

The nuns were always available, always patient, always supportive, and there was a deep sense of peace at New Hall underlying the high-spirited lives of the girls.

Pupils tending their 'little gardens' – early days of horticulture

ELISABETH (Liz) OLDING (née Marriner)
1952–1958

These were the days when heads were always covered in church. We all had white veils, on to which our School numbers were sewn, and they were kept in little wooden pigeon-holes outside the Refectory. They began the term pristine white but became grey by the end of the School year!

I have certain vivid memories:

– Saturday-morning shoe cleaning with S.M.Martha, who exacted a high standard.

– 'Running Round' after breakfast and before lessons. Up to the Plot and back along the Beech Walk, which I did not enjoy.

– No running in the corridors. I remember this as I am a 'last minute' person and have always needed to run.

– The smell of the exam papers when they were distributed at the end-of-year exams.

– Helping S.M.Magdalene in the Linen Room on the top floor. Sitting on a large cupboard helping to darn socks.

– Meeting S. Anne at the door to the nuns' side when she let me borrow a washboard for the group that Mary Taylor, Biddy O'Ferrall and I formed for a School show. We also had a tea-chest with string to make a double-base and went on the stage carrying lighted cigarettes, which we promptly stubbed out. And wearing maroon men's M&S cotton pyjamas; this was our bedtime fashion of the day.

– The Corpus Christi procession – another day off lessons. The altar on the Plot with the smell of the flowers (probably lupins) adorning it; also the wonderful gold monstrance and Benediction.

I remember sharing a room with Rozanne Lowe (Hippo) and Serena Goldsmith (Sena) – almost my happiest time and two friends who remain today. We had a room near Angels dormitory at the Gym end of the East Wing, with S.M.Dismas, our Housemistress, in the room dead opposite. No doubt she heard all the hilarity and probably every word that we said as we were full of beans. One night, I returned from the loo to find an apple-pie bed and the others roaring with laughter as

I tried to ignore it. S.M.Dismas made Rozanne and Serena remake my bed while I had to sit watching them. We kept quiet for the rest of that night!

On 12th March 1957, Teeny Redfern and I went up the water tower. I suppose I remember the date as the adrenalin was running high. It was a wonderful moonlit night and we could see down into the nuns' gardens.

I remember in my last days at New Hall helping S. Anne in the Sacristy. She became something of a buddy and I would spend quite a bit of time with her on several reunions.

My very last day was the day that the new altar was consecrated and the beginning of what seemed like an austere period when the nuns become more remote behind a grill at the back of the altar. I used to love all the Church music and singing the Latin Masses and being in the Choir.

I am the daughter of Pamela Marriner (née Webber), who was at New Hall in the 1930s, and the mother of Philippa (Pippa) Brown (née Olding) and of Joanna McCarthy (née Olding) who were at New Hall in the 1970s.

Choir, before the stalls were removed

TESSA TRAPPES-LOMAX

1952–1958

For the memory bank.

It's the simple things I remember first: the taste of water in the silver Liège beakers; the scent of warm ironing in the Linen Room; the clock striking every seven and half minutes; the distinctive swish of heavy black habits across floors which were endlessly re-waxed and buffed with outsize 'bumpers' – a word I've never heard before or since.

But mainly I remember the utter otherness. How crossing the railway line by the old signal box opened a hidden door into a parallel reality.

An Old Fish memoir of 1876 describes living in 'a mediaeval world' within the convent walls and then returning 'to the Victorian age' at the end of every term. By the 1950s, the lag was maybe only twenty or thirty years, but it was still a tight, self-contained cat's cradle of a universe. Beyond the boundaries of the grounds, the rest of the world vanished almost completely. Day-to-day School life was interwoven with age-old religious rhythms. Jokes and stories of the near and distant past were as close as yesterday. And every night, the nuns – those warm, funny, scary individuals who were part of every fibre of our daytime life – vanished down the creaky wooden passage which led to the veiled anonymity and silence of the mysterious 'other side'.

It was probably an odd way to grow up, even then. But we learned some long-lasting lessons: to get stuck in when something needed to be done, however messy or daunting it might be; never to tell lies (sometimes a real drawback later on); to value small things as well as big ones. And to understand what it meant to care about people and be cared for.

'History is that certainty produced at the point where the imperfections of memory meet the inadequacies of documentation . . .' (Julian Barnes, *A Sense of an Ending*).

JOAN KENNEDY

Teacher 1953–1957

I was a young member of New Hall's teaching staff for four years, teaching History, English and Geography, mainly to the Lower and Middle School, and I enjoyed my time there immensely. I was one of the few resident staff with accommodation in a wing away from the School but still part of the whole complex of buildings. Several members of staff came down from London for two or three days each week and had a room in the main School buildings, and two or three others lived locally and came in each day.

Mother Margaret Helen was our much revered Headmistress. She was an expert historian, well-versed in the annals of New Hall and its past Community, among whom she found two Sisters who probably belonged on my own family tree. Of the Community, S.M.Martha taught Science, and S.M.Dismas and S.M.Thérèse were also teachers. Full-time Lay staff were Miss Lane (History), Madame Widerkehr (French) and Miss Boyle (Latin). The latter went back every weekend to London, which she found quieter at night with all its traffic than

A classroom

New Hall with the mooing of cows in the next field. Both Mrs B. Kerslake and Miss Zoe Monteanu taught Music and were great characters. The two PE staff lived locally, one of them being Miss Ruth Raven. Nurse Baetsen, who was Dutch, looked after the health of the nuns, while Matron Frances Lynch, an Old Fish, attended to the health of the girls. I went to her wedding on the Welsh Borders – she was tremendous fun and used to drive a little green car at a time when not many young people had a car. (She sadly died a few years after she married.) Peg Peterson succeeded her as Matron.

There was an elderly retired Jesuit who was Chaplain and lived in a separate flat adjoining the teaching staff's accommodation. He was a lovely, gentle priest. I remember that he introduced me to *The Tablet*, the weekly Catholic periodical, which he left outside my door every week when he had read it. I also remember Percy, who was the School caretaker and looked after security. He and his wife and family lived in a house near the teaching staff's quarters and they had a large Alsatian, Jock, who was very fierce and struck terror into the hearts of many people although he was easily controlled by Percy's young children.

I well remember some of the girls I taught. The most distinguished was Gay Horton, who became S. Margaret Mary – little did any of us think that the eager young teenager would one day lead the School. Others I remember were Vicky Fletcher, Francy and Margie Reid, Ciaran Madden, who became an actress, and Vivien Lee. Helen Petre and Winnie Cardis were also pupils, although both were older.

The girl I remember above all others, however, was Flindy Atkinson. She was about 13 when she was diagnosed with leukaemia and, beyond the care of Matron Peterson, she was taken to Chelmsford Hospital. There was not a great deal that could be done for leukaemia in the 1950s and, after much suffering, Flindy died. As her parents were in Germany, with her father in the army and constantly moving around, they requested Flindy be buried at New Hall in the Community's cemetery. Flindy's Requiem Mass in the School Chapel was solemn and unforgettable. After the Mass, we all walked in procession with the coffin to the burial ground. It was a sad day but we were consoled by the fact that Flindy's suffering was over and we hoped that she had gone straight to Heaven.

I left New Hall in 1957 and since then I have only been back twice, once for a reunion and once for a three-day retreat in the Barn led by S.M.Stephen. While there, I was privileged to be allowed to visit Mother Margaret Helen who was then ill in the Infirmary, and we both enjoyed reminiscing.

Two things I have never forgotten among so many happy memories – the sense of joy and happiness in the School of both Community and girls, and also the big clock in the tower which struck the hour half an hour before it arrived as well as striking once between every quarter. On my first night at the School I thought time had gone mad.

I am very active in my parish in Eastbourne. After writing a history of Catholicism in Eastbourne from the Middle Ages, I read for a degree in Divinity at Maryvale, the Catholic Theology College in Birmingham, becoming the oldest student they had. I am now a catechist for the RCIA in the parish, a reader, and a member of the Catholic Women's League and St Vincent de Paul.

STEPHANIE LAWRENCE (née Jackson)

Pole 1953–1958

I came to New Hall from Goodings, which had moved to Denford where we had often gone to ride and pick snowdrops for Ruth Wade to sell at Covent Garden to raise funds. After Goodings, New Hall seemed very big. I did the flowers in the Guest Room and Ambulacrum for several years and looked after the guests. I spent many happy hours in the Green Room making costumes for plays which meant I avoided prep. I remember the great flu outbreak and being the eldest about downstairs, I had to organise an awful lot of things as we were short of nuns and staff.

I remember I sang so out of tune that I was not allowed to sing in the Chapel!

I spent three years in Australia before returning to England and working for Fenella Jeffcock's family. I married John Lawrence in 1966 and we farmed until 1985, when we moved to where we are now. I had two daughters and a son, who is now deceased, and have four grandchildren.

ROZANNE (Hippo) BARTON (née Lowe)

1954–1957

As I was 13 on arrival at New Hall for the summer term of 1954 it might have been difficult not to feel an outsider with everyone having formed their friendships, but of course the New Hall spirit prevailed and I quickly felt not at all lonely.

There were only 99 Fishes then, although my School number was 106. I discovered the yummy crusty bread with butter and jam. I couldn't have enough of it, and went from a skinny girl from Kenya to eleven stone in too short a time, thus acquiring the nickname Hippo!

The 1955 summer half-term I stayed at New Hall, which was such enormous fun as we were allowed unlimited freedom. A crowd of us, including Bunting (Zelie Morris), Tessa Crimmin, Peela (Angela Peel), Willy Earle, Ponty (Virginia Pontifex), Arna (Anna Plowden), Win (Cardis), Sheila (Dalgliesh?), Tink Jowett, Helly Petre and Lice Trappes-Lomax, all went down to the farm on a perfect summer's day with Pluto (the School dog). I spied the pond, some drums and some bits of wood and rope. We all went to work and ended up with what we thought was a fine raft. I climbed aboard – some bright spark (I think it was Bunting) insisted on attaching a life line – and I launched off

Girls on the farm

Senior Common Room

into the deep amid cheers. Short-lived triumph ended in disaster – it was not as stable as I had planned (I later married a naval architect to prevent a repetition). The drums filled, the raft sank and I climbed out in a very wet and muddy Art Room smock. Pluto enjoyed the scene, rushing around the bushes barking with delight. On slinking back through the West Wing door, I encountered S.M.Dismas who gave me one of her raised-eyebrow smiles and asked if I realised that pond was the School sewer. Was it, I now wonder?!

I climbed the water-tower with Trisha Crispin one night, and we flash-photographed each other smoking to prove it, but the most interesting night was when we went through the Art Room hatch into the roof and ventured right along to the 'other side', where we found some trunks stored. We opened one, shone a torch – and I found an album with a photo of my mother captioned 'Cow Campbell [because of her big brown eyes and long eyelashes] and Betty Cantopher'. We also ran around the roof after climbing out of the Cockloft skylight to enjoy the view from the parapets.

We swatted for our GCEs in the Cockloft. For about ten days before our exams we could all choose where to go and revise, and Lizzie Marriner and I reckoned we chose the best possible place. We really did swot hard, testing each other periodically – with the *1812 Overture* as stimulating background music (the Piano Room was beneath us), and I seem to remember it paid off!

The excitement of doing the Duke of Perth, and all the other Scottish dances, culminated in the thrilling evening when a boys' school dancing team was invited.

I dream of those wonderful hazy, lazy days of summer when the sun always shone, and we played tennis on the Cedar Plot amid the smell of newly mown grass.

Lacrosse we played on Six Acres – and I remember the day we played a boys' school: they led at half-time because they tucked their lax sticks under their arms and were difficult to tackle, while we played like the young ladies we were. After a half-time discussion we played dirty too – and tripped them up with our sticks! I can still remember the looks of horror on the faces of the nuns watching on the sidelines, but St Trinian's New Hall won!

We'd ride the New Hall Dragon – well, just sat on him – and gaze at the beauty of the Tudor building and the cedar trees.

Dear Miss Boyle, who taught us Latin (my favourite subject), would call out, 'Now *who* is that looking out of the window?' She would ask a question, look around the room, point at someone on her left but look at someone on her right, and say: 'Yes, *you* dear,' to get two of us answering, which really creased us up.

I played the part of Bolingbroke in our Sixth Form production of *Richard II*, with Ann Feighan as Richard – still my favourite Shake-speare play with all the best speeches which I have off by heart.

I remember making stink bombs with S.M.Martha in the Science Lab and having interesting and hilarious exchanges with S.M.Magd-alene and others in the Linen Room, putting the world to rights.

Any books brought into the School were checked and censored: I remember taking one entitled *Boldness Be My Friend* (a war story) to my Housemistress who threw it across the room exclaiming, 'And that is absolute filth. Have you read the bit about the coal mines yet?' No, I assured her. Years later, while cleaning the Head's study, I found the book (with my name in it) in her glass-fronted corner bookcase and retrieved it!

I was thrilled to be asked by Penny Gilbey to be her sponsor at her Confirmation. How I yearned to be 'made' in the Sodality! Everyone,

Confirmation group in the early 1950s, with Fr Butler (centre right)

but everyone, had medals or Asp ribbons except me (I wonder why?!). I longed to have the weekday medal on a cord that I could flick between my fingers like all the other Fishes. The week before I left, I became a Child of Mary, and I suspect S.M.Dismas, who was sympathetic, was probably instrumental. What joy! And I have said the prayer that came on the prayer card with the picture of Our Lady of New Hall ever since. It was right psychology and I left intending to be a better person, effectively banishing latent rebelliousness without curbing my restless energy.

CIARAN TYLER (née Madden)

1954–1959

I dream about New Hall once every two or three years. It generally involves high-speed running down the stone stairs from dormitories to classrooms. I was very happy there thanks mainly to the sweet-natured and good-humoured nuns. They were mostly young and English and used words and colloquialisms for everyday life that took some getting used to.

All my memories are cheerful ones – a couple stand out. Once, on a free afternoon, over a weekend, we were told we had to stay in and do extra prep. Rather disgruntled, we filed back into our classrooms to find our desks cleared away, a screen and projector rigged up and Greer Garson and Laurence Olivier waiting for us in *Pride and Prejudice*.

On another occasion, there was an inexplicable moment which found Mother Margaret Helen the Headmistress throwing handfuls of toffees out of her study window as the post-breakfast obligatory Runners Round trotted underneath. This was doubly charming because of her other-times stern demeanour.

The emphasis in those days was different. The success of the only Oxbridge candidate resulted in a whole-day's holiday for the School. Her subject was Spanish – as was her mother!

VICKY FLETCHER

1954–1958

When I was in Class One, I remember that at prep time in the evening, instead of working for the full-time, S.M.Dismas would take us up to the Lady Chapel where, if we had been good, she would read to us from books like *The Blue Flower*, *The Happy Prince* or *The King's Invisible Clothes*.

The Pageant – with Angela Morris as Henry VIII

For a treat on Saturday evenings, the whole School would get changed and come down in our dressing-gowns to sit on the steps down to the Ambulacrum. There we would listen to records of light classical music such as Gounod's 'Ave Maria', or 'Oh For The Wings Of A Dove', and even lighter music such as the album *Echoes Of My Fair Lady*, where each song was arranged in the way a famous composer would have arranged it. I have managed to get the record on the Internet after years of looking for it.

A different happy occasion was at the Easter half-term when instead of going home we stayed at School. Each house did a Tableau. Fishers did a hospital featuring an operation, for which we all dressed up in white sheets. And another time we did a guillotine scene out of *A Tale of Two Cities* with some girls crouching beneath the classroom desks with only their heads showing. I was Madame Defarge, sitting by the guillotine knitting with the hair of the corpses.

PATRICIA (Mary) IGNARSKI (née Schofield)

1958–1961

Things I loved:

– Plainsong, and learning how to sing it. It was taught by S.M.Francis. I don't think many of us admitted to liking it when we first started, but it grew on me, and now I love hearing it sung.

– Tuck Shop on Saturdays. I used to return to School with about £2 to last the term. S.M.Thérèse who ran the Tuck Shop, also tried to teach us Maths. We were supposed to ration ourselves to a few sweets a day, but my recollection is of 'pigging out' over the weekend with none left for the rest of the week.

– Sunday evenings in the Library. We would bring our eiderdowns to the Library and listen to records, sitting together and nattering with music in the background. I first heard Eartha Kitt singing *I'm Just An Old-Fashioned Girl*, and *Autumn Leaves* and *Smoke Gets In Your Eyes*, and these songs are all bound up in my memory of those Library nights.

– Swimming in the summer. Although the water in the outdoor swimming-pool was freezing I always looked forward to these sessions. We were allowed our own costumes (no bikinis), but had to wear

The outdoor swimming-pool was built in the 1950s

those ridiculous rubber swimming caps that made us look as if we were wearing eggshells on our heads.

– Learning to smoke! This of course was absolutely forbidden. A few of us managed to slip out of sight for the odd ciggy at weekends. To start with I wasn't included in the group but remember vividly an invitation to join in, which felt a great honour. Some of these clandestine sessions took place in Our Lady's Grotto.

– Watching films at weekends. The School was supplied regularly with good films, which I think was because Michelle Frankovitch, daughter of Mike Frankovitch (boss of Columbia Pictures?), was a pupil. I recall watching *High Society* and *Pal Joey*. Occasionally the nuns would hold a private viewing beforehand to see if the film was suitable for us.

– Chemistry classes (the only subject I was any good at). Chemistry was taught by S.M.Martha, who had been a student at London University.

Things I disliked:

– Having my nails inspected before needlework. I didn't like needlework (still don't) and I especially didn't like having to line up to have a nail inspection, knowing that I would be in trouble for biting them.

– The horrid hand-bell announcing that it was time to get up in the mornings, especially cold mornings. You could hear this bell tinkling

148

in the distance, knowing that it was only a matter of minutes before the person ringing it reached your dormitory.

– Scottish dancing. Enough said.

– Jasper, the School dog (a Gordon setter). I actually liked him, but the trouble was he had this habit of shaking his head and depositing strings of slobber all over you.

– Only being allowed to phone home about once a term.

– Not having enough baths – one every few days and then in not very hot water.

– Having to eat tripe once. Mass hysteria and rebellion broke out and the horrible stuff never appeared again.

Looking back it was a good and happy experience. The number of pupils was only just over a hundred and we knew everyone by name.

My parents died not long after I left New Hall and I immediately entered the Diplomatic Service on the lowest rung of the career ladder, ending up in Peking during the Cultural Revolution. I took leave to go to Cambridge University, married Jonathan and worked for the BBC World Service. In my early forties I had two children, Sophie and Marina. I made a number of good friends at New Hall and while some have got lost along the way, Patsy (Wells-Hunt, née Law) remained a good friend and was godmother to my younger daughter, Marina, until her sad death a few years ago. Our main home is a very small farm on the Isle of Wight.

Bedtime

RUTH RAVEN

Teacher 1956–1991

In 1956 I heard from my mother's cousin that there was a vacancy at New Hall. I must admit that until that time, although having lived in mid Essex all my life, I had never heard of the School. With great trepidation I applied to S. Margaret Helen, Headmistress – the trepidation was because my family was staunchly nonconformist and I had had no contact with *nuns*!

I need not have worried. S. Margaret Helen was charming and not at all daunting. We walked up the Beech Walk and chatted of this and that and I was shown the Gym, netball-court and two hard tennis-courts, and Six Acres which was the lacrosse pitch in winter and some grass tennis-courts in summer. S. Margaret Helen said that she would like to employ me, but could I please send her some testimonials and names and addresses of a couple of referees, together with a letter of application, 'just for the record'!

Old Fishes v. present Fishes – after tennis

S.M.Ignatius
Sketch done by Old Fish Georgina Palmer, née Butler

The School at that time consisted of 120 girls (all boarders), three resident teaching staff and the Community.

I had 35 very happy years as the School got larger and my role changed gradually from full-time teaching of Games and PE to being Senior Mistress.

I would like to thank the Community for their unfailing support, particularly my four Headmistresses – S. Margaret Helen, S.M.Ignatius, S.M.Francis and S. Margaret Mary.

The 1960s

What's going on in the world during the 1960s

The average price of a house was £2,530 and of a loaf of bread 5p / Cold War / Bay of Pigs / Vietnam / Labour in government under Harold Wilson / Swinging Sixties generation of fashion and pop

Twiggy

1960 Doc Marten boots / *Lady Chatterley* trial / Roy Orbison 'Only The Lonely' / Elvis Presley 'It's Now Or Never'

1961 Yuri Gagarin becomes first man in space / Elvis Presley 'Are You Lonesome Tonight'

1962 The audio cassette invented / Beatles 'Love Me Do' / Cliff Richard 'The Young Ones' / Elvis Presley 'Return To Sender'

1963 John Profumo MP resigns / Great Train Robbery / *Dr Who* arrives on BBC / Assassination of John F. Kennedy / Cliff Richard 'Summer Holiday' / Beatles 'I Want To Hold Your Hand'

1964 Nelson Mandela imprisoned / Radio Caroline broadcasts / *Sun* newspaper launched / Cilla Black 'Anyone Who Had A Heart' / Beatles 'A Hard Day's Night' / Manfred Mann 'Do Wah Diddy Diddy' / Roy Orbison 'Oh, Pretty Woman'

1965 *The Sound of Music* released / Post Office Tower opens / Funeral of Winston Churchill / Byrds 'Mr Tambourine Man' / Walker Brothers 'Make It Easy On Yourself' / Beatles 'Day Tripper' and 'We Can Work It Out' / The Who 'My Generation'

1966 England wins the football World Cup / Twiggy appears / *A Man for All Seasons* awarded six Oscars / Nancy Sinatra 'These Boots Are Made For Walking' / Frank Sinatra 'Strangers In The Night' / Beatles 'Paperback Writer' / Beach Boys 'Good Vibrations'

Left: Virginia Maskell in The Pageant in 1964

1967 First heart transplant by Dr Christian Barnard / BBC 2 colour / Jeremy Thorpe Liberal leader / Sir Francis Chichester sails *Gypsy Moth IV* single-handed round the world / Homosexuality decriminalised / Monkees 'I'm A Believer' / Sandie Shaw 'Puppet On A String' / Kinks 'Waterloo Sunset'

1968 Ford Escort replaces the Anglia / *Joseph and the Amazing Technicolor Dreamcoat* / Enoch Powell 'Rivers of Blood' speech / First Isle of Wight Festival / Louis Armstrong 'What A Wonderful World' / Beatles 'Hey Jude' / Scaffold 'Lily The Pink'

1969 First men on the Moon (Apollo 11) / Beatles last public performance / Bernadette Devlin in Ireland / *Monty Python* first episode / Marmalade 'Ob-La-Di Ob-La-Da' / Fleetwood Mac 'Albatross' / Marvin Gaye 'I Heard It Through The Grapevine' / Desmond Dekker & the Aces 'Israelites' / Rolling Stones 'Honky Tonk Woman' / Jane Birkin & Serge Gainsbourg 'Je T'Aime . . . Moi Non Plus' / Rolf Harris 'Two Little Boys'

What's going on at New Hall during the 1960s

New Hall continued to expand during this decade. The 1963 block went up; the Pavilion was demolished and Beaulieu was built; Science classrooms were created; the little gardens were grassed over; and at that time what is now the North Room was the Junior Home before it became the School Refectory (and then the Community Refectory).

Many Community members were working in the School, with key leadership roles taken by S.M.Ignatius, S.M.Dolores, S.M.Dismas, S.M.Francis, S.M.Martha and S.M.Thérèse

During this decade the Community decided to close the Junior School at Denford and to consolidate numbers at New Hall. In 1967 New Hall welcomed back Community members who had been based in Berkshire, and also pupils from Denford who were given a new base in Beaulieu.

Performing Arts at New Hall were very important and this decade saw the flourishing of The Pageant, starring Virginia Maskell and including music written by David Fanshawe.

The winds of change were blowing in society and new attitudes in the Church during these years were reflected in pupils' preoccupation with *Top of the Pops* and mini skirts!

ANNE HAWARD

Head of Classics 1957–1987

In 1957 the School must have numbered under 150, small enough to kneel for assembly on the cold tiles of the Ambulacrum and to line up in class ranks after break and lunch. As the School grew the versatility of the rooms in the old part of the buildings was amazing. Each autumn term brought fresh surprises. Where would the Sixth Form classroom and the Staff Room be this year? The East Wing probably holds the record for the most metamorphoses and the walls have echoed to Maths, Latin, Home Economics and Science. Dormitories became Homes, became classrooms, became exam hall. The opening of the first extension was marked with a Mass and lunch for the great and good; the lesser and not so good, who acted as waitresses, were found to be somewhat 'tired' after the guests departed. They had decided the way to clear up was to drain all glasses!

Anne Haward (right)

155

In my first years there was a delightful attitude that put celebrations of Ascension, Corpus Christi, St Francis Day (with the whole School's cuddly animals assembled on the front stairs) before teaching, but over time an increasing number of Lay staff began to mutter about lessons missed close to public exams. For big theatre productions, however, the timetable went out of the window and who is to say they were not worth it. The unforgettable Pageant of New Hall with Virginia Maskell seemed to take up every minute. Work must have gone on, for as well as playing a memorable Lady Margaret Pole, Elizabeth Butler achieved a place at Oxford, and academically this marked a change to more ambitious aims for the Sixth Form. Other outstanding dramatic performances included those of Denise Turner as More in *A Man for All Seasons*, Francesca Bedford as Hermione in *The Winter's Tale*, Fiona Adler in the title role of *Antigone*.

Inevitably major changes came with the growth of the School. No longer were nicknames obligatory (Gabriella Wizniewska had become G.Whiz within minutes of arrival) and the switch to subject rooms brought more formality to lessons. There was no more Latin in a practising room which the students were painting bright pink at the weekends. Most notably, the introduction of the tutor system meant that the easy relationship between teacher and pupil (the feature I most valued at New Hall) continued and flourished.

I still live in Essex, writing and Church Recording.

VERONICA HARRIS (née Capps)

1960–1971

We lived in Ireland. My mother had been to the Sacred Heart Convent, Roehampton, but for me my aunt chose Denford – she went on a recce and found the grass was well worn and there was a Riding School; she thought I'd fit in.

In 1964 I left Denford for New Hall. I remember waiting for the level-crossing gates and driving up the Avenue with my parents towards a magical place marked by cedar trees . . . Here life was a mixture of challenges and support – both were readily available. Life outside the classroom was cosy. I remember watching a 32mm film starring Stewart Granger, in the Hall snuggled up under eiderdowns. *Young Bess* was amazing – I'd like to see it again.

In the Sixth Year I was elected Head Girl. It may have been a controversial decision as I'd had a slightly chequered career and was not exactly academic. While I enjoyed the drama, I totally adhered to the ethos of the school.

The most amazing memory I have was the Autumn Ball, November 1970. It was a fund-raising event and as Sixth Formers we were co-hosts with the Community. It was hard to believe that our School was going to be so utterly transformed: the Quad was to be a 'Romantic Garden'; the Sid Phillips Orchestra was playing in the Hall; there was a disco in a classroom! A world was unfolding.

Just before the evening started, our Headmistress, S.M.Francis, announced that we could not avail ourselves of a glass at the champagne reception or of any drink in the multiple bars and we could not smoke! This was horrendous – we were over 18! The evening began. I was placed between the Prioress (S.M.Christopher) and S.M.Francis. My dress had been purchased in Chelmsford: I had been taken by a member of the Community to get something more suitable than the one planned! I felt a little bit like a meringue.

Music and champagne flowed as everyone moved towards the dinner. In spite of the ban, we had easy access to drink; parents we knew were very obliging. After dinner we students did a cabaret for the guests. I still have a photograph. My song was a re-take of a Joyce Grenfell number: 'I went to school in Chelmsford; where the cedar trees are shady . . . ' I sat on a bar stool smoking a cigarette in a holder – it was a prop! The evening continued – an incredible blend of the adult world you wanted to enter and the disco which you felt was your territory. I remember Mike O'Riordan – he was the DJ – and at one stage in the evening we were under the table getting acquainted.

The post-mortem was rigorous. I had to wait on a bench to see S.M.Francis. S.M.Christopher swooped into the Ambulacrum, her words to all of us I can quote verbatim: 'It will take every minute of every hour of every day until you leave to make up for what you have done!' I was demoted for three months. The Deputy Head Girl, Tony

Kavanagh, was my substitute. I did my penance and after three months I was reinstated as Head Girl. As I look back on this event, as a teacher in a Community School in Tipperary, I realise that I learnt an enormous lesson. I know that students are not their behaviour and I give my students every chance to move on from mistakes.

Veronica Capps in cabaret at the 1970s Ball

SUE STOKOE (née Carter)

1957–1963

I have many happy memories of New Hall. The Great Feast; doing a Tableau of Julius Caesar with lots of desks piled up and covered with sheets for the White Cliffs of Dover; lying on the Cedar Plot in the sun revising for exams; working with S.M.Bernadette in our little gardens.

I remember lots and lots of cleaning which, I have to say, has stood me in good stead. Stripping the beds and turning the mattresses and our 'run' down to the Lodge every morning after breakfast.

I've always been thankful to my parents who made sacrifices to send me to New Hall, and to all of the Community who made those years so memorable.

SARAH CICCHETTI (née Grindon-Welch)

1967–1974

New Hall was not only a school to me but also a second home. I dreamed of it often when I left – and occasionally still do.

That magnificent approach down the Avenue, the straight drive of lime trees acknowledging my arrival, both they and I growing a little

'Coppelia' in 1974 with Angie Prysor-Jones, Serena Debono, Jane Hennessy and Sarah Grindon-Welch

taller every year. There was a sense of welcome in the long arms of those royal cedars and the gorgeous Tudor Palace – I was a part of this historic place.

The Ambulacrum with its red-tiled floor, always highly polished, and the dark oak table to one side. S.M.Francis's room was to the left. Through into Aloysius Corridor and either down East or West Wing or over the old creaking floorboards towards the Refectory and that beautiful Chapel. Across the iron-grated floor, with pipes beneath reverberating to the tread of decades of school feet, shod with clicking Idlers, and on towards the wooden Figure on the Cross. I spent hours in the Chapel, directing so many prayers towards the Man on the Cross that it must have become imbued with my entreaties; it was a place made sacred by the devotion and the faith of so many.

I loved ballet and danced throughout my time at New Hall, even down the Avenue with Serena Debono, my lifelong friend. Mrs Ashcroft, elegant, ramrod straight, beautifully turned out, was always encouraging and keen for us to grasp opportunities. Apart from the discipline of making my body do things it resisted doing and not minding being called 'pea brain' by Miss Mitchell because I could not remember the routines that she danced out for us (I loved Miss Mitchell), I felt spurred on by their humour and muted kindness, I have two particular memories of what dance gave to me. *Coppelia* is one. I danced one of the friends, with Serena and Jane Hennessy. Sandra Debono was the doll, Sue Hennessy, Swanilda, and Karen Quinn played Dr Coppelius. All those rehearsals, the putting together and learning of steps to music, the costumes, make-up, lighting, the individual and group performances, all knitted together to create the story. At the centre of it all was the life of the Green Room. This was a hub of creativity, excitement, nerves and triumph; it was the sanctum out of which we stepped on to the stage. The other memory is of our taking a train to London every Saturday to attend a class at the Royal Academy of Dance in Kensington. There we glimpsed some well-known dancers and Sue and Jane Hennessy were accepted by RAD after they finished at New Hall. Despite my enthusiasm I was never good enough. Serena still does ballet, and has just been accepted by the Royal Academy to do a teaching course, forty years later – and it all started at New Hall.

I remember midnight feasts in the little chapel in Beaulieu, walks in the beautiful grounds, talks with friends, sadness and tragedies – the walled cemetery and little Emma. I remember escaping to the Art Room and S.M.Stephen when things became too much, an escape for a number of students I seem to remember, our little oasis at the top of the old house. Or not quite at the top because on the next floor up and taking in some of the depth of the same floor was the room of pianos, with cubicles in which small or great cantatas were played; another place of escape.

Living in our Houses gave us a sense of family. I was always an Owen, with S. Angela, S.M.Mark, S.M.Gabriel and Miss Impey as our House Mothers. S.M.Christopher was Mother Prioress and S.M.Magdalene was in charge of the Infirmary, which was another oasis because she was always so kind and approachable. There were many other Sister Marys I think of with fondness – Dismas, Andrew, Peter, David (Rose), Thérèse.

I had wonderful and inspirational teachers – particularly Mrs Jones (English) and Jean Hall (History of Art). There were the struggles and rewards of friendships, study, responsibilities – New Hall was a world within the world, real Life. I learned so many of the lessons that have helped me to live my own life. It gave me the philosophy and ethics I depend on. It taught me self-reliance. It helped me understand individual struggle and that we are all the same and also all different.

With day girls and boys now, it is good to know that the School is still doing well and that its main ethos continues to sustain successive generations. I feel sad the Community no longer lives on site, but I know that it is still connected to the School. I feel a sense of being defined by having spent my formative years in that beautiful place.

I did a degree in the History of Art and Psychology. I have four grown-up children and four grandchildren. I taught for the National Childbirth Trust for a number of years, while the children were small, before doing my Midwifery training and am still a midwife 18 years later. I have also done a number of Counselling qualifications and have fitted in volunteer counselling between work and family life – which becomes busier by the day.

School photo (with dog) at New Hall (1960–1)

CHARLOTTE WOOD (née Strutt)

1958–1963

On my arrival at New Hall I was immediately nicknamed 'Charlie' by S.M.Francis. I had arrived in the summer term because my sister Sarah was ill and, much to my fury, I was kept down the following term to be with my peer group. I took my revenge by never doing any work until I left – with just two O Levels!

I realised that the only way to get out of school was to be in a sports team and/or in a singing group. I managed to become part of the 2nd lacrosse team and to join the Choir. I particularly loved plainsong, and singing in choirs has remained with me ever since. When I was 15, in my final term, a few of us decided that we had to do something 'wicked' so we sat in the Ha-Ha instead of going to Benediction, which was my most favourite service. I don't think anyone noticed.

As an Anglican I shall always be grateful for being at a Roman Catholic Convent. There were 10 of us Anglicans, I think, and no concessions were made; we had to go to all services, just like the RCs, but of course we couldn't go to Confession or Communion. But on All Souls' Night, our prayers for the Souls of the Dead counted just as much.

Trip to Rome in the 1960s. Left to right back: Lavinia Scott, Sally Harben, Elizabeth Butler, Corinne Montgomerie, Francesca Bedford Front: Paula Lebono, S.M.Martha, Sarah Leyden, Lucinda Buxton, Sally Payton, Pam Ferrier

Gymnastics

NICKY SYKES (née Strutt)

1959–1963

I remember the smell of supper as we came through the front door into the Ambulacrum at the beginning of term: meat and cabbage, though it can't always have been, cooked up in those huge industrial catering urns.

Old iron bedsteads with a huge dip in the middle. No chance of ever rolling over and falling out.

S.M.Martha doing her stint in the cubicle off that funny little room on the landing at the top of the front stairs, which for some reason had a sign hanging from the light switch that said 'No Egg-zit', with a picture of an egg! If you were unlucky enough to need the loo in the night, negotiating your way across creaking floorboards and hearing that never-to-be-forgotten voice: 'Who's that?'

Running down the flipping Avenue, cradling a flipping lacrosse ball because the flipping games pitches were too flipping wet. The Avenue trees were saplings then.

The marvellous full and fun weekends. We felt we were the lucky ones. Oodles of young nuns in the Community, all very involved and very committed. Everything was accessible: art rooms, needlework, roller-skating, almost any activity you could think of, all before 'elf and safety and insurance premiums came along.

Best of all, the close-knit atmosphere. There were 90 or so of us when I arrived at New Hall and a few over 100 when I left. The whole school knew each other by name. We ate, slept, worked, played and prayed all in the same building.

The Litany of the Saints, sung on All Souls' Day, went on for hours. *Ora pro nobis.* I still love the sound of plainchant, church organs and church singing.

Book check at the end of every term – woe betide you if you had lost, mislaid or marked a textbook. S.M.Martha and that voice again.

The sign 'Adder at Work' on S.M.Ignatius's office door when she was totting up the internal exam marks (before calculators or computers).

Frances Amor getting 100% for her Maths exam. Elizabeth Butler ('Butty') coming top in most exams, in spite of reading racy (it was the '60s) novels on her lap during all lessons. And I should know, I sat next to her! She was the only one to pass Latin O Level that year.

Listening to records in the Library, in our pyjamas with our rugs or eiderdowns all over the floor. Ah–h–h–h, happy days!

VERONICA (Martini) CELDER-MARTIN
(née Martin)

Denford and More 1961–1968

Coming from Denford to New Hall we were the youngest and therefore had no responsibility, which the class above noticed, particularly when we all used to play rowdy games in the Gym after supper.

There was a lot of building in the 1960s and sometimes our classroom was the space between the piano-practice cubicles or in a sewing room between the Science Labs. We were streamed with fewer than 10 in a class and when I first arrived there was a marking system for Order, Conduct, Games and Work.

School trips were the only time we left New Hall. At the Tower of London our guide was Monsignor Goulder and the only interesting thing he told us was how the English martyrs wrote notes in invisible ink, using the juice of oranges. Once we went to Walberswick, where S.M.Thérèse strode right out to the end of the ruined pier, her habit flying in the wind, with all of us gleefully following her, something my parents had strictly forbidden us to do! We had other outings to pick blackberries for supper

We had the Latin Mass, which meant endless plainsong practice. There was a procession round the grounds for Corpus Christi, with children strewing petals in front of the Host, and stops at altars here and there, where we would kneel down and get up without brushing the grass cuttings off our knees. In Class I there was a craze for jacks, which we played all through Mass, until we were told to stop because of the noise of the jacks being thrown on the floor.

There were two gangs, the Big Gang and the Little Gang, based on how tall you were. I refused to be in either. It did not, however, stop me from being bullied for wearing a red ribbon on my ugly plastic hair slide, which I only took off for sports day at Miss Raven's bidding.

The Art Room was my refuge. It was a wonderful Aladdin's Cave of exciting things to do and beautiful books to look at. We beat copper, twisted wrought iron (my weathercock still does its job!) and worked with stained glass or clay, in addition to painting and drawing.

I did not mind wearing uniform because it was cherry red and I did not care about clothes anyway. In fact, when a few of us stayed on an extra term to take our Oxbridge exams, we were told we could wear home clothes – but we decided it was easier not to. We sat those exams in the Guest Room by the front door and what a fuss they made of us! We had sandwiches halfway through.

We used to have to walk down to Ockie's cottage every morning before breakfast and before A Levels I would walk down revising the *Aeneid*, Book Six, until I had the translation almost off by heart. One year we had a Canadian Games teacher on exchange who introduced cross-country running. In Class VI there was a choice of fencing or judo. I remember someone so intent on putting her opponent on the floor that she did not realise her trousers were round her knees!

There were clubs. I was one of three in the photography club,

Nuns at prayer in the Choir

developing in the dark room at the back of the Pottery Room. There was a debating society run by Mother Margaret Helen and we had debates with the local boys' school, the first organised contact with boys. No socialising or dancing, though.

S.M.Francis, our Headmistress, was very much in charge. She would come down the East Wing rooms saying goodnight to each of us and was amused once to find me listening to *Parliament Today* on my radio: I was taking my civic education very seriously!

For my first few years, we were woken up by S.M.Martha coming round ringing a large cow-bell, saying, 'Blessed be God,' and we had to answer, 'Praised be Jesus Christ.' At shut-down, it was, 'Father into Thy hands I commend my spirit,' to which we answered, 'Lord Jesus, receive my soul.' Lesson changes were marked by a girl ringing a large hand-bell, a task I observed carefully for when my time came – but it never did as we got the electric bell.

Building never seemed to cease, with the increase in numbers. The Community habit was simplified and we saw nuns' hair for the first time. We had more and more Lay teachers and even a man! Mr de Stacpoole taught History. Miss Smith, later Mrs Marquina, my Spanish teacher, inspired in me a lifelong love of Spain and everything Spanish and it is still my favourite language to speak. My best subject was Latin, for Mrs Haward's lessons were always lively and interesting. She would draw stick-men in battle formation on the board and we had long philosophical discussions after translating a couple of lines of Cicero. We had some good discussions too in S.M.Simon's lessons on religion. It was also a time of great changes in the Church. I remember writing an essay in favour of keeping Latin for the Mass.

After leaving, I went to Cambridge to read Modern (Spanish and Russian) and Medieval Languages. I became a conference interpreter, interpreting for the UN in Geneva. Spanish is my favourite language to work from.

EILEEN (Mouse) CRONK (née Andrews)
Pole 1961–1968

I have great memories of the summer term 1964, spent in preparation for the New Hall School Pageant (I still have the programme). Virginia Maskell and her husband, the photographer Geoffrey Shakerley, came to live at New Hall for a time with their two little boys, and one evening to my utter delight (I have always been besotted with babies), I was chosen to help look after them and spent a very happy hour helping to put the boys to bed.

During my Sixth-Form years, I remember relishing a greater degree of freedom. On one occasion in 1968, Geraldine Kirk (Jing – who became Lady Inglis of Glencorse), who was a keen motor-racing fan, borrowed her sister's Mini and drove four of us to Stratford-upon-Avon to see Eric Porter famously appearing in *King Lear*, with an overnight stay at Henrietta (Henny) Hudson's grandmother's house. Credit to our Headmistress, S.M.Francis, for allowing us out for what (in those days) seemed a very daring 'first'. No mobile phones, no seat belts then.

Henny Hudson was a very good friend of mine throughout my time at New Hall. I remember our first dormitory – Angels – and long chats in the Music Practice Rooms; serious sessions going through our stamp collections, and walks down to the farm to see the bull – Henny was a farmer's daughter so had a great deal to tell me! Some nuns did not approve of our friendship and tried to separate us, saying we were a bad influence on one another (we certainly weren't naughty – far too fearful to be so).

I made so many good friends at New Hall – among them, in addition to Henny and Jing, are Mary Clare Gribbon (née Baillieu), who is godmother to my eldest daughter, and Belinda Mitchell (née Ponsonby), who is godmother to my second daughter (as I am to her eldest son). We see one another rarely, but when we do meet, we pick up straight away from where we left off.

I worked for the Crown Agents in Bahrain, at David Greig in London and as a Personal Assistant at Rank Xerox. I married Julian in 1974 and have three lovely children and two granddaughters so far. I owned and ran a garden-toy business for many years while my children were growing up, and then took a degree in History of Art (First Class Honours!) at the University of Kent, and for over 15 years have run an antiques business from home.

Dancing in the Gym

GILLY YARROW (née Clarke)

Pole 1961–1968

My chief memories revolve around the fantastic productions I was happily involved in under the gifted Drama teacher, Sheila McGovern (not that we always saw eye to eye!). Productions like *The Vigil*, in which I played Mary Magdalene, and *The Winter's Tale*, in which I took the part of Leontes, opposite Francesca Bedford as Hermione, awakened in me a love of acting and public speaking that has been invaluable over the years.

However, the most memorable of all the performances staged by the school was The Pageant, which traced the history of the building and all that it had witnessed over the centuries. The costumes were fabulous, (I remember S.M.Benedict stitching away in the Green Room) and the star narrator was an Old Fish, Virginia Maskell. Her husband was a hugely handsome and successful photographer and, needless to say, we all lusted after him! Imagine my surprise when at a dinner party in Portugal last year I found myself sitting next to him! His memories and affection for New Hall and the nuns could not have been warmer if he had been an Old Fish himself.

After a BA Hons at Cardiff, then a PGCE at Kings College London, I spent the next nine years teaching history in a London comprehensive. I married Alan Yarrow in 1975 and we had two boys, Max and Guy. Max turned out to have special needs so I gave up hope of returning to work and instead got involved in local schools as Governor for Special Needs and Chair of Governors of Finton House School. Now I'm a fundraiser for Mencap, chairing an Events Committee for them. My husband of 36 years, Alan, is currently Sheriff of the City of London and we spend much of our week living at the Old Bailey with our Labrador, Nala.

HENRIETTA (Henny) McMILLAN-SCOTT
(née Hudson)

Campion 1961–1968

My first memory is of arriving and being told by Jo Cavanagh, Deputy Head Girl, that they had heard about me and would be keeping a close eye on me! (I had been at Denford Park, the Prep School.) The casual and unintended cruelty of those times I think may have determined the direction of my lifetime career. My final school report, which my mother still has, said I had 'come up under a cloud' – I still do not understand why.

I had the impression the nuns all thought I was going to end up as a drug addict or even worse. I understand the school has changed a lot, but what was not right then was a lack of recognition of the importance of academic achievement. We used to get points for our behaviour – conduct points were the most valuable and I performed dismally – my House was Edmund Campion (the Champions).

The memory that really stands out in my head is of something that happened in 1965, near the end of the term. I ended up being accused by S.M.Francis of 'consorting with local boys'! I subsequently found out that a school-friend of my brother's (they were both at the Oratory) accepted a bet that he could get into a dormitory at New Hall – and the proof would be provided by me who would confirm that he had. Anyway, he managed to get in and the first person he encountered was my friend, Titch. He asked her to take him to me. With some presence of mind Titch directed him out of the building. Needless to say the alarm was raised . . .

As it happened, I had left term early to have a plastic-surgery operation following a car accident. I was at home, and the first I knew about it was my mother waking me up 6.30am saying that S.M.Francis had rung up accusing me of 'consorting with local boys'!

What I cherish is the image, relayed to me by friends, of lots of nuns, wimpled and with their veils flapping in the wind, running round the swimming-pool and then down the Avenue after some adolescent prankster, whose name I cannot remember. No one ever apologised for wrongly accusing me. As it happens, I don't much mind about that,

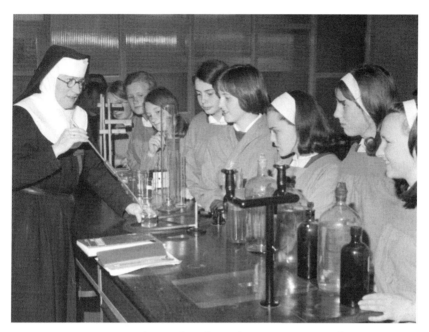

S.M.Martha with girls in the new Science Lab

because it would have been much cooler if I had known about it! I'm sure S.M.Francis thought I would turn out to be a serious renegade.

Eileen (Mouse) Andrews and Geraldine (Jing) Kirk have remained my lifelong friends. Academically I have always done well and am still very active as a working solicitor and appear in courts all over the country.

I have been married for 40 years and have two offspring and a third grandchild on the way. As a consultant solicitor on the Law Society Child-Care Panel, I represent children independently of parents and Local Authorities in care proceedings. Technically I may be an OAP but I am not stopping yet. My husband is Vice-President of the European Parliament with responsibility for Democracy and Human Rights.

PAULINE CROWTHER (S. Pauline)

1961–1968

The 1960s were a magical time. WWII and the dreary years of the 1950s were over.

We saw history being made in the rise of youth and pop culture. The *Six-Five Special* gave way to *Top of the Pops*. Cliff Richard and Elvis gave way to the Beatles and the Rolling Stones. Frocks gave way to the mini skirt and hot pants and nightdresses and Viyella pyjamas gave way to baby dolls and bikinis.

We Baby Boomers wanted it all and we wanted it now! Convent School girls we may have been but we were clued up and we felt the future was ours. We had a really good academic education from both the teaching nuns and from a significant influx of excellent Lay staff. Many of them are still going strong and many of us owe them a debt of gratitude.

New Hall has always had a strong theatrical tradition and the 1960s saw the revival of this powerful influence. The Pageant in 1964 celebrated the granting of the manors round Boreham to the Canons of Waltham Abbey in 1064. The music was written by the late David Fanshawe, the script by the famous children's author Barbara Willard, and the rising actress and Old Fish Virginia Maskell played Perpetua, the 'spirit' of the place. The Gym regained some of its former glory as a replica of the Garrick Theatre, with footlights, proscenium arch and raked stage. The backdrops, costumes and scenery were of the highest excellence. We learnt our stagecraft there. The standard of drama after The Pageant was notably high.

Sitting in the Chapel or in the Ambulacrum we learnt about the Church and the world. We were kept informed of the happenings at Vatican II. We explored the dialogue Mass and we learnt the importance of participation in the Liturgy as the priest turned to face us and we celebrated the Eucharist in English. We were encouraged to develop a mature and questioning conscience. We discussed Martin Luther King, Gandhi and Kennedy and were shaken by their deaths. We were excited by the discovery of DNA and the double helix. We were aware of some of the social issues of the time – housing, poverty, racism – and there was an embryonic NHVS to encourage us to step out of our comfort

The Pageant – finale

zone and visit people in need in the surrounding villages and in Chelmsford. We were marked by these events and opportunities.

The 1960s was a decade of change. We felt we had the best of all worlds: we had all that was good from the past and we had all that was best of the new world opening up to us. We left as well-educated and aware young women able to take our places in society and eager to make a difference.

Once a year chaos reigned! A fire-bell would wake us and we were told it was the Great Feast. No classes! Hare and Hounds with strict bounds and register, extra good food, the Tableaux, which involved begging straw from Mr Furze at the farm, and, at the end of the day, a sing-song in the Ambulacrum. I will never forget S. Philo (Philomena) singing to *In Trinidad There Lived A Family* and *Your Daddy's Not Your Daddy But Your Daddy Doesn't Know.* Younger pupils had soft toys and eiderdowns, and all finally filed up to bed with an individual blessing for each pupil from the Headmistress.

The 1960s may have been a turbulent decade but my years at New Hall left me with an inner serenity and a deep sense of belonging.

I was born in Abadan, Iran. After I left I did Teacher Training, then taught at St John Fisher's, Perivale, and St Bernard's, Slough, before

*entering the Noviciate at New Hall in 1982, taking final vows in 1991. I
did a degree and Masters in Religious Studies and taught at New Hall
until 2006. I now teach in Chelmsford Prison and work in the parish.*

GINA RIPPON

Fisher and Southwell 1961–1968

Having spent the era of the 'swinging sixties' at New Hall, it is sometimes hard to know whether some of my stranger memories are to be
relied on (quite a common dilemma for those looking back on that
decade).

I remember nights in Angels – a bare barn of a dormitory with an
intriguing 'platform' over the corridor which was strictly out of bounds.
S.M.Martha came round every morning with a bell to turf us out of our
beds and on to our knees (definitely not standard practice in the 1960s).

Food figures high in my memories. In later life I saw a TV documentary about a wonderful Essex convent school (New Hall, of course!)
that was at the forefront of all sorts of educational activity and there
was a shot of girls eating chips! 'We were never given chips!' I cried. I
do remember mashed potatoes – with eyes. Puddings were popular –
I'm sure there was a jam roly-poly called 'Reverend Mother's Leg' and I
definitely remember a chocolate pudding called 'Pus and Bunions'.

I have a memory of a whole summer term when we did nothing
but rehearse for The Pageant, even living in our housework overalls
(presumably the laundry nuns had become the wardrobe nuns?) which
meant that we had to be shooed up to the top of Six Acres if ever there
were any visitors. Ginny Maskell, the glamorous 'Spirit of New Hall',
came to live with us all, plus husband, children and dog. Other plays
too – *A Man for All Seasons*, *The Winter's Tale* – all intensely directed
by Miss McGovern.

Lessons? I loved lessons, but I was a shameless 'swot'. Was there really
a member of staff who fell down a hole in the ground? And a male (!)
history teacher who set us class quizzes with questions such as, 'What
was the name of Czar Nicholas the Second?'

Sport? Lacrosse – lots of it, with Miss Raven. Those voluminous

divided skirts . . . and very cold bare
hands were a target for your opponents'
sticks! If you could get into a team
you were allowed to travel on coaches
at the weekend to the rather limited
number of other schools that played
this ancient game! I don't seem to
remember winning very much but I
did enjoy the trips. And the journeys
back when we regaled the rather
bemused coach driver with a mixture
of *Panis Angelicus* and 'Oh, Sir Jasper!'

Gina Rippon

So perhaps my 1960s' experiences at New Hall were just the same as
those of others 'outside', or have I dreamed it all? But, I am right, aren't
I – we didn't have chips, did we?

*After a gap year working in the States, I did a BSc in Psychology and a
PhD in Psychobiology at London University. I have unadventurously
stayed in academia ever since, working at Warwick University and Aston
University. I mostly teach 'Brain and Behaviour' courses and do research,
using brain-imaging techniques, into developmental disorders such as
autism and dyslexia. I am married to Dr Dennis Bancroft and we have
two daughters and a grandson and live on the Warwickshire / Northampton-
shire border, near Rugby.*

VERONICA (Ronnie) WALD

More 1962–1966

After six happy years at Denford Park, September 1962 saw me arriving
at New Hall a day before anyone else . . . That first night I was to sleep
in one of the East Wing rooms and supper was with the resident
members of staff in their dining-room. Who was there, I don't
remember. What I ate, I don't remember. I was nervous and scared.
What I do remember is being visited by S.M.Christopher, at that time
Novice Mistress and later to become a much respected and loved

Reverend Mother. I have long forgotten her actual words, but the feeling of love, warmth and encouragement with which she welcomed me to New Hall I will never forget.

The following day, when the School arrived, I thought I knew the ropes and I'm sorry to say I felt a little superior to my fellow 'new girls', the majority of whom were also from Denford. I soon learnt there was a drawback to arriving at school a day early – the nuns had no difficulty remembering my name!

S.M.Francis took over from S.M.Ignatius as Headmistress. S.M.Martha oversaw prep in the evenings, sitting at a large desk so she could clearly see everyone in the three classrooms – made one by sliding back the 'walls'. After one of us was refused permission to 'visit the Aunts' and, embarrassingly, wet themselves, permission was never again refused, thus giving some of us a wonderful opportunity to slip quickly out to the orchard, in the dark, and pick apples off the trees. I have never eaten sweeter apples. Sadly the orchard was grubbed up to make way for new buildings. One dark night, following rehearsals for the Nativity Play, we heard strange cries which seemed to emanate from the building site. Miss McVey was discovered down an enormous hole. Unfortunately, she'd broken her leg in her fall, but to us merciless children, peeping round the Infirmary curtains to watch her being lifted out of the hole and taken away by ambulance men, it was extremely funny.

The principal acquisition was a new Refectory and we watched in wonder as S.M.Stephen created for it a fascinating and beautiful mural. We started using the Refectory before the mural was completed and had great fun naming the parables as they appeared and trying to recognise the nuns in the faces of the Apostles at the Last Supper.

Cardinal Heenan visited New Hall and gave us dispensation to eat meat on the day of his visit – a Friday!

S.M.Thérèse played the organ at the end of Sunday Mass; I always wanted to remain in the Chapel until the piece was finished – organ music remains my favourite.

Many times I woke in the night and lay awake waiting for the clock to strike the hour so I would know what time it was. It never occurred to me to switch on my torch and look at either my watch or my clock! I loved to hear the School Clock.

Refectory mural painted by S.M.Stephen, with, left to right, S. Bernarda (Turnhout), S.M.Magdalene and S. Margaret Helen in the foreground

I remember S.M.Simon taking us for 'Life of Christ' lessons in one of the Science Labs – our classrooms were always on the move.

A vivid memory is of the shock at hearing that President Kennedy had died after being shot while visiting Dallas.

Possibly my greatest memory is of the summer of The Pageant, even though I was only a bit player with three small parts, one of which was as an Avenue tree during the visit of the Duke of Buckingham to his new house. Oh! the sighing and beating of hearts when Geoffrey Shackerley visited us with his ethereally beautiful wife, the actress Virginia Maskell (an Old Fish), and the competition to be chosen to take care of their two sweet little boys – perhaps we'd get to spend time with Ginny or Geoffrey if chosen? Geoffrey took the photographs and Ginny played the 'Spirit' of New Hall, talking the audience (and pupils) through the building's rich history, from when it was first commissioned by Prince Harold in 1064 right through the royal – and otherwise – ownerships, to the eventual purchase by the Canonesses of the Holy Sepulchre and their setting up of a school for the education of Catholic girls.

But precious above all are the lifelong friendships I made at New Hall. Of the many friends I have gathered over the years, it is my New Hall friends who are closest and dearest.

I was born in Mahe in the Seychelles. I've had a rich and varied working life starting at the Bank of England – very boring – and moving on to working in a Carnaby Street shop. A few years later, after working and partying in St Tropez for a summer, I looked after a five-year-old boy in Paris – possibly the happiest period of my life. Back in England I worked for Dewynters Limited, which grew into London's biggest Theatrical Advertising Agency. I moved out of London and to the country in 1988 and now live in Puttenham (Surrey) with my cat Hannibal and dog Twiggy.

Mid-Essex Beagles come to New Hall in 1968

ANNE DOMONE (née Hennessy)

Campion 1963–1968

When I first went to New Hall in 1963, there were only 120 girls in the school and in the evening we would all gather in the Ambulacrum for a hot drink and a prayer before going to bed. I slept in the Sacred Heart dormitory, where Proudie, the school dog, got hold of my koala bear and bit off its ear and took some of the fur out of its back. I was desolate at the time, but thrilled when my mother-in-law restored it many years later!

I also remember sleeping in the Gallery overlooking the hall with two friends, Cathy Marshall and Maria Fitzgerald. We were fairly isolated from the rest of the school dormitories so were able to do our own thing, such as have the odd midnight feast without anyone knowing too much about it. I remember a box of Maltesers falling and hearing them bounce down the steps, one at a time.

I remember doing housework after breakfast every morning. We would don our blue overalls and, with polish and cloth in hand, set to on the wooden benches or the tiled or wooden floors, which were rigorously inspected when we had finished.

I remember my younger sister, Kate, who joined me at New Hall after Denford Park, locking poor S.M.Thérèse in the Tuck Shop cupboard at the top of the school outside the Art Room. This wasn't her only prank and I was often asked why she behaved in this way!

After a bilingual secretarial course, I did a degree in Languages in Cambridge (not the University!) and took a gap year with my parents in Uruguay, where I became fluent in Spanish. After my degree, I went to Uganda for two years, teaching English in a small International School, and there met and married my husband, John, in Kampala. He died in 2002. I have been living and working in Cambridge for many years in Academic Management, a job I still enjoy.

PENELOPE MARTIN

1965–1970

My teenage years were among my most difficult. Yet, looking back, I can see how they were 'redeemed' from disaster by the sheer kindness of the nuns, and of the Lay staff, despite, in some cases, our almost constant battles! My memories are random and are played out against this backdrop:

 – The inspiring teaching of some of the staff, especially Mrs Haward, who made Latin so enjoyable that one resented her sending one 'out and round' in case one missed something interesting. ('Out and round' was her remedy for yawning, and meant a quick run round the 1963 block to get some fresh air!)

 – The seeming continuous unpleasantness of some Prefects – and some who were not Prefects – who lacked the maturity to be kindly encouraging towards their more errant charges.

 – Nicknames: Mouse, Titch, Scrap, Ticky, Midge, Squeaker, Buddha, Martini (my elder sister, Veronica). There was a vogue for them and unfortunate were the Fishes who were landed with them on day one. Luckily, I was already Penny and nobody was moved to distinguish between a diminutive and a soubriquet!

 – Proudie! That bundle of ferocity and bullet-hard muscle that made up the school dog. I've never trusted bull terriers since. Black was the day when a large dog kennel was erected in the Quad to receive PROUDIE'S PUPPIES (what ensued was obviously too awful to remember).

 – The craze for the music of Joan Baez *et al.*, when everyone, including nuns, strummed a guitar, and when the whole School used to gather in the Ambulacrum for a sing-song, innocently piping its way through anything from *Where Have All The Flowers Gone?* to *Puff The Magic Dragon* and beyond.

 – Boredom. Extra-curricular activities hadn't really arrived at that time so, apart from spending time in the Art Room, I remember hours of just mooching around. I've never been bored since, and maybe that inoculation of teenage boredom was in fact much healthier than the over-stimulation which is a danger for today's teenagers, who are spoiled for choice.

SERENA MICALLEF-EYNAUD (née Debono)

Pole 1965–1974

I came to New Hall from Denford Park and have many happy memories, particularly those related to my dancing lessons, ballet mainly. Our teachers were from the Royal Academy of Dancing, Mrs Murielle Ashcroft, Miss June Mitchell and Miss Sue Danby; all were inspirational and have influenced the dancing of my life to this very day. I have never stopped dancing ballet, even though I am in my mid-fifties, mother to three daughters and grandmother to three granddaughters and a grandson to date.

I'll never forget Wednesdays, ballet day. On waking up, I would put on my leotard and tights under my uniform and fasten my hair up in a 'fancy' bun. It was obvious to all who saw me what day it was!

I participated in two ballet shows. When I was younger I was the snowflake in the *Nutcracker*, and finally, in the Sixth Form, I danced the big part of Coppelia's friend in *Coppelia*, with my best friend Sarah, Angela Prysor-Jones and Jane Hennessy dancing other friends. My sister

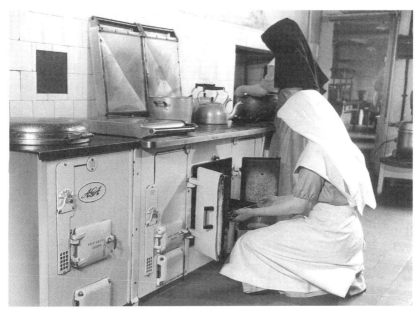

S.M.Magdalene, and S.M.James in the Kitchen

183

Sandra Morgan (née Debono), who was always a superb dancer, danced Coppelia, the doll.

So apart from the spirituality and strong friendships, ballet at New Hall marked my introduction to an art which fulfils me now as much as it did then.

I first worked at the 'White House' in Rhinedalin, Germany, a NATO base (my father was in the army), doing admin work, then I worked for a while in Malta, living there with my grandmother. Aged 23, I met and married my husband

Sandra Debono as Copellia

Martin Micallef-Eynaud, and we raised three daughters, Caroline-Alicia, Lisa-Serena and Alice-Serena. While they were growing up I worked part-time in a school as a Special Needs assistant. I had a cancer scare in 2002, which led to a total hysterectomy. I achieved a BSc (Hons) degree from the Open University in Health Studies and attended a wonderful graduation ceremony held at the Barbican in London. I am currently employed part-time by the Primary Care Trust as a Health Promotion Specialist. Most of these clinics are run in the evenings, which fits in well with caring for my grandchildren.

SYLVE PROVOT

Campion 1965–1970

New Hall has given me so many unforgettable memories. It was a haven of inspiration, serenity and beauty.

Aged 13 and living in France, I asked my father if I could follow my beloved mother who had run away to England, and when she had me with her, my mother sent me to New Hall. My first day was daunting, as I barely spoke a word of English. Slowly I found the words: 'Please, where can I wash my hands?' A tall uniformed stranger said, 'In your basin, of course.' I had not noticed it in the corner of my pixie cubicle, with its bed and chest of drawers.

After one energetic morning run up the Avenue we were gathered in the beautiful Ambulacrum for morning prayers – but for me everything went spinning round and I fainted spectacularly and dramatically. That brought about my first meeting with S.M.Augustine – S. Angela – who sat on my bed and said such comforting words I wondered if I'd died and gone to Heaven! She became the most influential person in my life. She once wrote on the bottom of my exercise book: 'Sylve – hope on, hope ever, after the darkest night comes the brightest light.' I have lived these words, and I am proud to say she and I are friends to this day.

I remember the sing-songs in the Ambulacrum, when we'd gather with our eiderdowns, the gifted seniors playing their guitars, while we sang our hearts out – *Kumbaya, Blowing In The Wind* and, of course, *Puff The Magic Dragon*.

I still have contact with Penelope Martin, who became a Carmelite nun, and has given me valiant support in times of great despair.

After training at Addenbrooke's Hospital I became a nurse then a social worker, until a bad car accident changed the course of my life. I live in Norwich, practising as a handwriting analyst.

Staffroom

ANNE (Pooch) SPILLER

Southwell 1967–1972

Mum had been at New Hall during the war and experienced the evacuation to Newnham Paddox. My first memory, visiting with her at the age of three, was of the long wooden-floored corridors of the East and West Wings which smelt of polish, and riding my little toys up and down them.

In September 1966 I arrived at Denford Park. S.M.Andrew greeted us, informing my mother that we were a day late! That year turned out to be most enjoyable – it was the last before the school amalgamated with New Hall. In the summer term of 1967, S.M.Dismas drove Class II pupils along country lanes, through London and out to New Hall.

We were greeted by S.M.Christopher (Prioress), S.M.Francis (Head-mistress) and I particularly remember S.M.Magdalene (Matron), who wore a white starched apron and served us with triangular cartons of creamy milk, with a straw, and biscuits from a trolley in the Hall.

As we toured the School, two places really stood out: the Refectory, with its amazing painting of the Last Supper by S.M.Stephen, and the Chapel: with the life-sized Crucifix hung below the inscription: 'The Lord is Risen. Alleluia'. There were creaky floorboards either side of a metal grid protecting the heating pipes up the centre aisle. Everything everywhere was highly polished. I can still see the ornate painted ceiling, the coat of arms, the organ, the large windows, the Chapel bellrope and the School Clock that chimed every seven and a half minutes.

I remember the massive works for the building of Beaulieu. During the first week the water pipes burst. The flood was discovered while we were watching the film *Cathy Come Home* and it was all hands on deck to mop up a river of water in the ground-floor classroom corridor – to save the new parquet floor!

After gaining a Diploma in Business Studies, I worked for the Midland Bank (HSBC) and Horse Trials of G.B., before becoming self-employed in the Bookkeeping business. After a year working at New Hall (1991–2), then in the North Wales Police Control Room, I became Bursar at St Brigid's School, Denbigh, where I have been for the past 10 years.

Lessons outdoors on the Plot, early 1960s

KATIE GRIFFITH-JONES (née Cathryn Stone)

1967–1972

No red jerseys allowed under your white sports jumper / My cubicle and Gumption – Inspection, please! / Sore throats and receiving 'tombstones' from S. Maggie Joe / Hiding in the 'Aunts' to avoid lacrosse / The whole-School sing-song in the Hall, with our eiderdowns / Writing cheques in the school Shop high up in the eaves / Playing Hare and Hounds on Great Feast Day / Skidding through the Ambulacrum (always thought it was the 'Anne Blake Room') in our Idlers / Ghost-hunting down the corridors and the Ouija-board scare / Shaking hands after Evening Prayers and Benediction.

After New Hall I worked in an antiquarian bookshop, and then went travelling with Christine Lampier (Macadam) in South America. For the next decade I worked for Reader's Digest Magazine *– first as a researcher and then as one of the editors. Now I'm back living in Essex, married to John and with two children. David just started at Oxford and Louisa is in the Sixth Form.*

CHRISTINE MARQUINA (née Smith)

Spanish teacher 1966–1970 and 1980–2001

My first memory of New Hall is of being brought coffee in the Guest Room before my interview with S.M.Francis and S.M.Ignatius. All the Community looked alike then to me!

Foundation Day celebrations were organised by the staff and it was hard work, but great fun – paperchases, 'It's a Knockout' competitions, treasure hunts in French.

There was outside Mass and the Easter celebrations, Passover meals and all the festivities involved the positive participation of the girls in the Liturgy. I particularly enjoyed doing flower arranging and cooking sessions with different groups.

I recall the last day of term and the classroom clean! We had to collect a solution of Ticky Tacky in what looked suspiciously like sick bowls, and then clean the classroom according to a strict list.

In my first year of teaching we wore academic gowns and the Community could not speak to you after 9pm; they would just disappear.

In the staff dining-room we were fed delicious home-grown food, prepared by S.M.John and served by little S.Teresa. If I overslept she would make my bed for me!

When I first started teaching in 1966 we studied Spanish Literature and I recall one Sixth Former, having completed a very difficult old Spanish text and really enjoying it, saying: 'Miss Smith – if you'll excuse the language – that was b***** marvellous!'

I was received into the Catholic faith in the Chapel, on what was a very special occasion, and our daughter Victoria was baptised there. We celebrated our 25th wedding anniversary in the Barn; and, on a lovely sunny day, we also held our daughter's wedding reception there.

Finding photographs of my mother's cousins in the New Hall photograph albums from the 1920s was exciting.

New Hall was part of my life for so many years and the Community continues to be very important to me. I value the Community's prayers and pray for their new ventures and different aspects of their service to people in Essex and London.

I first started teaching at New Hall in 1966. I married in 1968, and left New Hall in 1970 when our daughter was born. I returned in 1980 and retired in 2001. Now I'm living in a village near Nottingham, enjoying two grandchildren, playing bridge, taking on various church commitments, serving as Chairman of Christians Together in Radcliffe and teaching Spanish as a volunteer for the U3A.

PAT WESTERN AND MARJORIE JONES

Members of Staff (Pat 1967–1978 and Marj 1967–1980)

Marjorie Jones died on 6 June 2012, while this book was in the final stages of preparation.

It is almost 45 years since we first encountered New Hall. This was in the time before the A12 was improved to become a dual carriageway, so we trundled down the old road and had to negotiate a level-crossing over the main London to East Anglia railway line. Timing this was tricky, dependent on the punctuality of the trains and the cooperation of the man who controlled the gates. Eventually we saw the impressive

Post-A Level party in the 1960s

mellow brick façade lit by the low winter sun shining through the cedars.

At this time New Hall School consisted of a hundred girls, all boarders, some from abroad – mostly from Spanish-speaking countries. Things changed quite rapidly when the Junior School from Denford amalgamated with New Hall.

We were impressed by the small groups we handled and by having to teach in some lofty rooms, with special names. They lay down twisting corridors which meant we got lost at times. Another thing that confused us was the main clock, which instead of striking just the quarters struck every seven and a half minutes. This had some significance part way through the afternoon and, as there was no synchronised bell ringing to mark the end of lessons, things could go astray.

The teaching staff at this time was about half nun and half Lay, some of whom boarded at the School.

We have particularly fond memories of Mother Margaret Helen with whom we exchanged books and book recommendations, for she shared our delight in reading and we remained friends with her for a long time.

We also admired the indefatigable energy of S.M.Ignatius, whom we once accompanied on a field trip to Colchester. She had the year group working from the moment we left School, having issued them with individual questionnaires. In Colchester she divided them into three parties, each of us in charge of one; and while we did the walking tour once, she, as leader, did it three times over. At the end of the day we arrived home exhausted, but we learnt later that before supper she had checked all the questionnaires and awarded House points.

We became fond too of one of the Lay Sisters, S. Teresa. She served the Staff Room with morning coffee and afternoon tea and was in attendance at lunch for the Lay staff, whose dining-room was across the courtyard where fruit trees grew. We had damask napkins and personalised rings and so spent a civilised time together. S. Teresa chatted and often got hold of the wrong end of the stick. One member of staff was considering buying a moped to get to school. She called this a 'scooter'. S. Teresa thought for a while and then gave her view – was this a good idea? Surely one of her shoes would wear out much more quickly than the other . . .

Corpus Christi procession in the 1960s

The 1970s

What's going on in the world during the 1970s

Decade of strikes – The 'Winter of Discontent' – The Three-Day Week / Edward Heath and James Callaghan / Platform shoes, flared trousers and hot pants / The era of global travel with the first Pan-Am Boeing 747 and Concorde 1976 / Popular cars were Aston Martin, Triumph TR7, two-door Capri and MGB GT

1970 Computer floppy disks introduced / Edison Lighthouse 'Love Grows (Where My Rosemary Goes)' / Simon & Garfunkel 'Bridge Over Troubled Water' / Elvis Presley 'The Wonder Of You'

1971 UK changes to decimal currency / VCRs introduced / George Harrison 'My Sweet Lord' / T Rex 'Get It On' / Rod Stewart 'Maggie May' / Led Zeppelin 'Stairway to Heaven'

1972 Terrorist Attack at the Olympic Games in Munich / Watergate Scandal begins / New Seekers 'I'd Like To Teach The World To Sing' / Alice Cooper 'School's Out' / David Cassidy 'How Can I Be Sure' / Deep Purple 'Smoke On The Water'

1973 US pulls out of Vietnam / 10 CC 'Rubber Bullet'

1974 Haile Selassie, Emperor of Ethiopia, deposed / Terracotta army discovered in China / US President Nixon resigns / First domestic microwave cooker was sold / Abba 'Waterloo' / Charles Aznavour 'She' / David Essex 'Gonna Make You A Star'

1975 Arthur Ashe first black man to win Wimbledon / Pol Pot becomes the Communist Dictator of Cambodia / Rod Stewart 'Sailin' ' / Queen 'Bohemian Rhapsody'

Left: Assembly with S.M.Francis (Headmistress) and Ruth Raven

1976 Hottest summer / Abba 'Mamma Mia' / Wurzels 'Combine Harvester (Brand New Key)' / Elton John & Kiki Dee 'Don't Go Breaking My Heart'

1977 Elvis found dead / South African anti-apartheid student leader Steve Biko tortured to death / *Star Wars* movie released / David Soul 'Don't Give Up On Us' / Leo Sayer 'When I Need You' / Abba 'Knowing Me Knowing You' / Wings 'Mull Of Kintyre' / The Sex Pistols 'God Save the Queen'

1978 First test-tube baby born / John Paul II becomes Pope / Kate Bush 'Wuthering Heights' / Bee Gees 'Night Fever' / Boney M 'Rivers Of Babylon' and 'Brown Girl In The Ring' / John Travolta and Olivia Newton John 'You're The One That I Want'

1979 Ayatollah Khomeini leader of Iran / American hostages in Teheran / Margaret Thatcher first UK woman Prime Minister / Mother Teresa awarded Nobel Peace Prize / Sony introduces the Walkman / Ian Dury & The Blockheads 'Hit Me With Your Rhythm Stick' / Gloria Gaynor 'I Will Survive' / Boomtown Rats 'I Don't Like Mondays' / Police 'Message In A Bottle' / Pink Floyd 'Another Brick In The Wall'

What's going on at New Hall during the 1970s

In line with changes in education nationally, the School continued to open its doors more widely in more than one sense.

This decade saw the arrival of outside caterers, the start of NHVS (1978), the first 'Children's Holiday' (1979), Grahame Gardner School Outfitters, Residential School Easters, the Riding School (1975), the advent of greater numbers of boarders from far-flung countries, and . . . day girls in 1975!

Reel-to-reel films were shown in both the Lecture Hall and PE1, and the miners' strikes led to torches and candles being used both in classrooms and dorms.

Work continued on the building, with 'the dragon' being moved, Radcliffe being added, and the Chapel again being refurbished (1978).

S.M.Francis continued her long and remarkable period of leadership of the School during this decade, and responding to need as well as good practice, a Governing Body for the School was established in the second half of this period, led by Fr Patrick Barry OSB, to aid and support the Head.

Particularly memorable was Princess Anne's 1979 visit to New Hall, and especially to the School's Riding for the Disabled Asscociation facilities.

Visit of Princess Anne to New Hall in 1979

S. MARGARET MARY (Gabrielle Horton)

*The 1970s First Recycle (Part 2 of 3)**

Finally Professed and Teacher Trained, I was handed the Junior Class. I was thrilled. Two years taught me so much. I endeavoured to teach them every subject except French. (Madame wouldn't be surprised, but I'm sure S.M.Stephen raised an eyebrow at my teaching Art!) It was a challenge. Pupils were lovely but also energetic, permanently turning cartwheels. Not only 24+ children in our classroom but the gerbils kept reproducing – we didn't get the hang of the male and female thing. One was discovered giving birth under a sofa in Mores where Fr Eric was midway through giving the Sixth Form a lecture on virginity!

One memorable outing was to meet in a very personal way Mother Teresa. For many years following we did an annual sponsored walk in Colchester Castle Park, helping to raise funds for Mother Teresa's work.

I kept a little book of 'What they said' and 'What they wrote' at the age of nine. It is hilarious to read now:

Summary of Tudor times: 'Henry the 8 had seven wives. He was a bad king, all he thought was of ladies. He would get very cross if his wife had a girl four a child, he wanted a boy but it was girls he got. He did all he could to make it a girl but it was no good.'

'The worst thing in the whole world is having unhorsey parents.'

'If we are naked, hungry or thirsty Jesus will always be with you. He will dress us, he will give you a drink and he will feed you with steak, chips and peas.'

After a trip to a farm: 'I've made up my mind not to have any babies, ma'am. Ever since I went to the farm and saw that calf being pulled out of that cow with a rope by the feet, I promised myself I wouldn't have any. I don't want my babies pulled out with a rope by the feet, or by the head either.' (Fortunately not traumatised indefinitely – long since a mother of several children.)

From 1972 to 1985 I taught English and lived in Fishers House. Pat Western and Marjorie Jones were joint Heads of Department and adept at discreet tutoring of an inexperienced teacher. Their dry Welsh

* See page 125 for Part 1 and page 269 for Part 3.

humour kept everything in proportion, and together with Joan Jones and later Sybil Lock, as well as S. Stephanie, we made a convivial group.

This English teaching had to be accommodated alongside first Assistant House Mistressing and then House Mistressing in Fishers. I was lucky. I had a wonderful housekeeper in Heather, and a brilliant set of tutors who seemed to set no limits to the amount of support they gave. Rosemary Adams, Pily Bosley, Tessa Molloy, Margaret Murray (who has also undergone recycling and works with us now in Melbourne) and Helena Shepherd were long-term Fisher tutors. And we had some excellent Prefects. Our duties were catholic: when two

NEW HALL

New Hall School, Boreham, Nr Chelmsford,
Essex CM3 3HT
Telephone: Boreham (STD 0245-28) 588

FEES

(April 1973: Subject to revision)

Registration Fee £10.

Current Fees per term: Tuition £155 Total
Boarding £125 £280

The fees include stationery and use of school text books; library subscription; normal nursing and treatment; laundry.
For new pupils a charge of £15 will be made the first term to cover the use of linen and table-silver.
A travel float of £10 per child domiciled in the United Kingdom, and £15 for a child domiciled abroad is charged in advance to cover all travel, school outings and emergency expenditure.

OPTIONAL EXTRAS

Extra coaching	from £10	per term
Music: piano, violin,	£10.50	per term
'cello or guitar		
Dancing	£4	per term
Ballet	£5	per term
Riding	£8	per term

NEW HALL

New Hall School, Boreham, Nr Chelmsford,
Essex CM3 3HT
Telephone: Boreham (STD 0245-28) 588

STAFF LIST

Reverend Mother Mary Christopher, Prioress,
Chairman of Governors
Sister Margaret Helen, BA (London). Sub-Prioress,
Vice-Chairman of Governors
Sister Mary Simon, Dip Theo, Regina Mundi Rome,
Clerk to the Governors. Religion
Sister Mary Francis, BA (London), Post Grad Dip Ed,
Headmistress
Miss D. R. Raven, Bedford College of Phys Ed,
Senior Mistress. Head of PE
Sister Mary Andrew, TC & BA (London), *German*
Mrs M. T. Copsey, BA (Bristol), Post Grad Dip Ed,
Head of History
Sister Mary Dismas, TC (London), *Religion*
Mrs J. Douce, BSC (Reading), Post Grad Dip Ed,
Mathematics
Mrs M. J. Dutton, BSC (Durham), Post Grad Dip Ed,
Head of Biology
Mrs I. Z. Freath, BA (Cantab), *Italian*
Mrs M. French-Greenslade, AGSM, TC (London), *Drama*
Sister Mary Gabriel, TC (London), *Junior Subjects/
Needlework*
Mrs A. C. Gravina, BSC (London), *Physics*
Mrs J. M. Hall, BA (Cardiff), Dip Sec, *Business Studies*
Mrs A. E. Haward, MA (Cantab), *Head of Classics*
Mrs M. M. Howett, BSC (London), *Mathematics*
Sister Mary Ignatius, BA (London), Post Grad Dip Ed.
Head of Geography
Sister Mary James, TC (London), *Home Economics*
Miss R. E. James, BA (Cardiff), Post Grad Dip Ed, *Classics*
Sister Mary John, BSC (London), Post Grad Dip Ed, Cantab,
Biology
Mrs J. G. Jones, BA (Leeds), Post Grad Dip Ed, *English*
Miss M. H. Jones, BA (Cardiff), Post Grad Dip Ed,
Joint Head of English
Miss E. Knight, BA (Manchester), Post Grad Dip Ed,
Head of French
Mrs B. Lambert, BA (London), Post Grad Dip Ed,
Geography
Miss S. MacDonald, Cert Ed, Bathurst College, Australia,
Chemistry/Mathematics
Sister Mary Mark, TC (London), Dip Brit Inst Paris, *French*
Sister Margaret Mary, BED (London), *English/Junior
Subjects*
Sister Mary Martha, BSC (London), Post Grad Dip Ed,
Religion
Miss M. E. F. W. Mercer, BA (London), MA (Oxon),
History/Modern Languages
Mrs A. V. Miller, Bedford College of Phys Ed, *PE*
Miss A. de C. Neill, ARCM, *Music*
Miss S. Noel-Stansbury, TC & BA (London), *English*
Miss J. Preston, LRAM, *Head of Music*
Mrs E. Routledge, MA (Aberdeen), Post Grad Dip Ed,
History
Sister Mary Simon, Dip Theo Regina Mundi Rome,
Religion

donkeys strayed into the cesspit in the field behind the L shape, we all – Prefects, S.M.Bernadette and I – managed to lift them out.

Haverhill Fever was a big event during this time. It was very serious and affected a significant number of the School, staff and Community. The Notifiable Diseases people came in and the 'thought to be well' School members were sent home, and then, of course, several of them became ill; many children and some Community were out of school recovering for weeks, if not months . . .

House outings became annual events. On one occasion I was unwell with a dose of shingles and briefed the Prefects, telling them that the staff needed to be looked after and given a nice day out. So efficiently did they take roll calls, etc., that in the evening they sailed out of Walton, inadvertently leaving the Assistant Housemistress on the greensward. She returned by train.

Fishers House trip to Walton-on-the-Naze, 1975
Left to right: Rachel Culley, Diana Bellew, S.Margaret Mary,
S.M.David, Mrs Bosley (seated in deckchair), Melissa Gibson (back
view), Heather Haxton and S.M.Ignatius (checking her mobile?!)

One year the young photographer instructed the group of 11- to 16-year-olds all to shout 'Sexy' on the click of the camera. It was a very jolly picture that year!

House competitions were big in those years – Keep Fit, Gymnastics, Music, all the sports. In Fishers we had our own personal coach in Iain Mcleod-Jones, a sporty parent, until after too many years of winning too many cups the other houses shouted, 'Foul Play.'

There were those ghastly Saturday lunches for parents at Exhibition Weekend. Ampleforth found benefactors who supplied their offspring's House with smoked salmon and the like – we didn't! So the morning was spent spreading some sausage rolls and tired lettuce round paper plates.

March 1974 marked a sad time for the School and in particular for Fishers. On a dark, wet Sunday evening, Emma Cooke was killed in a car accident on her way back to school at the end of an Exeat. Her mother was driving. The shock was enormous. Emma was a bubbly eleven-year-old and a happy-go-lucky innocent. For me it was the second time I had buried a child in our cemetery. It rained throughout and the children were glad to have their hooded cloaks. I still have a vivid picture of that sight on the 15th of March.

My overriding memory of this time is of the House being a family group. Older girls looked out for younger ones; children found comfort when they needed it; in the main there was good role-modelling; parents were largely very supportive and appreciative; children of very different backgrounds and abilities found a place.

Over this period New Hall Voluntary Service as an organisation came into being and girls had increasing opportunities to become involved in Community Service. The Year of the Child in 1979 was celebrated by the first Children's Holiday. More than 30 years later, that continues. I was involved in that first holiday for children from London. It was a real eye-opener for us all. One aspect was easier then than now: Health and Safety hadn't been invented. I remember arriving on the beach at Frinton and the children rushing straight for the sea – their 'helpers' in hot pursuit!

In 1985 those years came to an end for me and I had a year to prepare for the next phase of recycling.

To be continued . . .

JOAN JONES

English Teacher 1970–1995

An abiding memory is of a line of staff, I am in their midst, in gowns and hoods coming into Assembly on Exhibition Sunday to the strains of 'Gaudeamus Igitur'. I always found it moving.

I came to New Hall in the most casual way. A university acquaintance, Mrs Jo Wing, rang me to ask if I fancied a job for a year, teaching English, of course. A chat with S.M.Francis and I was beginning a delightful part of my life. The one year became 25!

Just before I began in 1970 a new drive had been completed running parallel to the railway line, so no more 'because of shut crossing gates' excuses for being late. English then was taught in Beaulieu until Walkfares was built in 1992. There were around 300 girls in the School with the introduction of day girls. Teaching was easy, rewarding, and, as I was to say to Marjorie Jones, then joint Head of English with Pat Western: 'If I was any more relaxed, I'd fall over.'

And then, as I was to say in many editorials, there were the horses! Endlessly parading past my classroom window, both enticing and tedious.

Sixth Form photo with staff, 1981
Staff front row, left to right, Brian Harte, Pam Forrester, S.M.Thérèse,
Eileen Crossley, S.M.Andrew, Jean Hall, S.M.Augustine, Fr Leslie,
S.M.Francis, S.M.Mark, Jo Wing, S.M.Gabriel, Anne Haward,
S.M.Christina, Sue Feldmann, S.M.Dominic, Joan Jones

I remember singing with the Choir, standing next to Jean Hall (History of Art), a dear friend with whom I collaborated in the editing of the *New Hall Magazine* until her untimely death. I also recall trips to Stratford-upon-Avon with Year 11 as a treat after their exams, and becoming a tutor to the Sixth Form after being attached to Poles with S.M.John for some years. I loved teaching A Level English where the girls taught me as much as I them. The Community and New Hall became my second family.

I have been retired for 17 years and living in Old Harlow, occupied with church, NADFAS, bridge, tennis, etc.

JEAN WILSON

Head of Maths 1963–1988

From the time I started at New Hall, part-time and with only six O Level Maths candidates, to the time I left 25 years later with four complete Maths sets taking GCSE, New Hall and its trisection of people, Community, staff and students, has intrigued and fascinated me.

My time there expanded my horizons, literally, in that I found myself taking a party of Fourth Years on a skiing trip to Austria and enjoying the privilege of joining Sixth Form trips to the Holy Land, Russia and China.

Looking back, I remember:

– Seeing the Headmistress, S.M.Francis, with apron on, doing her housework, cleaning her own office on the first day of the Christmas holidays.

– Many special moments with Sixth Form tutees, sharing confidences and worries.

– Listening to the very varied opinions about everything in and out of school in the Staff Room.

– Having an Anglican Chaplain in a school run by Catholic nuns – very forward looking.

– The privilege of seeing my own sons learning to swim in the pool in the summer holidays.

Although I still think Maths is 'top of the list' of subjects, it was the people I met who made the world go round. Even in life after New Hall, their lasting influence is apparent in the voluntary work I do.

I am happy and busy living in Norfolk, doing voluntary work in village and county and tutoring Maths.

S. MARY GABRIEL (Angela Foley)

Staff and Community 1960–2005

Although my memories go back to September 1960 (the day I left my family and Glasgow to enter the Community), I am covering the period between 1969 when I started working as Assistant House-mistress in Owens House and 1989 when I stopped being House-mistress after 13 years.

Over these years I remember:

– Preparing the dormitories for the return of the children at the start of each term, making sure that everything was as clean and shining as possible. S.Teresa and I moving up the hill to Beaulieu the day before term began so as to be settled in.

– The early arrivals who had travelled from far-off and exotic places, sometimes accompanied by younger brothers. Greeting parents as they delivered their offspring into our hands; collecting passports, pocket money, fees, medicines; unpacking and checking what was there and what was missing, all helped by helpful House Prefects.

– Wonderful black cloaks with hoods lined in House colours (purple for Owens); blue overalls for housework and Science; visits from Grahame Gardner the School Outfitters; second-hand shop; Idlers and brown lace-ups from Mr Finch, lacrosse sticks and boots, tights and leotards.

– Hundreds of pairs of socks back from the laundry needing to be paired and always being left with odd ones; sheets to count before sending them to the County Laundry and counting them back in again on their return. And annual blanket shaking.

– School Assemblies in Chapel and in the Gym as well as House Assemblies; House Socials; Christmas Parties; Foundation Day celebrations, including special Masses and Inter-House Competitions.

– Summer evenings playing rounders on the Plot and, sometimes in the rain, sitting by the pool watching the children having fun and tiring themselves out before bed.

– Autumn leaves being a source of great joy for the younger children to catch as they fell to the ground and gather up and tumble around in; collecting conkers and blackberries from the fields to eat or make jam or apple crumble.

– The exquisite beauty of the cedars on the Plot in the early morning mists; the sight and sounds of the horses being brought up to the Stables from the front paddock; the morning walks down to Chapel before the rest of the world woke up.

– Snow on the front cedars and a helicopter flying over trying to disperse snow from their branches. The sound of a huge branch crashing down unable to bear the weight of snow any longer, and the sad day when tree surgeons came to bring down a whole cedar tree.

– Sunsets, especially behind the bare trees on the Beech Walk, stark and dark against blazing red and orange skies on winter evenings, and the more gentle ones to the west of Beaulieu late at night in summer.

I remember all the people who were a part of the life of New Hall – the estate, catering and household staff, teachers, tutors, Community and Chaplains and parents. And, most of all, the children – each of whom was special to me and from whom I learnt so much about life. So much giving and receiving, sharing and serving, forgiving and starting again, making and being a community. To each one I give thanks and for each one I thank God.

I entered the Community in 1960 and was one of the few at that time who had been educated at another school. I moved to Colchester in 2005 and am now at our present House on Greenstead Estate, where I enjoy being involved in the local community.

TERESA LENAHAN (S. Teresa)

Campion, Southwell and More 1970s and 1980s

Thinking back to my first impressions of New Hall I am reminded of the beauty of the place, the lively creative students and the very long hours we worked. Coming from a large Comprehensive School in South Wales, and after teaching in war-torn Uganda and then in another large Comprehensive, I found the girls-only environment a challenge. I missed the humour and fun of the boys. However, I quickly found myself at home.

From starting as Miss Lenahan I became Sister Teresa after joining the Community in 1975. Nelson Mandela's South Africa was on my agenda and no doubt I caused a stir by talking politics. One task was teaching everyone Drama – so 375 names to get to grips with in the first term. Deadlines were never my strength and the writing of reports was helped by very long nights with S.M.Francis keeping me awake with strong black coffee. The whole experience of Easter in my first year, with Fr Eric Doyle and the School present at the Liturgy, was involving, stirring and memorable. Indeed a feature of life from then on.

We were in our own microcosm up in Beaulieu – the flat roof was a temptation for some in the dead of night . . . No, the fire-escape doors did not set off the alarm when you went out that way! We all had ready access to the fields, the Riding School and tennis-courts and other places that I was not meant to be aware of ! House feasts, plays and concerts, with a lovely in-house feel, took up long hours and were a great alternative to 'square eyes' from too much television – although *Top of the Pops* and that long-running American serial were an opportunity for lovely quiet evenings for me.

I remember supper parties and the mad rush for tea, with teaspoons disappearing everywhere. *The Wombling Song* did not go down so well with the external judges at the annual House Gym Competition but S.M.Christopher and I smiled throughout. Pre-Haverhill days we had the rich creamy milk from the farm, Class 3 carrying those churns; all enjoyed the delicious hot chocolate. Ends of term were exhausting especially when I was meant to organise housework and packing and that was never a strength – but Gumption, Pledge and wet rags, puzzle brushes and a haze of dust flying from one place to another, gave everyone the going home feel and then the house went silent.

Yes, I also looked forward to the new term, hearing the stories of holidays and family time. That experience of working residentially and teaching was certainly a full-time life. There were sadnesses and joys shared – hard news to break sometimes, lessons to plan, lessons to teach, books to mark, prayer to lead, housework to check, clothes to sort, reports to write, tears to dry, chatting and encouraging and trying to be stern when the prank was really rather a good one. Parents to get to know and those were generally good experiences; the most challenging was when one 11-year-old started at New Hall and her father was in tears.

Moving to Mores was a change – at the same time taking on other works within the Community. The nights along the Strand with coffee and sandwiches, and a 'Drive in' McDonald's on the return. The Results days brought tears, whichever way the results turned out. Induction days, the Feasts, the barbecues, and having a surreptitious bar in the form of 'the Cupboard'. The Ball with the fire-engines in attendance and the helium balloons drifting around the ceiling of M1. The occasion when visitors, who had played rugby against each other during the day, then came to a disco at New Hall in the evening. Those Mores House Study Days on controversial topics – South Africa and Apartheid, HIV Aids, Homelessness, etc. Awaiting those who arrived back from somewhere rather late, then found the walk from the front door to the stairs more a circular than a straight line, and of course telling us how much they loved us along the route. The Leavers' Dinners – who would come? who would not sit where? – and all that followed at Exhibition Weekend.

Working alongside others in the Community in a shared venture based on Community, Service and Liturgy was really life-giving. Of course, it had its hard times, but overall it was a great privilege to be alongside those young people at such a formative time in their lives.

In 1997, I was a member of the first small group of Community who were living away from New Hall in Leytonstone, East London. I returned to New Hall in 2002, then moved to Colchester in 2005 and to Greenstead in 2009. I remain a Governor of New Hall.

CAROLINE RUSSELL (née Grant)

Denford and New Hall 1965–1975

My parents expected to be moving from country to country every two to three years, so sending me to New Hall was to give me stability, but in the end they stayed in Madrid. Nevertheless, New Hall became a sort of home from home and, yes, good friendships were formed that will last a lifetime.

One of my happy memories was going off at the weekend to help with the cows on the farm. I used to get them in from the field and help with feeding and milking. Once the milk had been cooled I helped the farmer take the big churns over to the school. All of this was, of course, before the Haverhill Fever scare after which the fresh 'green' milk was stopped! I knew all the cows by name. When it came to calving time, my hand being smaller than the farmer's, I was roped in to help pull calves out that got stuck. The calves that were being fattened up had to be fed with bottles, and there was one cow I particularly remember (I think she was called Patience) who had a fever, probably mastitis, and couldn't stand so I was dispatched to milk her by hand.

Little did I realise how useful some of those skills would be until years later my husband Hugo decided to take on a herd of 200 Boer goats!

After Madrid University I returned to London where I started as a secretary and ended up as PA to various MPs in the House of Commons (briefly including Jeffrey Archer). I married Hugo Russell and have been employed full-time bringing up our four children ever since – the pay is rubbish but you can't beat the job satisfaction! In spare time I breed Labradors.

GIG (Wiggy) MOSES (née Alexandra Whigham)

Denford and Owen 1967–1976

Denford Park will be with me for ever. I arrived in 1967 at the age of 10. My first dormitory was Kittens, sharing with Frances Beviere and Sophie Blyth, but beyond that all is a little cloudy. I recall spending many a night standing in the corridor as punishment for talking after lights-out. S.M.Joseph administered 'the slipper' from time to time – we never seemed to learn.

Roller-skating was my favourite pastime, on the cement court next to the little gardens. Celebrating Saint's days and Corpus Christi were always fun as it meant a day off and a picnic in the grounds. And I remember standing in a long queue to access our sweet tins after tea. We were only allowed to take three sweets at a time, so we all tried to hide extras up our sleeves. Break-time was sitting at our desks with quarter-pint bottles of milk and a couple of biscuits – the milk was frozen in winter and disgustingly warm in summer.

The School song on the Pack Coach was: 'Come to Denford, build a bonfire, / Put the teachers on the top, / Put the Prefects in the middle /

Lacrosse on Six Acres. Front left to right: Jenny Ryan, Clare Trappes-Lomax. Back left to right: Wiggy and Susan Wood

And burn the jolly lot!' When we arrived at New Hall it was the same song, but with a name change. I was in Owens up at Beaulieu. My Housemistress for the first years was S.M.Augustine (now Angela) and I was always in trouble: for things like not wearing my cloak and cubicle-hopping after lights-out, to – as I moved up the School – smoking, drinking, going to Chelmsford without permission and sneaking off to the White Hart. I even flew to France in the Lower Sixth on the pretext I was going to a christening in Kent!

When we moved down to the Main School, we had a new House-mistress, S.M.Mark, with S.M.Gabriel as her assistant. S.M.Mark had great faith in me and many of my misdemeanours stayed 'in House'. In my last year 1975–6 I happily held the position of House Captain with Christiane Amanpour and Marian Mullen. I remember the great rivalry of the Inter-House Competitions. Southwells led by Pippa Rose and Fishers led by Sarah Durkin were our major rivals but at the end of the year we had won the Gym, Swimming and Lacrosse Cups!

Australia is home and I have been director of the Moree Gallery for 15 years. I have two children Henry (23) and Lily (21) both at Sydney University. 'You can take the girl out of England but you can't take England out of the girl . . .'

Owens at Swimming Gala
Front left to right: Miss Cox, S.M.Mark and Christiane Amanpour
Back left to right: Pippa Symes and Alix Barclay

NICOLA SUTHERLAND

Denford and Southwell 1966–1973

Going back to Denford for the start of term meant finding a dozen nuns standing in the porch to welcome us. S. Teresa Magdalen always had a fabulous picture on the blackboard which she'd drawn in coloured chalk.

Moving to New Hall was a huge change. The Sixth Formers were so tall and frightening. We no longer had dormitories but cubicles, making it far more difficult to chat after lights-out, but it was possible by standing on the worktops. The curtains at the end would sway when one of the nuns was walking towards you to find out who was talking.

Do you remember those huge deep metal dishes we had on our tables, divided into eight? The only time we were exempt from eating something was if our parents wrote a letter. I was exempt from liver and carrots! If you misbehaved the Table Prefect made you stand up in front of the whole School.

Like most of the girls, I had a calendar on which to strike off each day until the end of term. I remember one of the nuns taking me to task, saying she thought it was rather rude to the Community: imagine how I would like it if she came to my house to stay and did the same thing!

Whenever my uncle, a priest in Ware, came to visit me, the nuns would invite us to have tea in their Refectory. It had a huge glass frontage, and my friends would try to catch my attention by waving and distracting me. The nuns used to say they had never known me so quiet.

I live in Salisbury, having moved there from Putney in 1999. I'm working in Reception and Customer Services and Administration in a private hospital called New Hall.

RACHEL KELLETT

Campion 1967–1976

I remember Henrietta Critchley-Salmonson taking care of me that first day, in her adult adept way, aged eight. And washing in cold water in basins somewhere with tall windows and uneven creaking wood floors. The scent of polish in the Ambulacrum. Lining up, height order, and being at the small end (I'm still taking up my trousers) and standing in the Quad blowing 'hot potatoes' into the back of the girl in front.

During the miners' strike, we were read *The Pearl* by John Steinbeck in candlelight in a Beaulieu classroom, while outside in the dusk the great cedar branches swayed in a westerly wind, echoing my own oscillating emotions, heightened by this unusual communal stillness and soft warm light.

I remember being caught smoking by the old sheds, and S.Stephanie's lesson on 'myself as other people see me'. And her unexpected warm hug after telling me Mary (a great friend) had died on the top of a Norwich to Dereham bus.

– Dancing lessons with Mrs Ashcroft, the Waltz of the Flowers from the *Nutcracker Suite*, the excitement in the Green Room below the stage. Piano practice from the Music Rooms at the top of the stairs. Mrs Kendal White's patience. The light from the Art Room. The free fall of experimenting with random forms in art.

– Sing-songs, snuggled under eiderdowns, girls playing guitars. Singing 'Kumbaya', and idolising Veronica Capps.

– Finding a worm in my salad, and after my righteously complaining, S.M.Stephen amusingly responding, 'Good protein!'

– At Choir practice standing next to S.M.Teresa, even smaller than I, the music sheet shaking in her delicate, liver-spotted hand; she, like all of us, was inspired by S.M.Mark, who once brought in a *man* to conduct us (for Handel's *Messiah*, I think).

– Conversations with Fr Eric, observing Germander Speedwells and reading *The Little Prince*. Laughingly being told by him I was a bit bossy. He was the first of many since.

– Our cubicle-curtain material, a brave psychedelic kaleidoscopic pattern.

– S. Angela's enjoyment of words, and her giving us 'pandiculate', which I still enjoy today.

– Being part of the 'Ping-Pong' Club behind the changing-room curtain in the Needlework Room, exclusively for those wearing bras (instigated by Wiggy perhaps).

– Fiona, Becky, Annie-T, Lori, Cathy, Marina (sampling another After Eight from her locker), Louise Simpson (how she made me laugh), Jane, Jo, Di, Christiane, Wiggy, Pippa, Sarah, Tessa, Heather . . .

My godfather, John Little, generously sponsored my 10 years at New Hall. After a gruelling 50-mile cycle to the Island of Mersea for the Duke of Edinburgh Award, I felt free, and would cycle to John Little's, often turning up unannounced, and always made welcome.

Letter writing on a Sunday remains a habit today. Laying out all our clothes for packing to go home left me wondering if I would ever

Charleston Girls
Back left to right: Rachel Culley, Leah Vierra, Emma Start,
Emma Birtwhistle, Rachel Kellett, Louisa Fernandez and
Jane Hennessy, with Lynn at the front

evolve to the neatness of Olivia Phillips. I never have but still lay out my clothes as then, a ritual which has been useful in a travelling life.

I am living in Suffolk. After a varied life with three professions – Teacher, Art Restorer, Computer-Support Manager, I spent 10 years travelling, mainly in India, initially helping to set up Greenpeace, then teaching and exploring.

ANGIE PRYSOR-JONES
Campion 1967–1975

The smell: of polish – 'big' housework done at half-term and the end of term – great fun if you got the job of putting dusters on your feet and polishing the Ambulacrum floor or St Aloysius; of TCP – if you got the loos and bathrooms in the Infirmary, I think from the jar the thermometers were kept in; of resin and sweaty leotards – when going into ballet lessons in the room above the Library; of Vick and Nelson's Inhalers in the dormitories – when everyone had colds in the winter; of toast in Mores – a treat, as we never had it lower down the School.

The feel: of the Ambulacrum – imposing and formal when lining up there to shake hands with Reverend Mother at the end of term, and cosy at Saturday-night sing-songs when the whole School gathered with eiderdowns (way before duvets!); of freezing – while jumping into the unheated outdoor swimming-pool and standing in the bitter east wind on the Six Acre lacrosse pitch; of boiling and itching in the nylon polo necks that went under the Sunday 'sacks', aka the new best dresses.

The sound: of the swishing of our Housemistresses' gowns up and down the dormitory corridors at night – apart from S.Stephanie's, because she glided; of the stampede from Chapel on Thursday nights as everyone rushed to get back to their Houses to watch *Top of the Pops*; of the nuns singing Compline while we filed into Chapel for night prayers after supper . . . and the creaking of floorboards on the way into Chapel; of the jangle of S. Magdalen John's enormous bunch of keys as she looked for one in particular; of the bell chiming the hours when you were in the Infirmary.

The sight: of the great cedars when coming up the Avenue; of the pigeon-holes in the House laundry rooms – that hopefully contained post; of the whole school 'running' to the Lodge Gates down the Avenue before breakfast (every day!).

The taste: of Sunday's roast lamb, sausages for breakfast (eaten with marmalade for some reason), apple crumble, Pus and Bunions (chocolate tart), snowballs (competitions to see who could eat more than six); of great chocolate-fudge birthday cakes cooked for you for your birthday by your Housemistress – S.M.Bernadette or S.M.James – and cider (which must have been mistakenly thought non-alcoholic).

After studying Archaeology at Reading, I worked in publishing in London then co-founded and directed the Oxford Literary Festival from 1997 to 2009. I founded and I'm now running Bookfest ('creating readers'), as well as working for HENRY (tackling obesity in the under 5s) for two days a week. I live in Oxford with husband Mark (Eastment) and two children, Dan (18) and Francesca (15).

THERESA LANE (née Byrne)

Pole 1967–1974

On my first evening, aged 11 years, I was paired up with Brenda in 'Ranks' to go into the Refectory for our first meal. ('Ranks' meant pairing up with someone and travelling around the school in a long crocodile line to go to Chapel / meals / Assembly, etc.). That meal is indelibly marked in my memory: a stainless-steel rectangular dish with eight poached eggs sitting in some slimy spinach. I felt far more homesick after that!

We had to do housework after breakfast every morning, which involved two duties: one was cleaning our cubicles and using lots of Gumption paste for the basin (I can still smell it), and the other was different every term, depending on which bit of the School we were given to clean. There was always a scramble at the beginning of term to see, 'What housework have you got?' I remember doing 'Radiators' one term!

There was the dreaded lacrosse which I absolutely loathed. The cunning bit was to choose your position down near the goal and make sure your friend was in goal so you could just go and spend the lesson chatting.

I remember having a beautiful gold chain that belonged to my grandmother (which I had just inherited) stolen from my cubicle on Prizegiving Day. And I remember being made to weed the grounds for hours after being caught smoking!

But I also remember crying all the way home from New Hall to Reading (no M25 in those days) in the back of my parents' car on the day I left. I had been very happy there and was inconsolable.

After leaving New Hall I trained as an Occupational Therapist and went to Australia for a year. Then I married Robin Lane and had seven years not working while having three daughters (Harriet, Emily and Alice). After living in Bristol and London I now live in Devizes, Wiltshire, and am working as a Community OT with Wiltshire Council. No plans to retire just yet!

JULIA AGUIRRE

Fisher 1967–1973

When I started at New Hall in 1967 things were in transition and everyone was talking about Denford Park. We were up in Beaulieu, which had not long been built, and in the first term the water pipes burst and flooded all the passageways. I have vivid memories of S.M.Francis and other nuns giving us piggyback rides to get us over the water.

I was in awe of some of the older girls, Robin Oldcorn, M.L. and Poz. They had a midnight feast in one of the entrance rooms at Beaulieu, and when they realised they'd been found out, someone tried to escape via the big swinging windows and set off the alarm. Later they all had to line up and apologise to Mrs Noblock.

Sport was never my thing, and still isn't. In lacrosse, I would hope and pray that I could play goalie, the only player who got to wear any kind of protective gear. We certainly needed it with the likes of Roisin O'Sullivan and Jehanne Andouze hurling that lethal ball around.

My fondest memories are of the hours spent in the Art Room. S.M.Stephen was a brilliant teacher, way ahead of her time. How lucky we were to have all those wonderful art and craft facilities.

During the last few years it's been wonderful to meet up with some Old Fishes. Sharing so many experiences together at New Hall, it was not difficult to start up a friendship again, even with a nearly 40-year gap in between.

I returned to Kenya in 1985 to become involved in my family Interior-Decoration Business, creating furniture and gift items made in Kenya in a home workshop.

STEPHANIE FISCHER (née Rose)

Fisher 1968–1977

Idlers would have to be the single most under-appreciated item of my youth. They fitted like a glove when new, and had smooth leather soles which, despite my parents' efforts with sandpaper, slid wonderfully on the highly polished School floors. This probably led to the 'New Hall Shuffle', best practised in the corridor stretching from the Library to the Language Lab (Aloysius Corridor).

Afternoon tea was one of my favourite times of the day. Unlike lunch or supper, it was a known factor: a cup of tea, two slices of buttered white bread with jam and a cake or bun. Sticky Willies were my favourite, partly because of their naughty name and partly because of the competition – who could take the largest bite?

I was never fond of exercise but did enjoy the game of lacrosse, much to my mother's horror for she was convinced that I would lose an eye! For a very brief moment I found myself in the school lacrosse team. I vividly recall Miss Raven running us up the Avenue and back practising our cradling; and the smell of the linseed oil that we used on the wood, while we rubbed the leather thongs with Vaseline. I lived in fear of Miss Raven: if my aim was to move as little as possible, her job was to 'torture' me with movement. However, in table-tennis lessons, Miss Raven taught me well and I had the opportunity to get to know and appreciate her.

In the summer of 1975 Fishers had a picnic party to say farewell to the leavers. Someone (Julia Cleland?) brought what must have been close to a whole Stilton! It was quite a feast, which I think we ate in the

Copse. As we left the House on a boiling-hot day, wearing our capes fully buttoned up to hide our goodies, we were stopped by S.M.Ignatius. She kept us for a while, asking where we were going and weren't we feeling a little warm, and then let us go. We felt very clever. Of course, she knew what we were up to! She was a wonderful Housemistress and I wish I'd shown her more appreciation at the time.

When I first went to New Hall, S.M.David used to take us out to play on the Plot in front of Beaulieu, and she was particularly good at French cricket. Other games I remember were British Bulldog, Red Rover and Queenie (Queenie, Who's Got the Ball?). The cedar trees used to feature in our games, either as 'safe' or 'home' locations or as providers of thick, gnarled trunks to hide behind.

The idea of staying at school for Easter did not at first impress me. But once I remember a Rabbi visited and led us through a Jewish Passover Seder. I'm still impressed with the open-minded approach of the Community, their willingness to embrace other cultures and beliefs and the positive effect this had on our development.

We had horse-hair mattresses which were thin, hard and full of lumps and craters. It was incredibly exciting when we were moved into cubicles with beds with sprung mattresses.

The Community seemed to be very fond of bull terriers. They were not particularly attractive or friendly and I well remember sitting in a group in S.M.Francis's office with the dog in the corner, 'scenting' the air and snoring away as S.M.Francis, rather graphically, explained the facts of life . . .

Mrs Haward always makes my 'most influential people in your life' list. As for the other staff, I remember how the Irish Science teacher, Miss Thompson, once gave us a stern lecture about safety in the Lab – while leaning up against the counter right next to the lit Bunsen burner, and the wire gauze hooked on to her Aran jumper! S.M.Joseph taught us to write acceptable italic, saying, 'Hold the pen lightly, never too tightly. Hold it obliquely . . . ' We used to write letters home on Sundays under her watchful eye. And the patience of S.M.Stephen up in the Art Room! I still have my mouse's ear, made from a lump of clay. My mother used it for years to store paper clips.

I can still remember the packing list: six Aertex shirts, six poplin blouses, two red twin-sets, two red uniform skirts, one gym skirt . . .

And, who could forget, the delightful red sports knickers? In the summer, we wore the white Fred Perry pleated tennis skirt and some frilly white knickers.

Blanket shaking was something I looked forward to because it indicated the approaching long summer holiday. And there was the excitement of the arrival of our trunks and suitcases from storage. Our packing had to pass inspection! Shoes and heavy items had to be at the bottom and spaces filled in with socks. Clothes had to be properly folded and layered correctly. I still pack this way and have taught my husband to do the same, but have given up with my son!

I left in 1977 and stumbled into the wine trade. Having studied for three deliriously happy years at the Wine & Spirit Education Trust in London, my future seemed set – Master of Wine and a lifetime of impoverished but enjoyable work. However, my path diverted unexpectedly and I emigrated to Australia. Knowing little of Australian wines, I went into Administration Management for Hong Kong Bank. I met and married Seth, and have one son. Our partnership also created our business, Filing Systems International. We thoroughly enjoy life in Sydney, for which we never cease to feel grateful and privileged.

The Duplicating Room (drawing by Susan Coffey)

JANE LIDDLE (née Davies)

Owen 1968–1978

New Hall was a real community. I had lunch with Anne Haward not too long ago and she said the nuns civilised us – I think she was right!

Here are some of my memories:

– Thinking all nuns moved on wheels.

– Sliding on the polished floors in Idlers.

– Breaking the sink off the wall and worrying where my wooden mouse was in the flood that followed (and S.M.Gabriel thinking I meant a real one).

– 'Pus and Bunions' for pudding

– Outings with the standard packed lunch of a Penguin and Dairylea triangle sandwich.

– Thinking Karen Quinn was the most stylish and beautiful girl ever and wanting to look like her!

Diana Bellew and Karen Quinn in Coppelia, 1974

Fr Eric Doyle OFM

- S.M.Augustine (S. Angela) telling me homesickness was *cotapaxia* and reading stories to us at night.
- Wonderful Fr Eric making Mass fun (he was a massive campaigner for women priests which I didn't know until recently).
- Watching *I Claudius*.
- The joy of toast in Mores.

I went to St Andrews to study Greek and Classical Civilisation and am now a partner in the law firm Overburys, in Norwich.

VERONICA SLATER (née Ogden)

Southwell 1968–1977

I arrived at New Hall in September 1968, aged just nine. As an overseas pupil I was somewhat overawed. I remember wondering whether all English schools had bedrooms in their Science Labs as I was shown to mine on the mezzanine of Middle Lab! Any fears about being left on my own in a new place were allayed when I met my new class teacher, S.M.Joseph, who was kind, intelligent, funny, fair and a wonderful teacher.

219

My memories are 95% positive. As well as testing the boundaries, I'm sure I tested those around me on occasion with resultant fallout, and there was lots of laughter among relatively few tears. Best of all, valued and solid friendships were made, which remain to this day. Two of these friends are godmothers to my children . . .

I remember: Southwells – S.M.Dismas's eyebrows – Southwells and Campions move to Beaulieu – the Beech Walk (especially at night) – shoe-cleaning on Saturdays – letter writing on Sundays – housework and inspection – bath nights – Foundation Day with Hare and Hounds and the dreaded sing-song – the cold, clinging curtains of the swimming-pool huts – changing the Chapel layout – Easter at School – the Green Room and S.M.Benedict's creative genius – guard-dog patrols – barley soup on Family Fast Days – House competitions and feasts – a power cut during the Choir's recording of the *Messiah* – cold, spooky Practice Rooms – queuing for the Shop – school cheque books – Fr Paddy – sliding along Aloysius Corridor – run-throughs of Prize Day with military precision – camel-hair coats and berets, Tricels and pinafores – the building of Mores House – toast in the Infirmary – lacrosse and chapped legs – boiled fish – The List – the Three-Day Week and being read *The Snow Goose* in candlelight by S.M.Andrew.

The Community were wily, far-sighted, caring, and much more human and 'with it' than we ever knew!

After leaving New Hall, I went home to Hong Kong and started working life in a ship-broking subsidiary of Kleinwort Benson. Thereafter I had a varied working life: a headhunter, director of a Motion-Picture Equipment Company, administrator of an International Music and Arts Festival and admissions co-ordinator for a primary school. Work brought me to England in 1986, when I was given a dog. I married its vet, Julian, in 1988, and Arabella was born in 1992 and Hugh in 1994.

These days I live between Newbury and Normandy, and while I no longer work in any formal capacity, my shorthand is in demand and I minute meetings for various groups on a voluntary basis.

BRENDA GOSLING (née Ludlow)

Pole 1968–1974

An event happened when I was in the Upper Sixth, which seemed unfair at the time, but now we all laugh about it.

It was my 18th birthday and my parents had given me a fantastic huge birthday cake, so we all decided to bunk off Games as it was May and it meant swimming in the old cold outdoor pool. Theresa Byrne, Sue Hennessy, Annabelle Henderson, and I were having a real party, singing and larking around eating cake and drinking cider at 3.30 pm. Suddenly there was a forceful knock on the door and we all froze like rabbits caught in a car's headlights. Slowly the door opened and there stood Fanny (S.M.Francis). She said nothing but walked in, picked up the cake and strode out. We were dumbfounded.

Later, at the end of term, S.M.Francis congratulated my father on having made such a delicious cake, saying the whole Community had enjoyed it for tea!

I studied Radiography at Addenbrooke's Hospital, Cambridge, where I met my husband, James, brother of Katy Gosling. After having two children, I returned to work at Addenbrooke's and St Thomas's in London. I now live outside Saffron Walden, and have branched out into selling antiques, and running courses in Antique Restoration and French Polishing.

CAROLINE BAILEY

Owen 1969–1972

I recall midnight feasts on the roof of Owens House and on one occasion a member of the Community catching us. Instead of punishing us, she joined us! I was Deputy Head Girl (with Anne Spiller as Head Girl) and Owens House Captain in my final year.

I have resided in America since 1975. I am most proud of working with young people when I was a Corrections Officer for Sarasota County. I'm now retired and living in Florida, visiting my brothers in the UK every other year. My hobbies include, kayaking, motorcycling, travelling, camping, reading, golf, bowling. I am widowed and my son Kent, who was born in 1981, is safely in Heaven.

MARIE-CLARE BRIND (née Daniel)

Fisher 1969–1978

The whole School expedition to the Treasures of Tutankhamen – meeting Mother Teresa and having my photo taken for the local press – the Saturday paper round (early recycling initiative!) – the Three-Day-Week – exercises at dawn to keep us warm in Fisher led by Iggy (S.M.Ignatius) – whole School being 'gated' to sand down the wooden desks on the Plot to get rid of graffiti – end-of-term 'big' housework – joint drama production with Ampleforth, and the Chelmsford Festival of Drama and Music – winning the Debating Society debate against the Edward VI Grammar School boys – PGL adventure weekend in the Brecon Beacons (never been so cold in my entire life!) – Classics trip to Pompeii and Rome – whole School fire-practice at night with the fire-brigade rescuing the Head Girl – the sad death of Emma Cooke – Choir Christmas concerts in Chelmsford and Christopher Walker visiting and composing works specially for New Hall – riding from the old stables down past the old farm and the new stables being built – Bradwell field trips – camel-hair coats, 'sacks' and berets, capes and red knickers – queuing for the telephone (one for the whole School!) – four-hour Exeat on Sundays between Mass and Compline – and no half-term.

After a gap year, I studied English & Classical Civilisation at the University of Kent, then worked for a London Commercial Property Company, trans-ferring to Chartered Surveying (Commercial Property Management) when I passed my RICS. I married Michael in 1986 and we have two children James and Charlotte. I ran a property company with my husband until 2008. I am now a Director of Sustainability-Plus Europe. I have lived in Malmesbury for the past 20 years.

ROSANNE BRODERMANN (née Gaggero)

Campion 1969–1976

My first memory was the bed – metal framed with a horse-hair mattress which had a huge dip in the middle.

There was the excitement of getting enough 'privileges' to allow you to walk to Springfield and visit the sweet shop there. On Wednesday evenings we went to the Tuck Shop up the narrowest, creakiest, rickety staircase, where we had our own New Hall cheque books. My weekly allowance for tuck was 40p, which, surprisingly, bought a fair amount. If feeling extra peckish, we would have to invent the birthday of a brother/parent/great-aunt which justified extra expenditure.

The food was great – most of the time. The only real horrors were the whole boiled onions! Biggest treat was 'Pus and Bunions' – chocolate on pastry and utterly delicious.

Outings and School trips were wonderful. I will never forget our trip to Rome and meeting the Pope. The Tutankhamen Exhibition was fabulous. Even the Science trip to the Bradwell salt marshes was exciting. It was there that I had my first and last cigarette.

My enduring memory is of the people: the nuns who looked after us with real care and such a sense of fun, the teaching staff who inspired us to be our best, and the girls, so many of whom remain my greatest friends.

I left New Hall for a year in Switzerland, then worked for the family firm for a couple of years doing press and public relations before beginning my career as an Industrial Editor, specialising in aerospace and defence and medical systems. I married a soldier (now happily divorced), produced three magnificent children, and moved to the country where I work as a Citizen Advocate.

MICHELE YVONNE JONES (née Congdon)

1969–1972

I started at New Hall in 1969 when my parents were living in Bahrain. My earliest memory was that the school seemed enormous, and I had to adjust to a completely different way of life after living at home and going to the local comprehensive.

My years spent at New Hall have helped me to cope with the many challenges that life has sent my way.

I started my working life in Bahrain, first as a Bacteriologist, then for IBM and lastly for an Animal Sanctuary. In 1988 I joined my husband in Japan, where my first daughter was born prematurely, a difficult challenge; later my second daughter was born. When we returned to England I was diagnosed with malignant melanoma but after five years I am now clear of any problem. My children have also had their problems, and have battled with autism, undiagnosed for many years. My elder daughter is due to graduate after achieving a degree in Biomedical Science. I am the main carer for my younger daughter, who is due to embark on an Open University Course from home.

SONIA BUCHHOLZ

Campion 1969–1975

End-of-term housework where, in our blue overalls, we cleaned the desks out on the lawn in front of Campion. I can still smell the Gumption.

New Hall puddings with incredible names, such as 'Pus and Bunions' and 'Sticky Willies', which I thought nothing off until my first term at Bristol, when I went into the local bakery and asked for a 'Sticky Willy'.

Our cider and marshmallow birthday parties (cider was about the only alcohol we were allowed), and, of course, the sumptuous chocolate-fudge cake.

Having biscuit duty on a Saturday morning after housework, and everyone getting three biscuits. If you were in charge you could have even more than three.

In the Sixth Form, frothing up coffee grains to get a type of cappuccino.

That really hard loo paper which was like tracing paper, totally ineffective as well as uncomfortable.

Racing up the lacrosse pitch cradling the ball in my stick, only to get to the other end and discover I had lost the ball a long time ago! All that in the freezing cold.

Looking forward to when my parents could come down to take me out for Sunday lunch at the place on the roundabout – the Army and the Navy.

Waiting at Paddington Station after half-term to get on the bus back to New Hall, all doom and gloom!

After studying German Literature and History at Bristol University, I worked at the BBC Language Service and then for a sports marketing company in London. I moved to Frankfurt in 1988 to work for a German sports marketing company dealing with Davis Cup Tennis and the PGA European Golf Tour. I've spent the last few years doing TEFL (Teaching English as a Foreign Language), and have just returned to the UK to live in Essex!

BERNADETTE BARBER (née Walsh)

Campion 1970–1975

I loved New Hall. My idea of heaven was the early-morning run down the Avenue and playing lax all afternoon in the winter, or tennis in the summer. Followed by Team Teas – the treats that were extended to us but denied others!

Sharing wonderful birthday celebrations with my fellow Campions – indulging in S.M.James's legendary chocolate-fudge cake with 'lashings' of cider.

There was a particularly memorable Easter when we all stayed in school to celebrate the Triduum with enactments on the altar and Easter eggs on Easter Sunday. Somehow it felt very special.

I have some wonderful friends from my schooldays with whom I am still very much in contact – 41 years on!

I did a Business Studies degree at Bristol Poly and then went to work in a London Advertising Agency. I married and had two sons. In the last few years I've returned to studying at Birkbeck University in Architecture and Art History and now volunteer at the V&A Museum and am a Trustee of the Friends of the V&A. I also do some consultancy work with Marriage Care, an organisation involved in supporting couples and family life.

1975 Sonia Buchholz, Susan Arthur and Bernadette Walsh with the Griffin

2011 Sonia Buchholz, Susan Beedle (née Arthur) and Bernadette Barber (née Walsh) outside the Colchester Community Home, with Kali the dog

PEGGY DEANE (née Anderson)

Campion 1970–78

Born and brought up on a farm, to me the idea of being away from mum and dad for weeks on end seemed like the end of the world. My first nights at New Hall were in the High Room, with appropriately high ceilings and with a sink for each of us.

I remember scrubbing the black marks off the bottom of our socks then hanging them over the radiator to dry. I am sure Heather Bonney was with me (I'll never forget those cartwheels and flips she used to do). We polished our shoes every night and left them outside our doors or cubicles for inspection.

We used to dry our hair standing in the middle of the passageway; Anne-Marie Augier's hairdryer looked like a silver rocket machine!

There were fire-alarms in the middle of the night. I remember filing out, or rather being marched out by S. Margaret Mary, in a long line and assembling on the front lawn under the cedar trees, awaiting the arrival of the fire-engines.

Yes, that's me with the frown on my face, behind Mother Teresa.

Mother Teresa with Peggy Anderson (behind), 1970

Was I lucky to be picked to take up the collection on to the stage! It made my day, and I treasure the picture still 40 years later. We had taken a coach to Ipswich and I remember especially what a softly spoken woman she was and how intently we all listened, full of admiration.

After leaving New Hall did a BTEC at Bishop Burton Agricultural College, then went straight into my first job for a farming and contracting business. I married in 1984 and had two girls. I'm currently working for a large family Farming Contracting Business and Leisure Park on the North Norfolk Coast. A few years ago I decided to return to studying for an Accountancy qualification and I'm also busy with Property Refurbishment and Lettings in the Norwich area.

ALIX JAPP (née Barclay)
Owen 1970–1976

My home country is Zambia. My parents decided that we needed an English education and so, after much correspondence by airmail and many phone calls to S.M.Francis, my sister Celia and I left Zambia at the grand old ages of 11 and 12 respectively. We were collected from Heathrow Airport by Mr Evans and arrived at New Hall by way of his minibus early one September morning in 1970.

Mum had been busy with her sewing machine and made us both lovely winter dresses that should have been preserved for posterity. Everyone we saw that first day remembers 'those dresses'. We entered our new school by way of the Ambulacrum, which was very impressive. After we were shown our new quarters in Owens House, we collected our uniforms, all labelled by one of the sisters, S.Magdalen John, I think.

We were asked to put on our 'wellies' and then taken for a berry hunt along the lanes, which was great fun as we got to meet a few other 'Fishes' while keeping busy picking the blackberries.

We got used to the food – 'Pus and Bunion' dessert for lunch, 'Sticky Willie' buns for tea, Refectory meals with Prefects dishing out food and stacking plates.

There were Sunday afternoons in the Common Room watching old movies. In the Sixth Form there was hot chocolate after study.

The Barclay family with S.M.Dismas: Amanda, Jacqueline, Celia,
S.M.Dismas, Alix, Mrs Thelma Barclay; and Theola in the front

I loved lacrosse and I tried running 800 metres one year for Inter-House Athletics (phew). I played a little tennis and tried netball.

I remember Prizegiving in the square by the Refectory under a big tent and getting the Deportment Prize.

As the years went by my sisters, Jacqueline, Amanda and Theola, also attended New Hall, so five girls through the School was quite an achievement for my parents. I feel we have done them proud.

ALISON BERNADELLO (née Clarke)

1971–1979

I remember being in the wrong uniform when arriving on my first day. And there was endless lining up everywhere. And hateful horse riding . . . I was terrified and bitterly disappointed in myself for being so. There was the Shop at the top of a hundred ancient stairs near the Infirmary on Saturdays. And huge slabs of toffee melting on radiators – no wonder I now have a mouthful of crowns. And the time I mistook S.Magdalen John for a monster in the middle of one night so loud were her snores . . .

229

DEBBIE WARWICK (née Turnbull)

Owen 1970–1977

I remember the Three-Day Week, getting up in the dark and dressing by torchlight. I was sharing a room with Nicy Shannon who had size 6 feet, seemingly huge compared to mine which were size 4½. As we went downstairs through the gloom I discovered that I was wearing one of Nicy's size 6 shoes. The Refectory was lit up like a Gothic castle, with candles on every table – we had a huge six-branch candelabrum on ours.

The second Three-Day Week took place in my third year. When dusk fell, S.M.Andrew would light a candle and read to us. She read slowly with her pronounced Austrian accent, her nose getting closer to the candle as she sought to illuminate the book.

At the time of the Autumn Ball in 1970, Owens occupied the West Wing bedrooms, which overlooked the so-called 'Romantic Garden', a courtyard which had been artistically converted. We were taken up to Beaulieu to be out of the way and watched a film, I think *Campbell's Kingdom*, with Dirk Bogarde. When it finished we were taken back, and I remember charging up the stairs to our bedroom windows to catch a glimpse of kissing couples.

At 4pm the bell went for the end of classes and we all hurtled through the corridors to be the first in the tea queue. But then we had to wait for the Sixth Formers, who staffed the operation, to arrive. They would saunter along, unhurriedly bypass the long queue of famished pupils and disappear through the Refectory doors. Eventually, the doors would open and we would all pile in. Jam, bread, a cake each and tea were provided. I remember 'Bird's Dropping', a round chocolate éclair, and 'Sticky Willy', an iced bun, being particular favourites.

Night prayers followed supper. We would line up, two by two, in the Refectory and then process over to the Chapel with our House Captain at the head. At the altar she would turn and bow her head and then we would genuflect in unison and file into our designated pews.

We had Scottish Dancing lessons, with Miss Raven getting increasingly exasperated because we couldn't get the hang of it. There was one complicated switching-location manoeuvre with Miss Raven bellowing, 'Pousette, pousette,' which Jane Davies and I were doing with great enthusiasm and concentration – only to find that we hadn't moved position at all. I laughed so much, I could hardly stand up.

TV access was limited but we were allowed to watch the Sunday Serial, which was usually a BBC costume drama. There were 60 of us in our House but a finite number of chairs, so the seat allocation was hierarchical and everyone knew their place. Class 5 had the comfy chairs. Class 3 and 4 had the wooden chairs. Class 2 and 1 sat on the floor at the front.

In the hot summer of 1976, Penny Kinloch would get up at 6.30 every morning to swim in the outdoor pool. We sunbathed on Six Acres and I'd foolishly rubbed Johnson's Baby Oil on to my skin. My legs were so sunburned that I couldn't bend them and walked like a penguin for days.

Mrs Sylvia Helsby, a graduate of the Royal College of Music, was our Sunday organist, and on special occasions she would play Vidor's *Toccata* as the School was processing out of Chapel after Mass. Upstairs in the Choir, we would stay to hear her play – six minutes of bliss. She made it seem so easy and effortless, making the sound that filled the vast ceiling of the Chapel and bounced off the walls.

Every time I hear a pigeon cooing I'm back in my room in the West Wing corridor, waiting for S.M.Gabriel to get me up, her habit swishing as she gives me a little shake and then swishes away again.

After Kent University I joined the NHS and held various administrative and management posts in central London, Kingston upon Thames, Harrogate and Durham. Philip and I met while both working at Harrogate Hospital. We married in 1993, having moved to Durham. I now work as a Learning Support Assistant at a college in Darlington, where we now live.

MARTINA HENNING (née Wolatz)

Fisher 1970–1975

I remember New Hall for its size and historic setting, and for the really good friends I made and have kept. I liked S.M.David because of her gentle aura as a House Mother in Fishers and I loved the Art Room and the atmosphere of the Ambulacrum – and, of course, the cedar trees! I remember an Italian cook who was small and round and had a good sense of humour. I think she came from Naples, and I loved her spaghetti Bolognese.

I will never forget a Chemistry teacher from Ireland who arrived for the first lesson on Monday mornings with signs of a hangover. Although not the greatest teacher, she was unconventional and never boring.

I particularly enjoyed getting away from school on closed weekends for tea and scones at the Brown twins' home in Little Waltham.

I went back to New Hall with my two sons and husband for the first time on my 50th birthday and have kept in touch since.

Brigitte Walker, Martina Henning and Louisa Fernandez wih the javelin

After studying languages, I worked as an international translator and did some photographic modelling in product advertising in the 1980s. I changed direction to study law, and I am now a Civil Law lawyer in Berlin. I'm married to Magnus and have two sons.

SYLVIA GOLDBECK (née Noronha)
Fisher and Southwell 1971–1974

Recently I returned to tour New Hall after almost four decades. The Avenue did not seem as wide or as long as I remember when we were required by Miss Raven to run its length on winter days. I was amazed at how large the School had grown. New buildings now stand where there used to be fields in which we roamed and feasted on wild berries. It was a treat to peek into the Chapel (in the process of being renovated), where I had spent many hours, clad in an ill-fitting red skirt, white Aertex shirt, Idler shoes and a red blazer whose misshapen pockets served as hand warmers and carry-alls. It was even more thrilling to walk beyond the double doors that used to mark the entrance to the Convent, and to be shown the rooms that individual nuns used to occupy.

S.M. Thérèse and S.M. Magdalene back to back

233

The nuns are no longer there, but to this day, their names are indelibly etched in my mind along with certain memories: Reverend Mother, S.M.Christopher, and her ever present, warm smile; S.M.Francis, a quintessential administrator; S.M.Thérèse, Bursar *extraordinaire*; S.M.Magdalene, always compassionate in our hour of need; S.Magdalen John and her efficient use of laundry bins (no child of mine would think of placing his/her laundry in the wrong hamper); S.M.Andrew and S.M.John and their high academic expectations of us; S.M.Stephen and her incredible artistic talent; Sisters Angela, Stephanie and Simon who attempted, with varying degrees of success, to teach us to be articulate and cogent debaters; S.M.Peter, and her orderly Library; S.M.Ignatius, S.M.David, S.M.James, S.M.Dismas, S.M.Matthew, S.M.Mark, S.M.Gabriel and S.M.Bernadette, who ran the Houses in which we lived, like clockwork, in spite of our best efforts to derail established routines; and S. Margaret Mary, who has sent me a birthday card every year without fail since I left New Hall.

Their example of living a life rooted in faith, integrity, humility and concern for others shaped me into the person I am today. For that I shall always be grateful.

After I left New Hall, I went to university in California, USA. In 1982, I married Andy and we are living presently in Edmond, Oklahoma. Andy is a University Professor while I continue to be at home, raising the last of our four children, a seemingly never-ending task.

DOROTHY PODMORE (née Trumpy)
Pole 1971–1979

When I think of my eight years at New Hall and reflect on the people I met, the friends I made, the games played, the lessons learned and the prayers prayed, the image that comes most often to mind is . . . the stairs leading from the Ambulacrum up to the Art Room!

Arriving through the front door as a timid ten-year-old I was awed by the long hall of gleaming red tiles with the staircase that stretched all the way to heaven, although in reality it led to the classroom I would spend my first year in. Its polished wood was worn soft by generations of feet which had walked, marched or shuffled up and down the six sections for hundreds of years.

The smooth feel of the banister, which was never, ever to be slid down. The little knobs, like small pine cones, on each of the corners, which I used to stroke as I came downstairs. As a Junior, I leapt the steps two at a time, trying to jump the last three and being told off. In my middle years, I sat on the warm stair wood when the whole School gathered in the Ambulacrum at the end of the Easter weekend for one big social. And I remember walking slowly up the stairs on the morning of my first A Level paper, knowing that the hour of reckoning had come.

Did Anne Boleyn ever walk up those stairs? A couple of us searched for her ghost one night at the other end of the School but all we found was an empty storeroom. Or did King Henry himself make some of the indentations in the wood as he swept down the stairs in his royal robes? We will never know their story; we can only remember our own.

After a BSc in Physics from Durham University, I spent six months travelling in South America, where I met my future husband. I worked for Lloyds Bank International, with postings in London and Portugal. We emigrated to Canada in 1994, by which time we had three children. After we had two more, I left paid work to become a full-time family slave and to enjoy the outdoor life on the west coast. Right now, we're making lists of all the exciting things we plan to do when we are finally child-free.

*On the horse: J. Scanlon, M. Bell, R. Gaggero, R. Jordan, M. Lavery,
G. McLeod-Jones. Standing: K. Maguire, C. Bennet, E. Holt
and E. Gurhey*

REBECCA JORDAN

Campion 1971–1977

I remember the mounting excitement and anticipation as you drove
down the Avenue for the new term. And the sense of height – towering
cedars, high ceilings, tall nuns.

– Going blackberry picking on the first weekend of each autumn
term as a distraction from homesickness. Although never homesick
myself, blackberrying has been forever tinged with sadness.

– Singing in the choir – the *Messiah*, Fauré's *Requiem*, St Francis's
'Prayer for Peace'.

– Being late for a meal and realising with a sinking feeling, as you
raced across the Quad, that S.M.Dismas was on duty. She could quell
you with a raised eyebrow.

– Gumption and 'second housework' – stable duty was more fun but
a mad rush.

– The backstage buzz of getting dressed and made up for *Coppelia*.

– The wonderful tranquillity of the Infirmary, with S.M.Magdalene
gliding around in her white habit . . .

236

– Worst food: lukewarm spinach and poached eggs; best: 'snot and bogey pie' (a pastry case filled with chocolate butter cream and cream on top).

– Collecting old newspapers with Mr Parsons, and one particularly unsuccessful Saturday afternoon when the Cup Final was on . . .

– Being looked after and nurtured by my Housemistresses: S. Margaret Mary in Juniors and S. Stephanie in Campions. And S.M.Christopher sitting by my bed all night after my grandfather died.

It was a unique and caring Community and a moral compass for life. My years at New Hall were in stark contrast to my Sixth Form in a boys' school, where it was commonly accepted that the girls were there 'to raise the tone of conversation in the classroom'! I realised, with hindsight, what strong, dedicated, inspiring and positive female role models the nuns were for us all.

After leaving New Hall, I went to the Sixth Form at Felsted, then South-ampton University and the Institute of Education. After a very brief time teaching, I retrained as a Solicitor, but after my children were born I set up a Gardening Business. I recently returned to Essex with my husband and two children to live on my family farm. I am delighted that my daughter now goes to New Hall.

DINA HIJAZI
Pole 1971–1976

After being told by Charlotte Douglas how babies are born, I was so horrified I told her she was lying – she seemed very pleased with herself! I remember missing my parents, crying hysterically every night until I was so exhausted I fell asleep. I was afraid to use the toilet day or night because I was too afraid of ghosts, having been told the King had cut off the Queen's head and she walked around carrying it.

I was told to say the Rosary so that I wouldn't cry and keep my room-mate awake half the night. I watched other girls see their parents at the weekend and felt such envy. I remember thinking that Sarah King was not upset by this place and realising her family was close by, and soon after her parents became my interim parents.

The curved staircase going up to 'Juniors' was stone and so worn that we could slide on it. The Sweet Shop was my favourite place but also frightening, with the narrow staircase that went up forever. There were the creaky floors of our bedrooms, and the loos where we pulled a chain to make them flush. And there was the Common Room where we could talk to each other and where I watched a girl eat a strange green thing with a big seed in it: Monika Lavery eating an avocado!

I remember the scratching cardigans and the stuffy Tricels, the shoes that never fitted me and the skirt I grew out of way too quickly. I remember drinking my first coffee because the big girls liked it. I remember being cold and the Biology Lab being a fascinating place to escape to. Of course I remember that vile food called shepherd's pie and to this day I shiver when I think of it. Such bittersweet memories!

MONIKA LINTON (née Lavery)

Pole 1971–1980

I remember meeting Dina Hijazi and Sarah King by the noticeboard with my mum on the first day, and mum suggesting we made friends. And Alison Clarke warned me of ghosts on the way to the loo with a story about Anne Boleyn with her head under her arm.

There was the huge climbing frame at the top of the Playing Fields where I loved going with Catriona Rankin. I remember the kindness of Catriona when any of us needed comfort or encouragement, her bun

Yakkety yakkety on the School pay-phone (drawing by Susan Coffey)

on the back of her head and her friendly smile. I loved walking round the back of the building, where the laundry went and where the working outhouses and the farm were – much more interesting to me than the posh front entrance!

I had a wardrobe of inappropriate and exotic clothes from Africa which my friends found strange, and which were never warm enough for England!

I remember sharing my first Junior House room with Claire Bennett and trying to be brave, with mum and dad far away in Nigeria. Those phone appointments in the office in Aloysius Corridor, in the company of the switchboard staff, when you were trying to tell your parents how you were . . . There was so little to say: you couldn't be honest, it was costing a fortune, and you had nothing in common because of the distance, and so conversations were usually about arrangements.

HELEN ELMORE

Fisher 1972–1977

School report Autumn 1972: Subject – Needlecraft
Helen has been rather distracted throughout the term; she demonstrates little interest in this subject. Her tie-dying was very good but her lampshade has been spoilt by untidy stitching. [Yes, I still have little interest in this subject.]

School report Summer 1973: Subject – House report
Helen must learn that a lively mind and a quick tongue are no substitute for hard work. [I am laughing so much.]

The School fees for the Autumn Term 1974 were £300. The bill included £2.31 for 'dissecting instruments'. A field trip to Bradwell-on-Sea was charged at £1.40.

After New Hall I lived in London (sharing a flat with Annie-T Eyston), and read English and Drama at London University. I've had a range of jobs over the years as a PA, office manager and, having moved into HR, in training and development. For the last 13 years I have worked in the NHS in Improvement and Leadership Development. I left London in 1997 and now live in Bath, Somerset.

EMMA GILBEY KELLER (née Gilbey)
Fisher 1972–1979

I now have two daughters of my own, Molly who's 14 and Alice, 9. They go to a progressive co-ed school in the heart of New York City. It's light years from Chelmsford. So how do I teach them values? What are my values? Recently I sat and wrote down all the bits and pieces that have informed my value system from my time at 1970s' New Hall. Here they are:

All shall be well . . . Lord make me an instrument of your peace . . . Forgive us our trespasses as we forgive those who trespass against us . . . This above all to thine own self be true . . . . Love is patient and kind . . . Love means never having to say you're sorry . . . Honesty is the best policy . . . Go placidly amidst the noise and haste . . . Pray inwardly, even if you do not enjoy it . . . In purer lives Thy service find, In deeper reverence, praise . . . Do as you would be done by . . . Work before play . . . Think of those 'less fortunate' than you . . . I am not angry, just disappointed . . . Don't let yourself down . . . Do not judge so that you shall not be judged . . . Kindness is the golden chain by which society is bound together . . . Love conquers all . . . *Think* before you speak! . . . Where is the Life we have lost in living? . . . No sex before marriage . . . Charity begins at home . . . Home is where the heart is . . . Be as you wish to seem . . . Two wrongs don't make a right . . . Do you reject the glamour of evil? . . . Is this your best? . . . A cynic is a man who knows the price of everything but the value of nothing . . . Like a bridge over troubled water I will ease your mind . . . The virtuous woman's price is far above rubies . . . Say not, 'I have found the truth,' but rather, 'I have found a truth.' . . . Love one another.

I studied English at King's College London and taught for a few years. I moved to Washington DC and became a journalist, working for ABC News. In South Africa, I wrote a biography of Winnie Mandela. Back in the USA, I wrote for most major US and UK newspapers and magazines. I married Bill Keller and we had two daughters. I wrote a second book, The Comeback – *seven stories of women who went from careers to family and back. I'm currently writing fiction for Middle School Girls plus contributing to the* Guardian. *I've just finished a brief battle with breast cancer. I won!*

BELLA PEREZ BUCHANAN (née Perez)

Fisher 1972–1978

Having driven up the Avenue and caught that first impressive glimpse of the building flanked by the stunning cedars, everyone in the family agrees that New Hall is beautiful.

There was also the Beech Walk where we trudged back and forth from Beaulieu in our winter capes, laden with heavy satchels. In spring and summer it was transformed into a lovely coppery tunnel.

I remember the sinister 'out of bounds' Wilderness which drew us like a magnet. As darkness approached, we would gather on the edge of it and dare each other to see who could penetrate farthest. It was terrifying!

Inside the floors shone, everything was clean and smelt of polish (not surprising with all the polishing we did!).

One of the loneliest experiences was the sound of the old clock striking the hour, when everybody else was sleeping, and then hearing a distant train . . .

I remember all my friends well as we started off in Lower One as a small closely knit group. We had most of our lessons in one classroom at the top of the house near the Practising Rooms, and for almost all of them we had one teacher, S. Margaret Mary (with whom we are still very close).

S.M.Ignatius and S. Margaret Mary were my Housemistress and Vice-Housemistress respectively and I am indebted to them both for everything they taught me, both academically and as a person.

BELINDA BREWIN
Southwell 1973–1978

I remember my first day at the School as if it were yesterday. Over the railway line, down the long tree-lined avenue and there stood New Hall, the Ha-Ha and the enormous cedar trees. I had longed to go to boarding school, imagining being one of the Famous Five, having midnight feasts, and I was surprised to find that not everyone felt the same. That first night, as some girls cried from homesickness, I lay in bed thinking this is going to be a great adventure – and so it was.

I didn't start off with the intention of being the naughtiest girl in the School but somehow or other it worked out that way. Early on when, late for Maths, I was told I had better have a good excuse for this tardiness, I said well actually I do, I got run over by a tractor on the Beech Walk, and am lucky to be here at all. I held up my mud-covered cloak that I had sat on over the weekend while probably smoking behind the cow sheds. My classmates all laughed and I got the first of many detentions.

Winters were cold and we used to sit huddled on the radiators and were told to get off them else we would get chilblains! Then there was the wind that blew across Six Acres and under the changing rooms by

A chilly swimming-lesson (drawing by Susan Coffey)

the swimming-pool – and the freezing water. Of course, the food was disgusting. One lunchtime I was forced to stay behind to finish the revolting semolina. It was a long afternoon.

In spite of two suspensions from school and even a week sleeping in the Infirmary, in the vain hope that I would somehow be cured of my appalling attitude, I actually remember school fondly. My great love for lacrosse, the camaraderie with my team mates and all the inter-house competitions, the hilarity of being together and of making great friends. Today, when I hear Fleetwood Mac's 'Rumours' or Bob Dylan's album *Desire*, they take me back to Southwells and my friends. My lasting memory is of my Housemistress, S.M.Dismas, an amazing woman, who never had to tell you what she thought, she just raised one eyebrow and you knew you were in trouble. I loved her and I am lucky I am still able to speak to her and to see her. Notwithstanding my appalling behaviour, I loved school. My only regret? Getting expelled, because I think the Sixth Form would have been even more fun.

NANDITA NELSON (née de Souza)

More 1973–1975

I came to New Hall in 1973 for two years in the Sixth Form – S.M.Francis was Headmistress and S.M.Christopher was Reverend Mother. It was the time of fuel shortages and it was freezing cold in Mores!

With very few Prefect duties, no uniform and studying the subjects that really interested me, I found New Hall a wonderful experience. I relished being in the Choir led by S.M.Mark, S.M.Peter's support during all those long hours in the Library, S.Stephanie's excellent use of English, classes for the Oxbridge entrants and S.M.John's lively Biology sessions. Tre Lenahan was one of the stimulating Lay teachers.

Alison Bowditch and I shared a room for ages and nearly 40 years later we still see each other regularly. She was my bridesmaid 25 years ago, and is godmother to my daughter.

Despite the cold, I have the warmest memories of the generous spirit of the Community.

I studied Physiology at Newcastle and then Medicine and have been a practising doctor since 1983. My speciality is Radiology and, having now taken an academic path, I am leading a research team at the Institute of Cancer Research and am Professor of Translational Imaging and Deputy Dean for Clinical Sciences at the Royal Marsden Hospital. My husband Steve is a Renal Physician. We have one daughter, aged 22, studying Music at Cambridge.

Nandita de Souza with Peggotty

HENRIETTA COURTAULD

Fisher 1973–1980

I remember:

– Maggie Mary, Iggie, Hippo, S. Magdalen John, Ollie, Miss Raven, Miss Cox, Mrs Hall; wonderful Fr Eric; Emma Cooke, who died in a car crash aged 11; and Dr Tamlyn.

– The shock of seeing the nuns without their hair covered.

– The echo (or squeak) of shoes on the floor of Aloysius Corridor.

– Dreading housework duties at the beginning of term – who was going to have to do the loos?

– The telephone booth, where I used to ring home every day, with a reverse charge call!

– Fr Barry singing 'Daisy Daisy' to S.M.Francis.

– Wireless on for breakfast, listening to Radio 4.

– Lacrosse and getting as muddy as possible in the winter. No such things as showers in those days, you just wandered about with dirty knees.

– The laundry baskets left out on the landings for dirty washing – rather smelly by the end of the evening.

– Washing our pants and socks every night and drying them on the tiny radiator in each cubicle.

– Polishing our shoes and having them inspected outside the cubicles.

– Putting a shoe outside my cubicle so I could be woken early to go to early-morning Mass.

– The dairy at the back and the stalls that we used to play in – wonderful smell of animal dung. The churns full of hot frothy milk, delivered to the kitchen.

– Tuck Shop cheque books. So grown up and taught us to budget. Then a Mars Bar machine was installed on the stairs beside the Refectory – disaster because we could buy sweets every day!

– School teas – originally the most amazing cakes (including 'Sticky Willies') but as the school got bigger it ended up just being slices of bread.

– The outside swimming-pool, and tiny cubicles for changing in. Miss Cox threatening to open the curtains if we weren't quick enough.

– Watching from Fisher as the beautiful and trendy Sixth Formers walked to tea – Emma Gilbey *et al.* – it was like a fashion show every day.

– Most traumatic memory is of being publicly weighed at the beginning of term – we had to line up by height and Miss Cox would yell out the weight so everyone could hear.

– The walk from Beaulieu to the Main School was jolly cold in the winter so we had to wear our capes with the House colours in the hood.

– The Nuns' Cemetery – within the walls and so peaceful and beautiful.

I'm fine and single. I have two children. Ranulf is starting law school, having just graduated from Edinburgh, and Lottie is in her last year at York reading an 'ology'.

JACQUELINE MAIN (née Barclay)

Owen 1973–1980

It is with affection and gratitude that I remember Mr Morgan the Music master at New Hall. Due to his encouragement and the efforts of his wife, who taught me singing, I joined the Madrigal Choir. Needed in one of the school productions, we proudly took our place on stage and performed with enthusiasm and pride. Sadly our efforts were not appreciated by the local press who felt that the 'Madrigal fell flat of its pitch' – my career in the limelight was not to be!

What inspired me, however, to love and appreciate the Performing Arts, arose from the fact that Mr Morgan had signed the school up to an amazing arts initiative, encouraging us to experience world-class live productions. New Hall had 12 tickets every term to a performance of Mr Morgan's choice in London. Sign-up sheets were in the main corridor of the school and my friend Susan and I signed up for everything. Every Tuesday, after classes ended, we would head to London with our 'packed dinner' of grated-cheese sandwiches on white bread with a packet of crisps. We visited the Royal Opera House where we were introduced to Wagner and Rossini. Ballets, concerts and opera were my weekly fix. The most memorable performance was Rudolf Nureyev in *The Sleeping Beauty*. I was mesmerised. He outperformed the *corps de ballet* and was absolutely magnificent.

I loved Geography because of S.M.Ignatius, and Church music because of the wonderful School Choir. Donkey riding at weekends was entertaining as we had to catch them first. They lived in a field full of nettles and, once caught, would take us to wander the grounds in search of mulberries. Having come from Zambia, I found the full-cream milk was like nectar – but it tended to disagree with me.

Returning to school after our holidays involved our being picked up from Heathrow, the long drive to Essex in the drizzle and then the final sweep around the bend as we entered the grounds. The magnificent view of the school from the Avenue was usually lost on me as the reality of another term away from our parents gave me an empty feeling in the pit of my stomach. The school was always immaculate with a wonderful welcoming smell of polish. Those highly polished

Mr Morgan conducting (drawing by Susan Coffey)

floors offered glorious opportunities to run and slide, and if you could add a crash into the swing doors and not get caught, you were a hero!

One night I bravely ventured out into the corridor, and rather than go past S.M.Gabriel's room to the main loo block, I went in the opposite direction towards Mores where there were additional bathrooms. On my return, creeping out and tiptoeing back, I was given the shock of my life: someone normally only ever seen in a habit came out of the bathroom, all rosy and pink after a nice hot bath, and with her hair loose and in considerable disarray. It was S.M.— !

SUSAN COFFEY

Owen 1973–1980

I remember the many school productions. I confess I dreaded taking part but it was regarded as an essential part of character building and everyone had to do it. I usually got away with a non-speaking role. There were plenty of budding thespians at New Hall but alas no boys then. The drama productions were the result of many hours of hard work by the Ronaldsons, a husband-and-wife team, who always smelled, not unpleasantly, of theatrical make-up and tweed. S.M.Benedict worked on the costumes.

On Sports Day 1978 I was 'Athlete of the Year' and look back fondly on having so much vitality and energy. I especially loved summer sports but was not keen on the winter ones like cross-country running. The red knickers were truly awful. Lacrosse was only for the brave and hardy.

We had some wonderful school trips. There was the Art History trip to Greece – the Acropolis with the lovely Mrs Hall. Our A Level trip to Hatfield to the studio of Henry Moore was a tremendous opportunity, although I felt too intimidated to speak to Henry Moore himself. There was a large sheep sculpture in a field nearby, surrounded by real sheep who seemed to like its shade and texture. On another trip we were introduced to Sir Howard Robertson, the architect of the Shell Tower on the South Bank (London). Working as a teacher in a state comprehensive with limited opportunities, I can appreciate how much we enjoyed privileged access to experiences like this.

Annual blanket-shaking took place on the ground between Mores and Owens. A significant part of our education was learning how to clean things and to understand seasonal, weekly and daily cleaning routines. (I suspect that it also greatly reduced the staff bill for cleaning such a large site.) There is nobility in all things . . . Duvets had only recently arrived on the British scene and we were allowed to have them as long as they went on top of our cotton sheets and blankets, which resulted in serious overheating. Eventually this was relaxed. S.M.Gabriel used to run her finger under railings and behind ledges to check dusting had been done properly.

For *The Beggar's Opera*, produced by Mr Morgan, I struggled with my newly learned bassoon part and can remember Mr Morgan's fierce brow lowering at me . . . None the less my fondest memories of New Hall are of Music being taught by Mr and Mrs Morgan. Mr Morgan was a man of many talents and just the one work suit – brown corduroy. He had built his own spinet and was enthusiastic about sharing his knowledge with us. He deeply inspired me. The peripatetic Music teachers who came in were marvellous, including the aptly named Mr Kitts who taught drumming. I started to learn the bassoon with the gifted Vernon Elliott, creator of the music for *Noggin the Nog* and a leading bassoon soloist. I learned piano with the elderly Mrs Kendall Whyte, but I didn't practise enough. Regardless of personal faith, collective singing in the Chapel and listening to the Choral Society and the singing of the Community was spiritually very powerful.

I got a degree in Typography and Graphic Communication at Reading. My working life included a wonderful spell at the English National Opera designing posters and programmes. When the in-house studio closed, my husband Andrew and I set up 875 Design Ltd in Reading, where we worked in partnership while raising our two daughters. I became interested in teaching and retrained as a Design Technology teacher, which is what I am now. The toughest job yet – but I have had a lot of inspiration, especially from key figures at New Hall, including: S.M.Ignatius (Geography); Miss Thompson (Chemistry), who said always own up to your mistakes and be truthful; Mrs Hall (History of Art); and Mrs Jones (English), who told me that one day I would appreciate Austen (she was right). Last but not least is S.M.Stephen, who always encouraged me in Art.

Prizegiving picnic on the lawn in 1980. The Fitzgerald and Coffey families with S.M.Francis and Mrs Wilson. Mary Fitzgerald looking towards the camera (photo by Susan Coffey)

LEAH VIERRA DESLAURIERS

Fisher 1973–1975

The winter of the fuel crisis was my first experience of cold weather. I arrived with two close friends, Gayle and Karen Quesnel, from Trinidad and Tobago, and we had never seen snow before. The school was without heat for what seemed like an age. I remember eating sandwiches and sleeping in layers made up of most of my clothes. But we survived. I did love the snow.

In the first week we somehow did not hear the bell for supper. Feeling intimated by S.M.Dismas (fondly known as Dizzy) and realising that everyone was already eating, we hid under a stairwell for the entire time and went hungry!

The teacher who influenced me most was Miss Mercer who lived in the cottage near the entrance. She was like a mother to me and I will never forget her. S. Margaret Mary also stands out in my mind; she was in charge when I was Vice-Captain of Fishers and she was a living example of unconditional love.

The horse rides back to New Hall I will never forget! As we entered the gate to the mile-long Avenue, the nun in charge of riding (who enjoyed a good gallop – which I did not!) encouraged us to let our horses go. As soon as you nudged those horses, they took off like wild things. I grabbed hold of my horse's neck and desperately fought to stay on its back, while branches from the trees lining the Avenue slapped my face. I didn't keep up riding, although I have enjoyed the times I have been able to ride over the years.

My time at New Hall began with the challenge of being severely homesick, but I grew to enjoy the friendships I made, especially with Yohanna (Hansje) Van Hellenberg Hubar and Bronwen Barker. I became independent and developed a love of travelling. I spent time in Germany, Spain and France, all arranged by the school. These trips, where we stayed with local families, were life-changing experiences I would not want to have missed!

After leaving I went on to Cambridge and then returned home to Trinidad. I ended up in Dallas, Texas, having married an American, and entered the

Travel Industry. I became Vice President of Sales and Marketing for a large travel company and got to travel to many destinations worldwide, an ambition that was born at New Hall. My last seven years in Dallas I had my own agency. David and I had a son and daughter and returned to Trinidad in 1999 where we went into the Land Development business, which our son is now taking over.

CLARINDA CUPPAGE

Owen 1974–1979

What a great name for a pair of shoes – Idlers. Were we actually allowed to idle in them? Mine – leather uppers and soles – were coveted by girls who had the rubber-soled variety, which lost their shape too quickly. I was teased by friends at home for my Idlers but at New Hall it was another matter. I have no idea who it was I passed mine on to, but I remember many offers.

Only at New Hall would our School reports include a page on 'Order'. Each term the final page reported on my housework and each term it

Victoria Twist, Clarinda Cuppage and Edwina Gurhy in the summer of 1979

said, 'Housework could be more thorough.' Some things don't change!

My love of arum lilies stems from those incredible vibrant flower arrangements in the School Chapel and the Ambulacrum.

I still remember the smell of Izal medicated toilet paper. Great for tracing Geography maps with, but not much else. I think I was on a School committee which lobbied for the introduction of softer loo paper – we certainly had lots of heated discussions over this.

The only prize for creativity I won at New Hall was for the design of a hat during Foundation Day celebrations, which I made exclusively out of cups. Quite fitting for the Clarinda Cup-page hat!

Being at New Hall was a happy and positive experience for me – it was a place where I got to learn about living in a new way. Responsibility was recognised and rewarded, participation and expression encouraged and support offered.

Many years later, I was invited to join the Board of Governors and I visited New Hall a number of times and briefly worked alongside the nuns, observing them in new ways. It dawned on me that I had been taught by some feminist nuns who were more political (with a small p) than I'd ever understood. It's been inspiring seeing how they have reinvented themselves, with each member of the Community finding her own individual way of expression, with some moving into social-action roles within the wider community.

Sitting in the Chapel while the Community sang the Midday Office, I understood that New Hall had offered me so much more than I had ever acknowledged. New Hall was not so much the physical place, but rather this loving Community of women whose enduring strength and connection I could tap into at any time from anywhere in the world. The Community offered so much more than an education: they offered a lifelong connection to themselves and their way of living, a guide to life itself.

I'm a Biodynamic Craniosacral Therapist working with people living with illness and the effects of trauma. I'm also freelancing in Communications. I'm a Trustee of a number of charities, including the MAP Foundation promoting emotional expression for people living with life-threatening illness.

DIANA (Dee) COE (née Foster)

Southwell 1975–1981

I remember:
- Standing in the old Main Hall in our House groups and year groups for Assembly.
- Taking part in a diving competition on behalf of the school.
- Playing lacrosse during the winter and swimming in the cold pool in the summer.
- Being confirmed in the Church of England and receiving gifts from S.M.Christopher.
- Fun lunchtimes, sitting at long tables in the dining-hall and having the Sixth Formers serve us.
- Cross country. We used to run down to the main gate but once over the hill, where no one could see us, we'd turn round!
- In the Lower Sixth having to do 'silver service' for the Upper Sixth during their end-of-year ball.
- Loving Sports Day and the last weekend of the term because our parents used to come with huge picnics which we ate on the lawns.

JANE ARNOLD (née Pate)

Campion 1975–1980

I'm a professor teaching Computer Science at La Roche College in Pittsburgh, Pennsylvania, USA. It's a Catholic co-ed with about 1400 students, and it's got the same feel as New Hall. It too was founded by nuns, and the nuns are still involved in the teaching, which makes it a really caring and nurturing environment.

I'd grown up in the USA and when my dad was assigned to Germany there was no school which really matched what my sister and I were looking for and my dad jokingly suggested we might like to try an English boarding school. We thought that would be an amazing adventure. We started at New Hall without any preconceptions. It was so different from what we'd been used to. In the States only very rich or troubled kids went to boarding school.

Having grown up sharing a bedroom with my younger sister, I was really pleased to have my own cubicle, with a sink in my room – that's so European and so useful! I absolutely hated some of the meals – stewed tomatoes, Brussels sprouts, fried bread, tongue and steak-and-kidney pudding and that horribly soggy thing with jello and cake. I was never a convert to the New Hall love of Marmite and chocolate spread. For me the highlight of the week was going to the Shop to buy chocolate bars.

The cold's another thing I remember. Coming from Florida, I'd never seen a cloak before. I found the school very draughty, and couldn't believe that we had to open our bedroom windows every morning. But I did discover hot-water bottles. I'd never had to shine my shoes or strip a bed every morning before I came to New Hall!

New Hall was pivotal in my career development. Mrs Wilson brought a computer into the classroom – it was the first one I'd ever seen – which began my fascination with them. New Hall also helped me develop excellent study habits and taught me how to handle extreme exam pressure. Things like evening study-periods are unheard of in the States in high school, and I'm sure the reason I got into a good university in America and had the success I did was because of my New Hall experience.

SARAH NAYLOR (née Drew)

Pole 1976–1983

S.M.John was Housemistress in Poles and I was House Captain with Jo Olding and Mubanga Musakanya.

I remember the rush for chairs for *Top of the Pops* after supper on Thursday evenings.

– Revising out in the sun with the House doors open and trying to catch Wimbledon at the same time.

– The Prizegiving picnic where a huge meringue got dropped in the grass . . . and was scooped up and enjoyed all the same!

– Hiding my supper yoghurt in my pocket, so that when a Prefect came to check the Chapel queue and I put my hand in my pocket, my fingers burst the lid and yoghurt exploded up my blazer sleeve!

– Cross country in the cold and wet. And House swimming and always getting cramp after the free-style relay.

– Carol singing in the Quad on the last day before the Christmas hols. And House entertainments, most memorably when I was Joyce Grenfell.

– School ski trip to Austria when the loos were blocked and it wasn't us!

– Chapel after supper when the School were told my brother-in-law had cancer and again when they were told he was cured.

– Melting Mars Bars under our study lamps. Hot milk and dropping a whole packet of Maltesers in to melt.

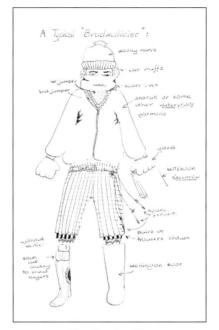

The Bradwellian
(drawing by Susan Coffey)

– Walking on the iced-over pond past the kitchen gardens, falling in and then sitting on our cubicle worktop with feet in the sink to warm them.

– Helping with a holiday for disadvantaged kids, and staying at School for the holiday and loving it.

– The Bradwell field trip, when Pole's Housemistress S.M.John didn't wear her habit!

– Being told I was to stop Latin and tearing up my verb book, then being told it was a mistake and having to rewrite *all* the verbs again.

I can remember so many of my teachers; I loved it all, and the memories keep on coming back in daily life.

I live on the Suffolk/Essex border with my family. I am a Practice Nurse and also work as a Travel Nurse Consultant. My husband James is in the wine trade. Life is good but scary, with three girls, Emily, Charlotte and Isobel, all reaching their teenage years.

REBECCA (Becky) NUGENT

More 1976–1978

Day one, Lower Sixth, new girl.

Housework allocation: Choir stairs and floor swept, banisters polished, job done. S. Anne Joseph on duty.

Me: 'I've finished my housework, ma'am. It was a bit odd because there was some grass on the floor behind the door.'

S.A.J.: 'Really? It's probably that old door hinge.'

Me: 'No, *grass*!'

S.A.J.: 'Yes, the door is very old.'

Me: 'Grass, green grass from the garden.'

S.A.J.: 'Aaaaahhhh . . . graaaaasss. I thought you said *rust*.'

Note to self: Don't try to explain anything with a Yorkshire accent because no one knows what on earth you are talking about.

Quotes from the Sixth Form dance:

'Mary Jane Mason . . . your brother has arrived and he is *not* wearing a tie.' (S.M.David)

'The lavatories allocated to the boys have been damaged. And I'm not surprised. Those poor boys didn't know what to do with themselves after you girls were all over them on the dance floor.' (S.M.Francis, the morning after the night before)

'Girls . . . if you give a boy your finger . . . he will take your whole arm.' (Mrs Bosley offering sensible dating advice)

PHILIPPA (Phil) BROWN (née Olding)

Southwell 1976–1982

My favourite meal was breakfast, when we would eat several bowls of cereal with milk fresh from the farm. The jugs were filled from a large vat and if you were lucky you would get the cream from the top. My next favourite meal was tea and I remember setting an all-time record by eating ten slices of bread and several doughnuts. I put on quite a bit

S.M. Stephen's Art Class

of weight in my first year at New Hall, which would have been recorded in the 'termly' weigh-in, an event we had to line up for – next to the Mars Bar machine!

The best dress was worn for Mass on Sunday, a shapeless shift of a thing which had underneath it a white Tricel, which made you itch and sweat.

On Saturday afternoon we were given our pocket money and went straight down to the Tuck Shop. I spent all my money on a slab of toffee which I would take back to my cubicle and put on the radiator to soften and would then eat all in one go.

After breakfast we had to clean our cubicles and then our House. Does Gumption exist any more? If you were unlucky enough to have a classroom to clean then you were expected to use wire wool to remove the ink spots from wooden floors and desks.

After Mass on Sunday was letter-writing time. Every week I would tell my parents how many goals I'd scored in Saturday's netball match and whether I had been mentioned for good play that week. Our post was handed out in the first break of the day, when we were given a glass of milk. It was always exciting if there was an envelope addressed to you and disappointing if there wasn't.

PHIL POWER and KATE PITT

Fisher 1976–1983

Playing rounders in the Quad / Trudging up to Beaulieu for double Religion / Pretending to operate on Foo Robertson in Fisher's Little Dormitory / Crying with homesickness into a basin full of pants.

Dusting, Dusting, Dusting.

Celebrating our netball successes / Jackie Knudsen taking it away on the drums / Standing on the Refectory tables belting out 'Our God Reigns' at Easter / Laughing / Crying every time we had to wear athletics shorts. They weren't shorts – they were just big pants. / The warning swish of S. Margaret Mary's habit as she swept down the dormitory / The fear as we took on Queenswood at lacrosse / Waiting for Foo Robertson to turn up for a midnight feast (we are still waiting) / Going home early for half-term as Haverhill Fever took its toll / Spongy white bread plastered with chocolate spread.

Sweeping, Sweeping, Sweeping.

The rare sight of a man not in Holy Orders – for example, the gardener mowing the lawns in the summer term / The sound of the bell marking time / The excitement of delicious food parcels arriving for Claudia Von Bismark / The Mars Bar machine on the way to the Infirmary and melting slabs of toffee on radiators.

Kneeling, Kneeling, Kneeling.

S. Stephanie's passion for English Literature / Mrs Locke's endless and impressive wardrobe options / Nuns you didn't mess with – S.M.Ignatius, S.M.John and, on a bad day, S. Margaret Mary / The excitement of the marquee going up for Exhibition Weekend.

Praying, Praying, Praying.

Kneeling among your stripped bedclothes mumbling Morning Prayer / Getting goose pimples every time we heard the descant to 'Lord, make me an instrument of your peace' / The laughter, the friendships and sadness of parting / What was Gumption and is it still available? . . . because it cleaned up a bath beautifully!

Phil Power writes: After New Hall I went to St Andrews University to read History, graduating in 1988. I then worked for Brunswick, a

PR consultancy in London, for 15 years, interspersed with some overseas travel. On returning to the UK, I moved into the charity sector, working for Help the Aged and the homeless charity, Crisis. I am now living in North London and am a freelance Communications Consultant.

ANON

1976–1982

There are so many funny stories and recollections of friends, nuns and teachers that I have considered writing about, but, in the end, I keep coming back to the fact that for so many years New Hall was my anchor.

I know from the bonds formed with so many at New Hall that while my experience is perhaps unusual, it is certainly not unique. My parents lived abroad. I was an only child and there were difficulties in their marriage which were fuelled by alcoholism (which neither of my parents have ever faced up to). New Hall truly was my salvation. The routines, the expectations, the support and friendship from staff and Community as well as my peers has made me who I am today. My husband often says that the very best thing my parents ever did for me was to send me to New Hall. Whenever I drive down the Avenue I feel as though I am coming home, and I think I always will.

Until the age of 11, I believed that adults made empty promises and then let you down – and I blamed myself for that. At New Hall there were three people in particular who I can honestly say never let me down and each had a huge part to play in my development. One was my Housemistress, S. Margaret Mary, who remains an inspiration to me today. The second was my personal tutor, who once threw a blackboard rubber from the front of the classroom on to my desk at the back in a vain attempt to stop me from talking but who always encouraged me to trust my own judgement and to do my best. The third was S.M.Matthew, who ran the Infirmary with a balance of discipline and love which was, as she is, extraordinary.

And finally, New Hall gave me my best friend. She will know who she is and we have shared everything, both then and now. We have juggled work, family and animals and, most importantly, after over 20 years, we can laugh just as much now as we did then.

JOANNA McCARTHY (née Olding)

Pole 1976–1983

I bet you are finding it quite a laugh to read who smoked behind the tennis-courts and what other naughty things we all got up to!

Here are some of the things I remember:

– Joining the Choir in order to miss night prayers on Thursday evening so we could watch *Top of the Pops*.

– Unscrewing the U-bend under someone's basin, because they had given you an apple-pie bed the night before.

– Mr Morgan trying to get us interested in classical music – I remember him telling us that when we were older we would appreciate classical music. We almost fell off our chairs laughing – but you know what? He was right!

– Having to linseed-oil and Vaseline our lacrosse sticks. I still have mine in excellent condition although looking at modern sticks now I think it should be in a museum.

– Listening to the School Clock chiming at night; being driven mad when I couldn't sleep, and mad at being reminded every quarter of an hour that I was still awake.

– Changing for swimming in the outside cubicles, where the curtain would fly up in a strong breeze and expose us to the waiting teachers.

– Climbing the wall and skinny-dipping one evening.

– Tie-dying a piece of fabric in the Needlework Room. Having learnt to wind a bobbin and thread the newly introduced sewing machine, we created a case for our Biology dissecting kit. I still have mine with all the instruments.

If we felt ill we went to visit the Infirmary (and were invariably given a spoonful of salt in a plastic cup, some sticky red cough medicine and Strepsils). Hairy Melon (who taught us how to do hospital corners) would check our cubicle housework. In our state of innocence, I'm not sure we really gave much thought to the meaning of these names; they were more a term of endearment, along with Maggy Mary, Gabi and Johny.

And the farm! Whatever happened to the farm? I used to go and visit the kittens, and those buildings, if I remember correctly, were opposite where we used to do Saturday paper sorting. New Hall was far ahead of its time in paper recycling!

Best of all though were the lifelong friends I made in my seven years at New Hall, some of whom are godmothers to my children.

After New Hall I worked in Personnel for Saatchi and Saatchi, then Freshfields (Solicitors), where I met my future husband, Paul. We have four children, Ben, 18, Nicholas, 16, and twin daughters Charlotte and Isobel, 14 years old. We live near Sevenoaks in Kent and have a holiday home in Southwold, Suffolk, where my grandmother (Pamela Olding, also an Old Fish) lives. One of my most recent and biggest achievements was to climb Mt Kilimanjaro in January 2011.

ANNABEL HARRIS (née Moll)

Fisher 1978–1982

Things I remember:
– Wrapping ourselves up to keep warm in our long black cloaks with Fisher's red hood-lining.
– Waxing our lax sticks or having a sing-song in the Gym on wet PE days.
– Sneaking down to the Refectory during the night to forage food, usually dry Alpen!
– Bright pink Gumption for cleaning our cubicle sinks.
– Hideous blue housework overalls and enormous brooms for sweeping the floor.
– Rushing to get a front-row seat on a Thursday to see *Top of the Pops*.
– The swish of a habit down a corridor.
– Writing letters home and waiting for post to arrive – the excitement of getting a letter or parcel.
– Having my sister, Suzie, to look after me while I settled in.
– Meeting some fantastic people who became good friends for life.

HENRIETTA BOND

More 1977–1979

It was the sunlight glittering off the highly polished wooden surfaces and the carefully waxed stone floors that did it – and the flower arrangements and the central heating. 'This will do very nicely,' I told my parents. We'd viewed more than our fair share of bleak boarding schools and New Hall was by far the most welcoming.

I didn't know then that I'd be part of the mechanism that kept the School looking so shiny. Even today, when I hastily tackle the bathroom with an impregnated chemical wipe, I remember being taught to scrub my sink with Gumption, and wipe it clean with my towel. Nor did I anticipate that as a Sixth Former I'd be required to serve meals, supervise Lower School bedtimes, perform 'milk duties', answer the phone, lock the doors at night . . . As for 'supervising' other people doing housework duties – I was severely told off by S.M.David, for my incompetence at that task. (But I still adored her.)

While the housework skills have eluded me, some of those early New Hall habits have stayed with me. I still put Marmite on less than delicious apples. And I feel the need to keep others fully informed of my whereabouts (woe betide anyone who left their room and didn't pin a card on their door!). And the importance of wearing tights, even in exam rooms on the hottest of days, has left me with a lifelong aversion to nylon. I still can't eat breakfast with wet hair without wondering if someone will send me back to my bedroom . . .

New Hall was also a place of nurture and security. How could I forget the hushed beauty of the Chapel at night, tiptoeing across the upper balcony, fearful of disturbing the nun kneeling motionless before the constant light on the altar. That sense that as we curled up in our beds the heart of the Community was as constant and solid as the ancient walls that housed us. Is it any wonder that after my parents died, New Hall became for me a 'safe place'? So the Community's move to their new location unsettled me deeply. But since I've visited that vibrant, sun-filled house in Colchester I now have *two* incredibly special places which provide me with a much needed sense of 'home'.

New Hall left me with an appreciation of the diversity of 'success'.

Coming from a day school that frowned on extra-curricular activities as a distraction from exams, I was delighted by the way New Hall promoted the fullness of human experience, valuing its artists, dancers, athletes and riders. Perhaps most of all I valued the way New Hall saw everyone as a precious individual and rewarded the triers, the kind-hearted and thoughtful as much as anyone who brought home the prizes.

I am married, and have two cats, a hamster and a retired horse. I live in Yorkshire where I combine writing fiction for teenagers with being a Life Coach, Journalist and Communications Consultant. My 'big issue' is supporting young people leaving foster care and I've written a number of books on this subject.

Princess Anne's Visit in 1979 (drawing by Susan Coffey)

The 1980s

What's going on in the world during the 1980s

Thatcher / Yuppies / Big shoulders /
Big phones / Bright socks / Swatch
watches / New Romantics / AIDS /
Rubik's Cube / Olympic boycotts /
ET / Hip hop and rap

1980 Zimbabwe moves to black
majority rule / John Lennon
shot dead / Ronald Reagan
elected President of US /
Solidarity formed in Poland /
Iran–Iraq war breaks out / Blondie 'Call Me' / Pink Floyd
'Another Brick in the Wall'

1981 First space shuttle, *Columbia*, lifts off / First IBM computer
launched / Prince Charles marries Lady Diana Spencer / MTV /
The Police 'Don't Stand So Close to Me' / Kool & the Gang
'Celebration'

1982 Falklands War / Channel 4 begins transmission / Raising of
Henry VIII's flagship, the *Mary Rose* / Dutch elm disease kills
20 million trees / Survivor 'Eye of the Tiger' / Haircut 100
'Love Plus One' / Human League 'Don't You Want Me?'

1983 Front seat belts made compulsory / Microsoft Word launched /
Greenham Common protests / Dexy's Midnight Runners
'Come On Eileen' / Michael Jackson 'Billie Jean' / Billy Joel
'Uptown Girl' / Lionel Richie 'All Night Long'

1984 First Apple Mac introduced / Indira Gandhi assassinated /
Bhopal disaster / Miners' strike / Brighton and Harrods bombs /
Band Aid 'Do They Know Its Christmas' / Tina Turner 'What's
Love Got To Do With It?' / Wham 'Wake Me Up'

1985 Mikhail Gorbachev elected leader of Soviet Union / Greenpeace's *Rainbow Warrior* sunk in New Zealand / Live Aid concert for Ethiopian famine relief / Katrina and the Waves 'Walking On Sunshine' / Madonna 'Material Girl' / Bruce Springsteen 'Born In The USA' / Dire Straits 'Money For Nothing'

1986 Chernobyl nuclear power disaster / *Challenger* space shuttle explodes on take-off / Prince Andrew marries Sarah Ferguson / Porsche 959 is the fastest car / Robert Palmer 'Addicted To Love' / Run DMC 'Walk This Way' / Bananarama 'Venus'

1987 Terry Waite kidnapped in Beirut / Great Storm kills 23 / London City Airport opens / Whitney Houston 'I Wanna Dance With Somebody' / George Michael 'Faith' / Los Lobos 'La Bamba' / U2 'With Or Without You' / Level 42 'Lessons In Love'

1988 Pan Am Flight 103 blown up over Lockerbie / Digital mobile phone invented / Pound note ceases to be legal tender / Pubs open all day / Clapham rail crash / Pet Shop Boys 'Always On My Mind' / UB40 'Red Red Wine'

1989 Fall of the Berlin Wall / Tiananmen Square protests / Exxon Valdez oil spill / The Bangles 'Eternal Flame' / B52s 'Love Shack' / Fine Young Cannibals 'She Drives Me Crazy'

What's going on at New Hall during the 1980s

Many initiatives and changes characterised this decade – some things came; some went. The latter included the Riding School, which closed despite the protests and the memorable sit-in!

The Barn opened as a Pastoral Centre for the Diocese and this became a second significant apostolic commitment for the Community.

The Smokers' Bench began at the start of the decade – and was relegated to the roof in the latter part of the 1980s before disappearing altogether before the decade ended! The famous fire in the bin area coincided, not surprisingly, with this 'smoking era'.

'Family Service' in the School Refectory gave way to a cafeteria system and greater choice of food – and greater waste!

New Hall's involvement with the Government Assisted Places scheme brought a new influx of pupils.

S. Mary Francis's Headship ended (1963–86) and S. Margaret Mary began her 10-year tenure as Head.

This was the era of the sensitive fire-alarm system which seemed to sound regularly from the Home Economics area; it was also set off by hairspray aimed at the detectors or by smoke machines at the newly inaugurated Sixth Form discos, dances and balls.

Much of life in this decade was immortalised in the BBC film documentary which was made at New Hall in the early 1980s, eloquently narrated by S.M.Francis in particular.

In 1987, the cedar at the front of New Hall was damaged in the Great Storm, together with others on the Plot. In 1994, after another storm, the cedar was so badly damaged it had to be felled. We all watched. Crosses were made from the cedar wood by a parent, Chris Fell.

Previous page: CAFOD Rich/Poor Lunch in the Ambulacrum

S. MARGARET MARY (Gabrielle Horton)

Headship 1986–1996 (Part 3 of 3)*

I remember a strange sensation on the first day of that September term 1986 – everything just happened. I don't know what I thought I had to do to jump-start the term but I didn't have to do anything.

One memory that stands out from any other is of the last years of the life and the death of Jane Anderson. Over a period of about two and a half years Jane and her family lived in an extraordinarily courageous way with Jane's cancer. My contact with Jane and her parents through this time had a very significant effect on me and on so many of her contemporaries. An amputee, Jane was training for the Paralympics swimming squad when she died. I had accompanied her to Lourdes. We travelled by train together and I had to swallow hard as the false leg was hurled up on to the top bunk before she hoisted herself up. Those days in Lourdes were profoundly spiritual, and

Jane Anderson

* See page 125 for Part 1 and page 196 for Part 2.

included a round of parties for Jane. Sharing her parents' vigil around her death-bed soon after her 16th birthday and her good GCSE results was probably one of the most deepening experiences of my life. She was entirely peaceful as she gave instructions as to how everything she possessed was to be shared out. A few hours later she was dead and our Chapel saw yet another funeral of a young person.

I worked with a great body of staff during these years. It wasn't an easy time for the school, since the recession of the late 1980s and early 1990s hit us hard and we had to pull together. There were a few particular people who worked closely with me. Margaret McGhee, my PA for the whole period, was and is brilliant. She bailed me out on so many occasions, sweet-talked upset parents, added 'pleases' and 'thank-yous' to letters (although, occasionally, I was very cross about this!) and often disrupted the peace with her raucous laughter coming through the double doors from her office. She is a mainstay of our Melbourne Toddler group to this day – and is still laughing. Jack Magill, Deputy Head for most of the ten years, also bailed me out on occasion and, among so many other things, defused – with incredible ease – a short 'sit-in' when the Riding School closed. And Ruth Raven, by then Senior Mistress, was an invaluable support to me, to whom she had taught the rudiments of lacrosse more than three decades earlier. We are long-term friends.

Naturally, over these years, there were many pranks. One of the best was discovered early one morning in the staff loos. The skeleton (George? or Henry?) had been brought down overnight and was sitting on the loo, empty whisky bottle under one arm, fag in mouth and a nun's sandals (Patricia's, I think) on his feet. Poor Miss Hilliar, the piano teacher, who discovered it was close to needing resuscitation!

I missed the children over those years – first-hand dealings with them and not just the naughty ones! I had to keep reminding myself that someone needed to be doing the job I was doing in order to facilitate everyone else's contact with the children. Of course, I had Heads of School and Prefect groups – several outstanding ones. I tried to make my style of leadership keep me in as close contact with the children as possible. For most of those ten years I knew each child and most parents by name. That was important for me.

What was I thinking about as I did that job? Yes, academic

achievements, bank balances, improving facilities, inspections, but, in the main, I let others take those forward. I wanted the School to be true to its Christian identity. I wanted it to reflect the priorities of the Religious Community. The prophet Micah's words, 'This is what Yahweh asks of you, only this: that you act justly, that you love tenderly, that you walk humbly with your God,' were perhaps my theme over these years. I was convinced that the only justification for us running an expensive independent school as Religious was that we should make every effort to help our young people become aware of their immense responsibility for those who did not enjoy the same privileged education as they did, and that that responsibility was a lifelong one. NHVS and the profile given to it, the support for the flourishing Justice and Peace group, the priority in terms of content for the Sixth Form General Studies and RE programmes – these all reflected that deeply held principle. This could never have been effective without many other adults, Community and Lay, being convinced as well. We found a memorable diagram at that time: the two feet of Christian Service – one foot looks to the urgent needs of those around them

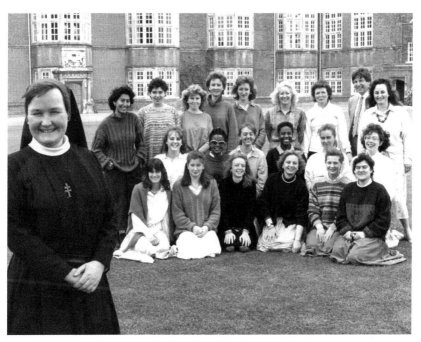

S. Margaret Mary and the Sixth Form, 1987

(NHVS) and the other foot looks beyond and below those needs to structures that are responsible for those symptoms of injustice in our world, seeking to change them. An inclusive Community: that was what we sought to be, and initiatives, policies, school events, all were tested to see if they served that purpose. How far any of that was effective, others will judge. That was what Community and School was about for me.

But 1996 came and it was time for further recycling.

S. MOIRA (MO'S) (Moira O'Sullivan)

1980s (Part 1 of 2)*

When I was in my early teens, some girls from St Bernard's in Westcliff, (where I was at school) went to New Hall, and that was the first time New Hall came on to my radar. They told stories of having to eat bananas with a knife and fork, and of calling the members of the Community 'Ma'am'. Such a strange place. When my school reports were less than they might have been, my father's new threat was that if I didn't buck my ideas up I would go to New Hall. A good enough threat for me – years later I was a Lay teacher at New Hall!

I have many fond and challenging memories of New Hall in the 1980s – a very strong sense of community and purpose, perhaps not always in equal balance with academic rigour! Coming from teaching at a grammar school, my teaching needed new strategies and that was the start of the infamous vocabulary sheets that many of you will remember.

Working in Mores at that time was a great opportunity to share life, idealism and faith. We had wonderful CAFOD days; rich/poor lunches; days on poverty, AIDS and apartheid; Taizé prayer vigils; sleep-outs and fundraisers. The RE and General Studies sessions in the Sixth Form tailored by Mr Glynn and others were second to none in their breadth and challenge.

There were memorable trips abroad. To France, of course, including some interesting 'homestays' in Paris! Also the headline trips to Russia and China. Clare Black, Judith Lynch, Anne Moss, Chinye Asiodu and

---

* See pages 306–8 for Part 2.   *Right: Trip to China in 1989*

Trip to Russia. Left to right: Kirsty Bell, Sophie Robinson, Sarah Bell, Candy Courtauld, Lizzy Amanpour, Sophie Thomasson

others – trading jeans for Lenin pins in the street; ice creams and sunbathing in the sub-zero temperatures; the 'developing friendships' between New Hall and boys from a London school – which had Mrs Newton and me keeping vigil in the stairwell all night. The trips to places of cultural interest when we struggled to stay awake; the all-

night train journey through Russia when they insisted that the train windows could *not* be opened before May 1st – because that was the rule! The plethora of bikes in Beijing, including the cyclists who cycled right into the auditorium during the five-hour-long opera.

There was a lot of idealism and hope around in the 1980s. Staying at New Hall for Easter really meant something to many students and was a time of creativity and searching for meaning. A Level French Literature lessons too were great times for debating the deeper meanings of life with integrity and intent – was Antigone a selfish young woman or an idealist? What was Meaulnes' nostalgia for things past really about?

FELICITY WARREN (née King)

Fisher 1977–1984

For me, as a member of the Liturgical Choir, one particular event stands out – the weekend when Christopher Walker and Paul Inwood came to New Hall to teach us their new works. At the time, I didn't much appreciate working at weekends, but now, as I sing the exact same music by Paul Inwood at Mass each Sunday, I see it was a privilege to have been part of that experience.

There were those School Shop queues up those narrow wooden stairs above the old Infirmary, ping-pong on a wet Saturday afternoon, playing lacrosse for the Mohawks on a Sunday when they were short of players . . .

My son has just started at New Hall, which may be why I am feeling nostalgic about my own schooldays and appreciative of the opportunity my parents gave me.

Since leaving school, life has been a whirl of activity driven by the major milestones of university, friendships, career, lots of travel, meeting my husband Simon, setting up home and becoming a mum – to Mark. I still work full-time for a cutting-edge technology firm, but now in the picturesque environs of Windsor where the pace is less frenetic.

OLIVIA BEDIER (née Scriven)

Owen 1978–1982

In my first term my aims in life were clear and simple: to have front row seats for *Top of the Pops*, to get to the table before anyone else at Refectory tea and to be first in line for School Shop.

Top of the Pops only occurred if S.M.Francis or, more likely, Kasia Giedroyc, the unsurpassably wonderful Head Girl, uttered the glorious words, 'There will be no evening prayers in Chapel tonight,' triggering a frenetic stampede to the various Houses. It was remarkable how quickly you could move from Main School to Beaulieu on a full stomach when Sting or David Bowie was awaiting you in the Common Room.

The race to afternoon tea was even less lady-like, involving elbowing, jostling and shoving your best friend to the ground in pursuit of prime position through the Refectory door. The goal: to get your hands on the bag of sliced Sunblest before anyone else, rip it open and coat one piece of bread with butter, chocolate spread, Marmite and/or strawberry jam and cram it into your mouth while repeating the process with the next piece. The most practised participants would then charge off to join the back of the queue for a second round, mouth still crammed full. The only time I attempted this trick I was spotted and sent, shamefaced, back to my House.

The happiest, most rewarding objective, however, was to be the first at the top of the back stairs queuing for School Shop. There, waiting for S.M.Thérèse to open up, I would forget my shyness and strike up friendships with my elders and betters, united as we were in our hunger for sugar. Clutching my orange cheque book, I would make straight for the slab of buttery toffee I knew would keep me going for the weekend (if my teeth didn't fall out first). 30p a week, I think we had, 10p of which had to be kept for Sunday Mass. If you felt really desperate, you could buy cough sweets out of your 'Necessities' allowance, meant for stamps and toothpaste. Later the Shop moved down to the main Quad and cheque books, percentages to the Church and Necessities became things of the past. It was never quite the same.

Sadly I had to leave New Hall after O Levels due to lack of funds! After that, my education was precarious and I ended up, aged 18, in London, drifting through jobs in publishing, interior design, estate agency, recruitment consultancy and as a sales assistant at Harrods. I was saved by my future (French) husband. We now live in Paris, although three of our four children go to Ampleforth. At the grand age of 46 I am finally embarking on my first career – in journalism.

JANE STANTON-COLE (née Stanton)

Southwell 1979–1986

Wearing the blue smock overall to do housework – and feeling indignant that the girls who came to school by train were excused, and thinking we should have a reduction in the school fees for our hard work!

Wearing four-inch black patent stilettos with steel heel caps that used to make a wonderful noise in Aloysius Corridor – these combined with my shoulder-length, permed hair used to aggravate S.M.Mark, who was Head of Sixth Form.

After a Business degree, I travelled around the world, came back to work for Mobil Oil Company and then for the family car-dealership business, based in Essex, and finally expanded into property. I now live in Gloucestershire with my husband, two children, two cats and 10 chickens.

ANYA HINDMARCH

Owen 1979–1986

We loved that fabulous building that gave 'presence' to everything and we loved staying for Easter, with the specially written music and candlelight vigils.

As for the Community – we loved your habits, which were fascinating, and we spent hours talking about what hairstyles you had underneath, or whether you actually had any hair at all. We loved the atmosphere of your side of the Convent.

Best and worst was 'the Smoking Bench' – how progressive it was for a Convent and how bad for our health! But good friendships were made there.

I remember desperately waiting for the post and queuing for the phone to buy British Gas shares, when that was all the rage. I started a newspaper-delivery service and remember being cross because I wasn't allowed to reinvest the profits! I remember being really excited about having a New Hall cheque book for the Tuck Shop that S.M.Thérèse ran from when it was originally situated above the Infirmary. I also remember spending a night in a room next to the Chapel and I am certain it was haunted. I was petrified.

I cannot overestimate the importance of the great friends and inspiring teachers and the wonderful insight and sense of spirituality that I got from School and Community. I often tell my children what S.Angela said to us in my first class: 'If you realise that in life you will never be fully satisfied, then you will have a very good life indeed.' She was damn right.

I was a terrible student and stroppy teenager but I was inspired, and although I didn't fare well academically, I have just (incredibly) been awarded an Honorary Doctorate, so I got there in the end!

CANDY ROBSON (née Courtauld)

Fisher 1980–1987

I remember the smell of the bleached dormitory at the beginning of term and parents lugging the suitcases up the stairs panting. Then unpacking and arranging all my ornaments in a line on the ledge by the bed and trying to dust round them every day.

– Sister Margaret Mary's sense of humour, charming and handsome Dr Tamlyn, and begging for one of Mr Glynn's ghost stories in the middle of RE lessons.

– The excitement of going to Springfield, having our Exeat card signed and waving at passing cars from the bridge over the A12.

– The School Dance and Mrs Crossley telling us we had to stand a balloon's width apart from the boys.

– Disabled riding and some of the ponies: Blue Peter, James, George.

And being able to have our ponies to stay in the summer – cantering down the Avenue.

– Waiting, with dread and embarrassment, in a long line, to be weighed at the beginning of term. And oh, the horror of gym knickers and especially of the Tricel top, really itchy and made by Courtelle.

– Being ill and not being able to have a bath and S. Stephanie washing my hair in the sink, which made me feel like being in a dolls' world.

– Having a midnight feast on Good Friday and realising, once we got caught and had a talking to, that perhaps it wasn't a good idea.

– Singing in the Choir – with S. Angela's lovely voice and Christopher Walker coming to teach us his songs.

– S.M.Ignatius' funeral and walking to the nuns' graveyard.

– The fantastic trip to Russia with MO'S [Miss O'Sullivan], and going on a brilliant pastoral retreat.

– S.M.Thérèse running the Shop and how we spent happy hours browsing the 1p chews. And there was the long queue to use the telephone box just outside . . . And the creation – and abolition – of the Smokers' Bench . . .

– Fire-alarm practice in the middle of a snowy night when I smuggled teddy under my nightie.

Shelter sleepout

278

I recall the Fishers' roller-skating competition; going on the 'Anglican' bus with Rev Turner to Baddow Church; the hierarchy of where to sit when watching *Top of the Pops*; and having my sister as Head of House. And my school report saying I was far too scruffy. And, of course, my friends – now godmothers to my children.

CLAIRE VAN HELFTEREN (née Golding)
Pole 1980–1982

The Avenue; scrambled egg and peas for supper; building a snowman during study leave for mocks; speaking in French at dinner to intimidate the First Years because we were so cool! Dropping to our knees at 7am for prayers on a cold, hard dorm floor; Gumption; PE knickers; the muddiest All England Schools' lacrosse tournament; tennis with a dislocated shoulder; trying to convince the Games

Lacrosse team

department that hockey was a far better sport than lacrosse; Exeats and long weekends; the peace of weekday Mass; making friends for life; the Quad on a sunny day; Mrs de Grey Water making sure I got my Maths O Level; Campion House; NHVS, which enriched my life beyond belief; a trip to Lourdes in the Jumbulance; Drama lessons . . . And, above all, feeling I belonged.

After A Levels I did a BSc (Hons) in Sports Science. My career has been varied, mainly involving sport, marketing and charity work. I am married to Antonius and we have two children, Luc (23) and Alexandra (21), who is also an Old Fish!

CLAIRE MERRY (née Fisher)

Owen 1981–1988

Friends spring first to mind, when I think about New Hall: Kirsty Brewer, Sophie Banning, Annalise Coady, Jacqui Heuer, Rosie Hodge, Jeanette Bamford and Alison Brown.

Claire Fisher on the cross-country course

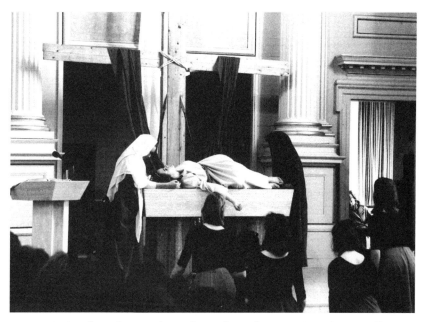

1986, Good Friday – taking down from the cross (Deidra Swaffield)

Then there is the Avenue that when you arrive seems never to end, but by the time you leave has become deceptively short.

Being a non-Catholic day girl, I did not expect to be given an important role during the Easter weekend celebrations. However, the honour bestowed upon me was not due to my honourable behaviour! I was in an RE lesson and thought I had mastered the art of whispering without moving my lips, but S. Teresa saw, and asked me to stay behind at the end of the lesson. Awaiting a demerit, I was stunned to be asked if I would hold the Holy Cross during the Easter Sunday Mass. For over an hour I held that Cross!

Although I enjoyed sport I didn't attain the dizzy heights of sporting stardom. My mother – a Suffolk tennis champion in her day – was delighted when I was picked to play in a tennis match against another school. She watched me being absolutely annihilated by my opponent. I remember the humiliation of having to be in the shot-put team for Owens on Sports Day (our star shot-putter had broken her shoulder) and coming last! I did manage to redeem myself in the school riding team and to this day I have a photograph of my favourite horse, in pride of place, jumping the cross-country course.

After an LLB Hons in Law and a year at the College of Law in Guildford, I took the solicitors' professional exams. I then spent a year in Italy, mainly in Florence. In 1995 I qualified as a Solicitor and practised in the West End of London, specialising in Personal Injury and Clinical Negligence Law. In 1997 I became head of the Personal Injury Department. Both my daughters, Kate and Lucy, now go to school at New Hall.

ALISON BATES (née Brown)

Fisher 1981–1986

I remember climbing out of my cubicle on to the Refectory roof during a study break and getting caught sunbathing; I did have my English book with me! Then there was the massive water fight in the Quad which started fairly tamely but got slightly out of hand . . . The nuns were horrified as they were entertaining the Governors in their Refectory and all our antics were on display.

When I started at New Hall all pupils sat at tables in mixed years, which I hated, but I absolutely loved the arrival of the carousel, especially with Wiener schnitzel.

I have many happy memories, particularly of Dancing – coming second in a dance competition with Jennette Bamford, and dance routines in Fishers with Jacqui Heuer, Juliet Gibson, Bernadette Brennan, Nicky Kennedy and Chinye Asidou.

I loved going into the Wilderness and would volunteer to retrieve balls when they disappeared from the tennis-courts. And I remember walking to the pond in Generals Lane when it was icy and feeding the ducks – our favourite was the one-legged duck.

The summer before I left, some of the Community told us why they became nuns. For the first time, I realised they were all human and had had lives before they came to New Hall.

When I think of New Hall I think of peace and that feeling is overwhelming. They were good days and talking about it makes me want to go back.

Having looked after children from inner London during one summer holiday, I realised that I would like a career in childcare and, fortunately, that is what I am now involved with.

CECILIA MAXIMILIA (née Willey)

Fisher 1981–1989

I arrived in a red hooded jacket with a roller skate on the back, taking my mother's hand and wondering what on earth life was going to be like without her. After saying our prayers that night, fear overcame me. I ended up in S. Margaret Mary's room crying all night and keeping the whole dormitory awake.

Once settled, I began to enjoy my studies immensely. My best subjects were Fine Arts, Drama, Dance and Languages – Biology and even Mathematics were fascinating because the teaching was so good. I couldn't have asked for a better education.

In the Sixth Form, life became even more interesting. We were allowed to wear our own clothes and were treated like adults by teachers and tutors. I'll never forget winning the dance competition, and taking part in theatrical presentations. Our Drama classes were completely avant-garde. We used to call it entertainment but, for me, it was really serious and shaped my personality to make me what I have become now: a multi-media artist.

New Hall felt like a second family to me. I am happy. I was brought up to believe in God and the importance of Jesus in our lives; my beliefs have been reinforced by recent trying life experiences. They have helped me to focus as an artist as I deal with communication and human behaviour. Even though I do not have children, my art is my child whom I continue to nurture.

On leaving school I went back to Italy and studied Fashion Design in Rome. Back in the UK I studied Dance Choreography in various different jazz styles and Music Technology. Arranging Latin jazz music took me to Paris where I worked in an Advertising Agency for six years as a multitask agent. I spent five years in Brazil executing my own project of 24 canvases in oil representing the people of South America. I am now in Barnes, London, and teaching English to overseas students – with my art exhibited in a restaurant nearby.

KIRSTY McGINN (née Brewer)

Southwell 1981–1988

I was a day girl, and very pleased with my cape with its blue-silk hood-lining. I also liked my lacrosse stick, although I couldn't play at all well. But I could have done without the horrible brown lace-up shoes we had to wear!

I remember Carmen, the lovely Spanish lady who cleaned Southwells. We still had to do housework and even the day girls had to put on their blue overalls first thing in the morning. We stayed at school to do homework for the first few years, so had tea at school, but, as soon as Claire Fisher and I could drive, we left school the minute the last bell went.

I remember the Science Labs and the smell of pickled locusts, which we had to dissect. The swimming-pool was outside and freezing. For the Bronze Duke of Edinburgh Award we walked 20 miles and camped out on Danbury Common. It was cold and wet and I have never camped since. The trip to the Soviet Union in 1987 was brilliant.

During O Levels there was revising outside to get a tan, and looking forward to the trip after exams to Chartwell. Foundation Day was good, no lessons for a day and wearing home clothes. At lunchtime, we would walk up to see the horses – unless it was Wimbledon, when everyone would crowd around televisions to watch a match.

JEANNETTE WRIGHT (née Bamford)

Owen 1981–1988

One of my most memorable recollections of New Hall is of a school trip to Rome. The first hotel we stayed in was dreadful; there was mould on the walls and we had to walk through the dining-room to get to the shower. It was the first and last time I tasted squid-ink soup! We had a packed lunch made for us – hard rolls and eggs – and were eating it on the Spanish Steps when an over-exuberant local came up to me and I threw the hard roll and egg to make him go away – it worked! I was ill with flu, but the plan to return was scuppered as the airport was on strike . . . On strict curfew in Sorrento, we became stuck in the lift – only a few moments (later exaggerated) . . .

My sporting claim to fame was to be in the shot-put team, but it was short lived as I had a riding accident, falling off Boysie and breaking my shoulder.

Other memories include S.M.John handing out lots of demerits; Mrs Haward throwing chalk or blackboard rubbers and chanting: 'bam, bas, bat / bamus, batis, bant / vi, visti, vit / vimus, vistis, verunt.'

ROSEMARY THOROGOOD (née Hodge)

Southwell 1981–1988

Easter at New Hall: we were all sceptical about spending extra days at School but the activities, meals and preparations for the Easter service brought everything and everyone together. I can still remember the songs Christopher Walker taught us.

House keep-fit competition: we did ours to the Wombles' song, much to Miss Cox's disgust! I remember turning up the volume of

S. Teresa in class

285

Frankie Goes to Hollywood and then either S.M.Christopher or S.Teresa marching in and turning it down!

Refectory: the salad bar was a good alternative to the hot meal, and when the grated cheese wasn't put out, some of us would go round the back of the refrigerated units and help ourselves.

The outdoor pool: we had to change in cubicles with curtains which whipped around our wet legs when the wind blew . . . And Nikki Kennedy was chased around the pool by one of the staff when she refused to get into the cold water.

Who could forget the school dance when the fire-alarm went off, and we all had to line up beyond the Ha-Ha for the register to be called? When the fire-brigade turned up, they were loudly welcomed with cheers and . . . where was Lara MacDonald? Time to 'fess up' methinks . . . !

ANNALISE COADY

Southwell 1982–1988

The 1987 School Trip to Russia: We travelled to Moscow and Leningrad (as it was still called) during the Easter Holidays in 1987. The USSR was just opening up and it was a time when you could exchange packets of gum for a Moscow University T-shirt. We visited Red Square, took in St Basil's, filed past Lenin, went through the laborious purchasing procedures at the GUM department store, toured the Kremlin and somehow managed to miss Margaret Thatcher, who was on an official visit. But my overall memory is that everything and everybody seemed grey, while in stark contrast, the New Hall group stood out in bright jewel-coloured, shoulder-padded coats in true 1980s' style. We were from another world and attracted a lot of attention.

We travelled by night train to Leningrad. My compartment crew – Sarah Ducharme, Stephanie Jeavons, and Kirsty Brewer – and I filled up on vodka and champagne and I don't remember much food. It was a raucous night with people carousing throughout the carriage, singing, laughing and over-indulging. Things then get a little fuzzy . . . The next thing I remember is waking up to a commotion; there was blood all over the floor and Kirsty valiantly trying to mop it up with a tiny tissue. Sarah had fallen out of the top bunk and somehow hit Stephanie's nose on the way down. I vaguely remember Mr Stevens trying to sort out the chaos. When we arrived in Leningrad, I'm proud to say most of us girls managed the early-morning tour around the city. The same cannot be said for some of the parents!

Perhaps one of the most important life lessons we learned at New Hall was: 'There are no mistakes. The events we bring upon ourselves, no matter how unpleasant, are necessary in order to learn what we need to learn; whatever steps we take, they're necessary to reach the places we've chosen to go.' (These are the words of Richard Bach, the writer of *Jonathan Livingstone Seagull* – a 'must read' of the time.)

After graduating with an Honours Degree in Materials Science and Engineering from Leeds University, I worked as a journalist before joining the British Government's Office of Science and Technology. Having been engaged in strategic communications for over 20 years and living in London, San Francisco and the Middle East, I currently live and work in Toronto as the President of High Road Communications, a leading North America PR and communications agency.

NINA GUMOES (née Firth)
Fisher 1982–1987

Naughty Nina's Belated Confession
  When Nina arrived at New Hall School / The nuns were very kind, / But Naughty Nina had one thought / In her devious little mind . . .
  Her cubicle she surveyed / For any nooks and crannies, / And there she hid her contraband/ Like sweets and tuck – and trannies.
  Nina thought it would be fun / To take the horses for a run, / So out she stole, while the nuns all slept, / And to the field young Nina crept.
  Once out of sight, the fence she climbed / And a bright bay cob she spied. /On she leapt and rode him fast / Till both were very tired at last.
  Then flushed and very full of fun / From her exciting midnight

run, / Back she went to the darkened dorm / And slid in bed all snug and warm.

Sophie was a nice young girl, / Who strove hard at work and play. / She studied all night long/ And never did any wrong.

Nina told her she'd snuck out / Away from the nuns and far from sight, / And down the drainpipe she had shinned / Then ridden the horses round at night.

Nightfall came and the dorm fell silent / And the girls' great escapade began. / But as Sophie tiptoed down the hall / A darkened shadow loomed so very tall.

Poor old Sophie, trembling with fear, / In Margaret Mary's scary office –Nina nowhere near. / She yawned aloud, fingers crossed out of sight. / 'Sleepwalking,' she said. 'What a fright!'

To her honour and her credit / She never said a single thing. / Sophie never breathed a word / About their crazy midnight scheme.

To a naughty girl who didn't deserve to get away / With a crime so large that the nuns might allay / The kindness they had shown / To a child so very feral, like none they'd ever known.

But no-one saw the change begin / In Naughty Nina's demeanour / As, after that, she pulled herself in / And worked with greater vigour.

So thank you, Sophie – greatest friend – / Who on that night took the flack, / And saved my neck – on that depend! / How ever can I pay you back?

BRIGID COADY

Southwell 1983–1990

That First Year is a jumble of images. Thinking how sophisticated the Sixth Formers were blackberry-picking. Always last to get a seat to watch *Dynasty*. Having one line of dialogue as a stoat in the play *Toad of Toad Hall* and, through nerves, delivering it with an American twang the first night, very English on the second, and settling for mid-Atlantic on the last night. Getting caught out of bed and being made to stand on a chair in the laundry slip in the dark.

Second Year we Southwells thought we were too cool for school. There was my first Silk Cut in the small alley between the PE hut and

Riding School

the wall. Soon I was making regular forays to a ramshackle barn, a can of bodyspray up one sleeve, a tube of Polos and pack of Cartier cigarettes up the other. Then of course there was the great night when S. Teresa, upset by the amount of cigarette butts on the fire-escape, declared an amnesty. I was in my cubicle, keeping my head down. I hadn't reckoned on Cindy Seabrooke, who wrenched back my curtain and stood there saying, 'I never took you for a coward, Brigid.' I added myself to the back of that queue.

Third Year meant graduating to the lower dormitory. Reading Mills & Boon novels under the bench in Physics. Being Lab partners with Rachael Kenny and flouting the laws of physics by having our thermometer go down on heating rather than up.

Fourth Year and the beginning of GCSEs. How many times did I hear the phrase, 'I think this is on the syllabus.' More acting in *Oh, What a Lovely War!* Jumping up and down on Carole Pendle's new Barbour to give it that lived-in look.

Fifth Year and suddenly we were scattered around the dormitories in charge of our own little sections. Panicking about mocks and then GCSEs. The whole of Southwells Fifth Year being obsessed by *Dirty Dancing*. I remember being summoned to see Miss Cox with Genevieve van den Boogard and Clare Padfield at Eastertime and saying if it was anything to do with House swimming we were going to refuse. As it turned out we had been made Sports Captains for the School. I was Swimming Captain. Not only did I have to do House swimming, I had to organise it!

That first term in the Sixth Form was hard; everyone was breaking into different groups of friends. Then I met Jacqui Moulds and Catherine Donnelly and things were never the same again – what with my being indoctrinated into Bon Jovi, Dogs D'Amour and Skid Row, as well as becoming adept in the art of backcombing and the use of black eyeliner. Our joint obsession with *The Breakfast Club*. The joy of a bubble bath, two cans of Miller and a Mills & Boon . . .

What New Hall gave me was the freedom and belief that I could be anyone I wanted to be, as long as I took up the challenge. It wasn't until I left that I realised I had received a gift that not many people are given.

Having graduated with an Honours Degree in Materials Science and Engineering from the University of Leeds, I had various jobs before becoming a Project Management Consultant, first in IT, then in the building industry, then in the education sector. I am currently living and working in London as the Operations Director for the British Council for School Environments and as a freelance management consultant. I have also worked as a Voice-Over Artist and as a Country-Music Radio Presenter and am working on my second novel.

ENYIDIYA ONWUKAH ODU

Owen 1983–1990

I was always breaking the school rules and getting away with it. Any time it was housework I would fall on the ground and start crying and Gabi [S.M.Gabriel] would come to comfort me, thinking that I was homesick. And there were the midnight feasts we had after lights-out . . .

My best times were PE times. I represented Essex in athletics, winning gold medals and getting into the local newspaper for breaking the Essex long-jump record – which was a great joy. On Prizegiving Day I was awarded Best Athlete of the Year. I thank Terry Cox for always believing in me.

Because my family was in Nigeria, friends took me with them to their homes during the holidays and I had great times with them and

Gymnastics

their families. Times which remain glued to my heart! Thank you, Anna Fox, Catriona and Eleanor Pearson, Victoria Cole, Sarah Finn and many others. I love you all and will never forget you.

KIKI PEARSON (née Victoria Blum)

Pole 1983–1989

Being a day girl, I found staying for Easter in the Third Year, and so being away from my family, quite a painful experience, but it was also special and exciting. With the bonfire on the Saturday night, it felt like a real celebration.

I remember finding the Fourth and Fifth Years achingly cool, and to think now that they were only 15! I could *never* seem to find my gym kit, and I remember trying to hide from S.M.Peter because I thought she was going to give me a demerit . . .

And swimming outdoors – trying to get changed in those tiny freezing cubicles with flapping curtains. The Children's Summer Camps at Southwells and Owens were lots of fun – and showed me New Hall in a more casual light . . .

There was a rumour that there was a pike living in the pond by the Barn, which someone had seen drag a duckling down under the water.

Going horse riding I loved – I was so sad to see that the Riding School was gone when I visited later.

KELLY POULIKAKOU

Southwell 1983–1988

My favourite times were spent *not* in class but wandering around the fields and farms surrounding the school. I especially liked it when the calves sucked on my thumb; it felt very odd but pleasantly funny. And there was the Wilderness – where, against the rules, we roamed and spied through the gates of the Sisters' Cemetery, all of us too scared to go in, hearts pumping in expectation of seeing ghosts. We'd run back to Six Acres out of breath, scared to bits.

Octagon and horse rider

Sister T. [Teresa Lenahan] was like a mother to me, kind and under-standing, willing to get me out of trouble, a confidante and ally. I hold her dear in my heart to this very day.

JULIA BLACKBURN (née O'Donnell)
Campion 1983–1988

Aha, the scary Wilderness! And swimming – why was it always the first period? It always seemed to be freezing, no lovely warm balmy after-noons for us, just cold, cold, cold – and trying to get out of it by saying it was my period at least twice a month. Miss Raven was the scariest woman I had ever met. Tea-time was my best time. I have never experienced scones or sticky buns as delicious since.

Twenty years on, I still remember the beauty of the place, and the cedar trees as you drive down the Avenue.

ALEXANDRA (Alecky) BULGIN
Campion 1984–1989

Ever since my older brother, Tom, had gone to Felsted, three years earlier, I longed to experience midnight feasts, Saturday sports matches and Tuck Shop visits. For weeks beforehand I paraded around the house, swishing about in my black cape complete with yellowy-gold hood – as I was to go into Campions. I even minced about in those ghastly granny shoes which I spent the next five years despising and doing my best to scuff up.

One small disappointment was that in one regard I had to be unlike Tom, who had the most wonderful trunk with his initials boldly stencilled on. New Hall insisted on suitcases. Mine was grey with black trim, bought especially as I'd never been away from home for much longer than a week. It had a matching small suitcase in which I packed a multitude of bits and bobs to decorate my cubicle: plastic frogs, china hamburgers, Athena posters of girls with pink hair, blowing bubble gum, and sewing kit (untouched to this day). Even miniature bottles of gin and vodka that I must have smuggled in when I was

293

older. Everything was new, even my duvet. I'd never had a duvet before and thought it the height of sophistication. It was white with pastel-coloured dots. Little did I know, as I proudly unpacked it and put it on my bed, how well I would get to know those dots over the next few years.

As I put up my posters, a beautiful Spanish-looking girl popped her head round the curtain to welcome me. She would have been only 15 but seemed so grown up and glamorous. I'd never met anyone like her before. I'd come from a small day school in Old Harlow where everyone was born and bred within a 10-mile radius. Here there were people from all over the world. When I went downstairs to the Common Room, around the table was gathered a fabulously colourful and exotic collection of 11-year-olds – they could have been out of a Benetton advert. Once my mother had hugged and kissed me goodbye I barely looked back, as I was so looking forward to learning more about the life-changing hand I'd been dealt.

After training at the Mountview Theatre School, but unable to find acting work, I set up my own theatre company called Recorded Delivery. Our first production, Come Out Eli, *won the Time Out Award for Best Production on the Fringe. Since then I've pursued writing with notable success and am currently working on various projects for theatre and television.*

SEANIN GILMORE

Fisher 1984–1990

The bells; arriving alone from Ireland and standing in the car park with my suitcases, with absolutely no idea where or what 'Fishers' was; 'Tell Out, My Soul'; nuns gliding into Mass, heads bowed; the Second Year dancing competition; my wonderful piano teacher, Mrs Stevens; Claudine and Caroline, always first to breakfast; Pottery with S.M.Stephen; *Stabat Mater*; lying on cushions on the floor in Fishers watching *Dallas* and *Dynasty*; sleeves pulled over hands; Mrs Auralswamy and her black book (and my name in it first); Grainne, Etain and Natalie giggling; Benetton jumpers and Burlington socks; birthday parties with cider; S. Pauline and the Wool Pack; *Cantique de*

Jean Racine; *Oh, What a Lovely War!*; the skiing trip; the Little Chef; gargling salt; Liturgical Dancing for Cardinal Hume; sharing rooms with Sam and Pippa; Mr Magill and W.B.Yeats; S. Stephanie and Milton; instant coffee (and S.M.Thérèse's admonishments for drinking way too much of it); S. Angela singing; pork choppies; deep and meaningfuls with Carole; *Ubi caritas*; our dear darling friend M-C and her pride in being Head Girl; Fauré's *Requiem*; joyous Easters; faith, hope and lots of love.

I read English Literature at Cambridge and then qualified as a barrister. I now practise as a barrister and sit as a Deputy District Judge and a Tribunal Judge. I am married to Graeme McPherson and we have three young children: Bella, Eliza and Patrick. We live near Stow on the Wold, Gloucestershire.

Colchester walk in aid of Mother Teresa with S.M.Helen

SARAH FIELD (née Cole)

Pole 1984–1991

The school brought together girls from all over the world and the friendships I made will last for ever. Eighteen years on, a small group of us meet up and reminisce and when we are together it seems it was only yesterday we last saw each other . . . I remember peanut-butter sandwiches, doughnuts, chocolate spread . . . The school Infirmary filled me with horror but when I see Strepsils throat lozenges it makes me laugh, as these were the cure for all illnesses. There was a unique fashion all New Hall girls followed – stripy tights, baggy cardigans, bashed-up brown school shoes and official red pants!

So many important lessons learned, lifetime friends found and countless, happy memories that will never leave me . . .

GRAINNE GILMORE

Fisher 1986–1993

All it takes are the opening bars of 'For the Beauty of the Earth' and the memories come rushing back: surreptitiously scuffing the regulation 'clod-hoppers'; grappling with Gumption; sitting on the worktop in my sister's cubicle; watching the nuns file into Mass; scoffing Exhibition Weekend picnics; marvelling at Mrs Jones's pronunciation of Chaucer's medieval English; reading over Natalie's shoulder during break-times; failing to learn backstitch; wrinkling my nose at the smell of croquette potatoes; arguing earnestly with Etain about the meaning of 'character is fate' in Hardy's novels; dawdling on the way to violin lessons in Walkfares; catching horses with Helen before housework; sitting on Mores landing with S.T. and S.M.Thérèse; sourcing biscuits for Mores Prefects; meetings with Moon and Patricia; quizzing S.M.Stephen on all sorts of topics after Evening Prayer; sneaking late into morning Mass on Fridays; brewing strong coffee during study in the New Wing; dancing with Anna and Yvonne in Fishers; admiring the yellow fields of rapeseed in the summer; hosting discos with Mandy in the East Wing; waiting for the buzzer outside S. Margaret Mary's

Picnic (photo by Seanin Gilmore)

office; rushing to ballet lessons with Emma and Mary; donning blue overalls for Pottery or housework; visiting the elderly; projecting my voice when reading lessons during Mass with S.M.Christopher; learning to windsurf during double period Monday mornings – in the winter term; lamenting the static of 'best' white shirts, and waiting by the radiator for Natalie and Kirsten . . . The hymn is soon at an end, but I am still smiling.

KIRSTY WAYLAND (née White)

Pole 1987–1991

I remember lying awake on my first evening at New Hall and thinking I would never get used to the sound of the Chapel bells but then leaving at the end of term and finding nights a bit quiet! When I have been back, I have found them oddly soothing.

I was Infirmary Prefect, which wasn't exactly regarded as 'cool', but I loved it. I particularly liked being able to walk through the top balcony of the Chapel and being able to pause to reflect, each night.

I was never a fan of the uniform, and now only occasionally wear red! My big frustration was arriving and discovering that the legendary big red knickers were no longer compulsory – having come equipped with a bag full!

There were specific New Hall words and phrases when I started; I felt as if everyone was speaking a different language. I thought the number of posters in Poles with 'TY' at the bottom meant there was a busy person with those initials at work behind the scenes. Apparently it was the way the Community always wrote 'thank you'.

What stood out for me was the encouragement by staff to consider people who were struggling in a whole range of ways. I have strong memories of the day-long activities in the Sixth Form on homelessness and on El Salvador, and of NHVS, and of sending Christmas cards to prisoners of conscience through Amnesty. I have tried to take the message of 'acting on your social conscience' into my adult life.

There were so many people who stood out for me, and I continue to value my relationships within the Community.

I moved to Cambridge to do a Music degree at the then Anglia Polytechnic. Stayed to work in the voluntary sector and somehow am still here, now working at the University of Cambridge in a role promoting Staff Development. I'm married to Matt.

DEBORAH LEEK-BAILEY (née Odysseas)

Head of Drama 1987–1996

Driving my car up the sunny tree-lined Avenue and seeing the stunning view of the Boleyn family home for the first time something deep inside me knew that a special chapter in my life was about to begin. It was 1987 and I was attending an interview for Head of Drama, with English. My sister, Lydia, accompanied me on the journey and, as the house came into view, I said, 'Don't ask me how I know this but one day I am going to live here and have a party.' Five years later I became a residential member of staff, taking responsibility for Child Protection – and yes, we had many parties!

Everyone at New Hall welcomed me. The pupils were so independent

Red knickers

that they excelled in practical activity. New Hall allowed them to be themselves and as I watched their confidence grow, I knew that I was privileged to work in such an unusual place.

At that time the religious Community were in key positions within the school, S.M.Luke as Head of Campions, S. Teresa as Head of Sixth Form and S. Margaret Mary was Headmistress. I struck up a particular friendship with S.M.Christopher, which lasted until the day she died. Both Margaret and Christopher encouraged me to aim high and I am convinced that I became a young Headteacher myself because they and my colleagues, Jack Magill, Brian Harte, Joan Jones, Andrew Fardell and Duncan Archard, gave me belief in my ability to succeed. S.M.Christopher had a remarkable memory and would regale me with tales of New Hall during the war, the impact on school life of the Haverhill Fever epidemic and ghost stories that had transcended time.

Enjoying birthday cake

She was a very brave lady who never complained when her health deteriorated and would find new ways to communicate with me when her eyesight failed. I remember her once saying, 'I know that you are a good Christian but how good a Catholic are you these days?' and finding myself straight back at Church the following Sunday, having missed Mass for more than a few weeks!

Certain memories are particularly poignant, such as evenings when the fire-alarm would go off and we would have to congregate by the Ha-Ha in our nightclothes, or when I walked into my Drama Studio to find Sir Harry Secombe getting changed before 'Songs of Praise'. And the amazing celebrations surrounding the 350th Anniversary of the school that had everything from helicopters to fireworks that illuminated the night sky. And I remember how, when the hurricane struck and destroyed some of the beautiful cedars, the Community innovatively had tiny crucifixes made from the wood and distributed to staff and pupils. Residential Easters with Fr Jim made everything so meaningful.

When I left after nine wonderful years, pupils organised a surprise meal for me and my husband, and we entered the Drama Studio to candlelight and a fully laid-out table, complete with music. That evening typified life at New Hall, with everyone investing in one another and our lives coming full circle.

Having left New Hall in 1996, I became Deputy Head and Head of Sixth Form at West Heath School. I was then appointed as Head Teacher of Babington House School, where I have remained for 14 years. I am married to Colin and am mother to Gemma, and my two stepsons, Josh and Jacob. We live in Chislehurst, Kent.

Professor Martin Harris (Vice-Chancellor of the University of Essex) at Exhibition Day, 1988

The 1990s

What's going on in the world during the 1990s

Dawn of the Information Age / Dissolution of Soviet Union and end of Cold War / Steady economic growth / 24-hour shopping and Sunday trading / Britpop / Wonderbra / Puffa jackets / DVDs / Digital cameras

1990 Nelson Mandela freed / Hubble Space Telescope launched / East and West Germany reunified / Iraq invades Kuwait – Gulf War begins / Margaret Thatcher resigns / Madonna 'Vogue' / Vanilla 'Ice Ice Ice Baby' / Sinead O'Connor 'Nothing Compares To You'

1991 World Wide Web available to public / Three million computers connected to Internet / Break-up of Soviet Union / End of Cold War / R.E.M. 'Losing My Religion' / Michael Jackson 'Black or White' / Nirvana 'Smells Like Teen Spirit' / Chesney Hawkes 'I Am The One And Only'

1992 Yugoslavia breaks up and erupts into civil war / EU forms under Maastricht Treaty / First nicotine patch produced / *Punch* publishes final edition / Whitney Houston 'I Will Always Love You' / Eric Clapton 'Tears in Heaven' / Red Hot Chilli Peppers 'Under the Bridge'

1993 US and Soviet Union agree to reduce numbers of nuclear warheads / First Dyson bagless vacuum cleaner sold / Radiohead 'Creep' / Whigfield 'Saturday Night' / Mr Blobby 'Mr Blobby' / The Proclaimers 'I'm Gonna Be'

1994 National Lottery launched / Sony PlayStation arrives / ANC wins first multi-racial election in South Africa / Rwandan genocide / Take That 'Sure' / Green Day 'Basket Case' / Wet Wet Wet 'Love Is All Around'

Left: Steel-band workshop in 1994

1995 Channel Tunnel begins service / Barings Bank collapses / Brixton Riots / Oasis 'Wonderwall' / Pulp 'Common People' / Bjork 'It's Oh So Quiet' / Blur 'Country House'

1996 10 million computers connected to internet / BSE (Mad Cow Disease) / Dunblane massacre / eBay up and running / Los Del Rio *Fiesta Macarena* / Boyzone 'Words' / Jamiroquai 'Virtual Insanity' / The Prodigy 'Firestarter'

1997 Dolly the sheep is first mammal to be cloned / Death of Diana, Princess of Wales / UK hands sovereignty of Hong Kong to People's Republic of China / Kyoto Protocol / Tony Blair becomes Prime Minister / Spice Girls 'Spice Up Your Life' / Aqua 'Barbie Girl' / Celine Dion 'My Heart Will Go On' / Supergrass 'Sun Hits the Sky'

1998 First MP3 player on sale / Good Friday Peace Agreement signed in Northern Ireland / Clinton–Lewinsky scandal / BMW buys Rolls-Royce / Google founded / Starbucks arrives in UK / Green Day 'Good Riddance' / Fatboy Slim 'Praise You' / Vengaboys 'Boom Boom Boom' / Robbie Williams 'Millennium'

1999 Euro adopted by EU / Self-rule restored in Northern Ireland / World population passes 6 billion / Millennium Dome opens / Prince Edward marries Sophie Rhys-Jones / The Queen opens first Scottish Parliament for 300 years / Paddington train crash / Britney Spears 'Baby One More Time' / Westlife 'Flying Without Wings' / Backstreet Boys 'I Want It that Way' / Lou Bega 'Mambo No 5' / S Club 7 'Bring It All Back'

What's going on at New Hall during the 1990s

S. Margaret Mary and S. Anne-Marie were Heads for this decade – the last decade to see Community leadership.

There remained some Community members teaching and in Pastoral roles, but Lay presence in key posts was paramount, with all Houses being headed by Lay staff by the end of the 1990s.

In the early part of the decade, the Prep School was re-established on campus, housed again in Beaulieu, and led by Gerry Hudson, the first

Lay Prep Head. The Prep established itself quickly and securely under his guidance.

Along with the changes to the buildings necessitated by the arrival of the Prep School in Beaulieu, there were further significant site developments with the building of Walkfares, phases 1 and 2, not only to house academic classroom needs but also to be a prestigious home for the popular Performing Arts Departments.

It was in 1992 that the Community and School celebrated the 350th Anniversary of their Foundation in style, with such memorable events as the release of 350 red balloons, the Service of Thanksgiving at Chelmsford Cathedral and Turn-the-Clock-Back Day.

It was in 1998 that the open-air swimming-pool graciously gave way to the indoor pool, dedicated to the memory of Jane Anderson.

It was in the latter part of this decade that there was a major overhaul of the House structures and the familiar House names of Southwell, Fisher, Owen, Pole and Campion were assigned to newly designed Vertical Groups, and the House buildings in the L-shape were renamed Hawley and Dennett.

S. Anne-Marie and pupils having tea in the 1990s

S. MOIRA (MO'S) (Moira O'Sullivan)

*1990s (Part 2 of 2)**

I have many memories of Modern Language trips during these years – some of which came before the whole Health and Safety regime reached its height! These memories include ten years of visits to the Castel d'Ailly in Normandy: Le petit train, the Bayeux Tapestry, the bowling, the snails, the cheese farm. And who was it that got stuck in the bedroom and could only be freed with an axe? I well remember Amanda Green's phone call home from one trip. She sobbed: 'Sister Moira says to tell you I am enjoying myself!' Choir trips to Belgium and Italy – especially the time I remained in Venice looking after two girls who were taken to hospital on the way to the airport (no names – but you will remember if you were there!).

There were also the famous French dinners with KEGS (King Edward Grammar School) and other schools, when the Ambulacrum was turned into a lavish dining set and a French meal was served accompanied by French-only conversation. It seemed to work well until the relationship needs outweighed the desire to speak French!

Trip to Normandy

* See pages 272–3 for Part 1.

Choir trip to Belgium and Holland in 1992

The tutor groups were key to life in these years and I have very happy memories of the close relationships that were built up among us. So many characters and such diversity – and great humour. Natalie Sharrock's reindeer antlers appearing at the classroom window during a particularly serious moment is something I shall never forget!

Persuading and encouraging girls to be reliable and engaged members of NHVS was a particular challenge for any tutor and as one of the NHVS leaders it was one close to my heart. 'Doesn't the V stand for voluntary?' was a question that someone out there will remember asking! Yet nothing gave me greater pride and satisfaction than seeing girls caring for others and making real the essence of New Hall's Christian identity.

Debating and Public Speaking really got off the ground in these years – first with Mrs Webb and then with Mrs Clark. We won many cups and awards and together we trailed around the country relishing the opportunities to look critically at key moral and social issues of the day. There were some fearsome debators in Zeynep, Lucy, Katherine, Frances, Catherine, Sasha, Jacqueline, Amy, Sascha, Celeste and many others. There were also the balloon debates on a Sunday evening when Mickey Mouse battled with Jesus Christ and Shakespeare to remain in the sinking balloon. Although times were a-changing, there was still room for girls to be girls and have fun and share laughs. Whenever we had debating practices after supper, I could be sure that a gaggle of girls would be hiding behind the curtains to jump out to give me a fright – all aged about 16! Could that happen now?

ANNE SPARROW (BYATT) 'Mrs B'

Librarian 1974–2006

Were you to walk through the churchyard of Chelmsford Cathedral in summertime, you might see a bed of red roses and a brass plaque commemorating the 350th Anniversary of New Hall School. This was our gift to the Borough of Chelmsford and surely a symbol that in 1993 we were very aware of how important were our links with the town.

Over the next years, with a declining interest in boarding education, the words 'marketing' and 'public relations' became common parlance. Our concern that the name of New Hall should be seen and heard and be synonymous with everything good in education increased. Putting New Hall on the map became essential.

Concerts, Book Weeks, Literary Dinners, with eminent writers such as Salley Vickers, Philippa Gregory, Gervaise Phinn and Michael Holroyd, and Foundation Day lectures were chances to share our wonderful facilities with other schools and many guests. We invited students from Chelmsford schools to hear speakers such as the poet Simon Armitage and the novelist Fay Weldon. We hosted concerts as part of the Chelmsford Cathedral Festival. All these events brought visitors to experience the hospitality of our school, and for many it was their first chance to see what lay at the end of that mile-long drive. We became members of the Essex Chamber of Commerce and entertained business contacts from across the county. The inspirational leadership of successive Headmistresses encouraged a wider partnership with the town and county.

When Dr David Starkey spoke at the Literary Dinner in September 2003, he told me that he had long wanted to visit New Hall and to see the famous façade of what had been one of England's most amazing Tudor palaces. When he spoke for more than an hour to 220 enthralled guests, his erudition and wit delighted everyone, and highlighted the small part we have all played in the fascinating history of our school.

I'm enjoying my so-called retirement! I am a trustee of two charities, I go to the Cathedral School each week to hear early readers, and I run a Book Club. I am a grandmother, and happily have more time for my family, my friends, the opera, theatre, entertaining and taking wonderful holidays, and visiting various European countries with the London choir my husband sings with.

In the library with Anne Byatt (Sparrow)

LYDIA BAZZARD
Southwell 1987–1994

I started as a withdrawn and unconfident slip of a girl with a strong Essex accent and left as a more confident, more accomplished and better spoken young lady with a string of qualifications.

I can still hear the swish of her habit as S. Anne-Marie swept down the corridor muttering, 'Right,' under her breath, sweeping curtains aside with a, 'Come on, Lydia, time to wake up,' and the scraping of twenty-odd chairs as bleary-eyed girls knelt outside their cubicles for morning prayers.

When I was feeling particularly homesick a friend, Natasha, comforted me by saying it was 'visiting night' – which I imagined involved leaving School to visit an old person; but it turned out to be getting up after lights-out and going into another girl's cubicle for a very hushed, whispered chat.

Conversations about underground passages and scary ghosts of nuns, monks and priests had been going around for some time. It was while visiting one particular night that following such conversations Lucy and I spontaneously concocted a plan to scare the others witless. We would draw a cross on their heads, while they were sleeping, in brown regulation shoe polish, and so as to remain undetected, would draw one on our own heads too. We managed this without disturbing anyone and gleefully retired to bed looking forward to what we thought would be a terrified and awestruck response to our clever trick. Everyone was very upset particularly as the shoe polish didn't come off after scrubbing with soap and water and we had to spend the day with brown splodges on our heads. We may have got away with it if Lucy's sister Sophie hadn't seen through us and told S. Anne-Marie at breakfast who was responsible for this violation. To say we got punished was an understatement, although we did deserve it. No swimming for a term. Not allowed to go home for the weekend all term, a demerit in our journal and worst of all we had to polish eighty pairs of shoes. Plus in our cross-drawing merriment we had found it funny to cover the feet in shoe polish of a girl who was snoring really loudly. She had woken the next day to a bed covered in brown stains and thought she was dying. Our penance to make amends was to tidy her room and take her sheets to the laundry, explaining how they had got that way.

I was fascinated by the laundry. It was a hive of activity run by a nun whom I liked because she reminded me of Mrs Tiggywinkle.

Despite it being a comfortable environment there was always the urge to escape, purely because you weren't allowed to. One night a friend and I ran away to McDonald's, in our nighties, without any money. It was a bit embarrassing once we arrived. We hadn't thought it through at all. So we just came back again. To avoid the security van down the Avenue, we jumped into a ditch. We made it back undetected.

My fondest memories are of my friendship with Jackie, a funny, tall girl I had a lot in common with. Our families were both fans of *Monty Python* and we had many hysterical moments re-enacting favourite scenes.

If there was something I couldn't understand I could always go to Jackie and she would explain it patiently; she understood how frightened I was of being 'a thicky' so she would pretend she was a woman called Sheila whose job it was to explain things in very simple terms to a boy with learning difficulties called Marvin. But the greatest help Jackie ever gave to me was the time she bravely saved my life. It was during Easter celebrations in the Chapel. We had all been given candles to hold, and while I was earnestly singing a hymn, my hair caught fire. Without hesitation Jackie grabbed the flames in her fist and put them out.

For a long time after I left I had a recurring dream that I had to go back to school – it was so realistic I would wake up happy until I realised it was a dream.

JACQUELINE SILVER

1987–1994

The journey back to New Hall ended with us sweeping up the majestic, mile-long Avenue, racing the trains before turning the bend to count the pairs of sentried trees and comfortably sleeping policemen.

Mornings began with sweeping classrooms, or trudging through muddy fields to pick out horses' hooves, clad in royal-blue overalls.

Break-times were filled with gaggles of laughing girls, arms linked, kilts flapping in the wind, sauntering unhurriedly down the Beech Walk.

It was a world where nuns glided through curiously coined corridors: the Ambulacrum, Aloysius Corridor, the Grey Passage. Where horses clip-clopped happily past the windows while girls daydreamed through their studies of the prospect of their lunchtime riding lesson with a real-life colonel and ponies with names like 'Wiggy Turbine'. Here netball matches involved loitering in the shooting circle when playing against opponents from local schools who made such opening gambits as, 'Is it true you all go to barn dances and go to bed at four o'clock here?' Of course not! Four o'clock was for study in the Octagon.

The Octagon was a rare instance of accurate nomenclature. Six Acres is not six acres. And who condoned naming the Reception the Red Room and then kept it steadfastly painted primrose yellow? And why during the 350th Anniversary year was there a flurry of duplication and every corridor in the school seemed to be re-christened the Susan Hawley Wing?

Who decided that the wood that houses mossy grottoes and the nuns' graveyard – that is strictly out of bounds – should be tantalisingly called the Wilderness? Could they blame the sneaky smokers and those engaged in the thrill of the trespass?

Irresistible mischief, antics and adventures. 'Girls, where are my twenty-two copies of *Wuthering Heights*?' piped a certain Scottish English teacher plaintively, desperately rifling through her desk drawers and every cupboard in sight, before a sheepish student, abandoned by her cowardly classmates who had originally egged her on, eventually climbed through the window to retrieve them from their outdoor hiding place.

To exacerbate a certain Geography teacher's anguish at his beloved paperweight (a stone with a painting of Great Britain on it) going missing, one new replica a day would appear overnight on his desk, over a period of two agonising weeks. We had created a fleet of forgeries, sized in gradients from the tiniest pebble all the way through to a giant painted rock . . .

There was a Latin prank that resulted in a pupil being taken as, at the very least, unconscious, if not dead, having feigned a fainting fit.

312

The well-planned, whole-class escapade had gone too far and she was too scared to rise, as if from beyond the grave, at the appointed time.

In a grand-scale costumed plot we tortured the spooked-out group of Scandinavian drama students who were unfortunate enough to be using the building for a Summer Camp while the annual Children's Holiday was underway. We appeared in their dormitory, as the bell struck midnight, dressed as a troupe of convincingly made-up, top-hatted, ghoulish undertakers, bearing a pallid, shrouded body – having raided the school's unrivalled costume cupboard – still the only place to this date where I have actually tried on vintage Chanel.

And if you ever hear tales of two novice nuns on the loose in Chelmsford who got into Dukes for free and were never rumbled as frauds, it wasn't they who borrowed veils from the nuns' washing line, where they flapped innocently and happily to dry.

It was a magical, mysterious, marvellous microcosm. Where adventure, parody and wit prevailed and character and the extraordinary triumphed. A unique world, fuelled by love for a special place and special people, and filled with a zest for laughter, life and learning. Education, achievement and personal triumphs, all the more prized because we were truly looked after and accepted as individuals and ourselves. A precious, privileged, unequalled seven years of education and inspiration; where personalities were formed, nourished and allowed to grow, and where friendships were forged to flourish.

EMMA LAWLEY (née Collin)

Southwell 1987–1994

On my first day I approached the Avenue with a healthy combination of fear, respect and excitement.

It was a privilege from start to finish. When I started, the fields were full of horses and many of my teachers were members of the Community. By the time I left, both the horses and the Community had receded.

I started as a day girl and finished as a full boarder and Head Girl. From the small quiet child who sported regulation red knickers and 'fashionably' scuffed 'granny bashers', I graduated through the extremes of skirt length (from bottom-skimming gym skirts to ankle-skimming kilts), sledged the snow-drenched ditches on black bin liners, shivered on the icy hockey fields and flirted with fencing. I learnt all that I was and all that I would grow into (definitely not a dancer or musician, possibly a scientist or historian?). By 1994 I had travelled through my teens and emerged as a woman ready for the next great adventure – brave enough to tackle India on my own and follow my heart academically.

There are precious moments that I will never forget. When the magnificent cedar trees fell in the storms of 1987 and we wept and mourned the passing of these majestic ancient friends – I still have the cedar cross we were each given in celebration of 'their' lives. Tea at the end of each day – racing to get the best buns, 'Sticky Willies' (and that was a name from the staff!). The thrill of netball fixtures outside school, NHVS visits to the elderly to share tea, biscuits and heart-warming stories of the past and the present, and the Gold Duke of Edinburgh Award (oh, the blisters!). Easter at School – moving, inspiring and deeply heartfelt – moments of community and shared spiritual passion. Mixed with a healthy dose of reality, like the singeing of my hair in Chapel and the 'Mexican wave' of wrinkled noses as the smell wafted down the aisle to the altar.

Exhibition Weekend – the culmination of all the year had been – with strawberries and cream, and lazy Saturdays with parents flushed

Granny bashers

by the sun (or the wine) as they watched their daughters struggle to master the Fosbury flop and hurl the shot in the name of House athletics, perform marvellous matinées and generally 'exhibit' all that was excellent, extraordinary and exciting.

Here was an environment that allowed each of us to flourish in her own field, and though led by a discipline of Catholic doctrine, was never exclusive or preclusive of other denominations but embraced an essence of community in every sense and above all else – and this is most of all my abiding memory of New Hall – a place and people full of warmth, kindness, generosity, sharing – of magical moments that informed and created me.

Earning money as a chambermaid, I went to India for seven months, before studying English Literature at Bristol University. After a period of working on the Essex Chronicle *I moved to London and into Television Distribution – in which I still work – travelling from Vietnam to LA to South Africa. I am currently Director of Programming at Indigo which I co-own with my husband, David.*

Exhibition Weekend picnic in 1998

KAY WINTERSGILL

Head of Careers 1988–2004

In the early days it didn't matter when you went into the school, there was always someone about to have a chat with and a cup of tea; you always felt that there was a friendly face to greet you. It was a wonderful feeling of family and belonging.

Driving up the Avenue made you feel good. I love the grounds and the Chapel and feel privileged and proud to have belonged to New Hall. It was always easy to find your own space and a little corner of tranquillity.

Tea in the nuns' Refectory was a treat and we had some great 'whole New Hall Community' Christmas parties at the end of term. It was all-inclusive. I particularly remember when the nuns came out of full habit one or two of the Sixth Form feeling outraged.

I never felt that being a non-Catholic excluded me from anything; we were a community that cared for each other and rejoiced in our differences.

The parents were very supportive in general and I led some amazing trips all over Europe.

I was sad to retire seven years ago but never really lost touch as I came back to teach Cookery and other subjects.

It has been interesting to watch the school develop, first with prep and now fully co-ed, but my warmest memories are of the 'old' days with the nuns and the girls and a tight-knit community that I loved.

LIZZIE FOLLOWS (née Tomlins)

1989–1997

Queues for doughnuts at afternoon tea; PGL in the Ardèche with Miss Morrow; warm evenings playing tennis, cricket and relaxing under the cedars in front of Owens; a very cold swimming-pool; trying to get away with wearing our PE kit all the time; the horrid brown uniform shoes and nappy-like PE knickers. Strawberries and cream at Exhibition Weekend, while everyone crowded around the

TV to watch Wimbledon; Pottery Club in our blue overalls after lessons – much better than being in the Octagon doing homework; Owens and Southwells turning into the Prep School, and having to move down to Hawley House.

After a gap year teaching English in Thailand with Project Trust I went to Nottingham University to study Medicine. I lived in New Zealand for six months before doing my GP training in the West Midlands. I married in 1996 and, after our daughter Leah was born, I continued to work part-time as a GP in Redditch. We live in Bromsgrove, just south of Birmingham.

ELOISE MASTER JEWITT (née Master)
1990–1997

Following the excitements marking the 350th Anniversary of the Foundation of the Community and School, we were in need of some cause for further celebration and so came the arrival of Nibbles, the hamster, on 31st July 1993.

1993 was also the year that S. Moira became my tutor and Assistant Housemistress simultaneously. We never quite saw eye to eye over which clubs I should participate in, she proposing the Debating Society while I happily joined Pets Corner Club, where I could visit Nibbles, giving her fresh sawdust which was paid for out of the £5-a-term boarding fee for hamsters.

Henry, another hamster, was destined to be the love of Nibbles's life. When I returned one day to find both had been let out and were on the floor together, I feared the worst. The Community heard of the unwanted New Hall pregnancy, and I was distraught (such were the small worries of my life at that time). S.M.Gabriel was extremely comforting whilst S. Moira, I think, just laughed.

Now, more than 15 years after her passing to hamster heaven, I can divulge a few of her secrets, such as her love of the Meditation Room to run around in and the night she stayed in my cubicle as it was so cold I was worried she would freeze! Oh, and the time Mrs Rickford was ill and Nibbles came to S. Moira's French lesson in my pocket.

LIBBY SEARLE

Southwell 1991–1996

An enchanting place – not only did the building have its own unique splendour, but the people, ethos and atmosphere were special. You could be a nobody yet somebody, normal or abnormal, you fitted in. We felt cocooned in a place where you could be 'you' and were supported in that.

I am currently the Head of Boarding at New Hall School; I have worked at New Hall since returning to Essex from Cambridge in 2007. I attended New Hall and then went on to study A Levels at Haileybury. After a year at finishing school and then completing a History Degree I worked for a while in the City. I have two children currently at New Hall.

SASCHA WILLIAMS

1991–1998

As difficult as it is to pick one time among so many in seven years, one that would certainly make my Top Ten involves the Liturgical Choir around 1996. The magnificent music, the unfailing camaraderie, the fact that members were allowed into the Refectory early for lunch, what wasn't to love?

The moment Mr Fardell told us we'd be going to Rome, to perform in St Peter's Basilica itself, felt very special. Months of practice ensued, often accompanied by excited squeals that we'd finally get to wear those Red choir gowns we'd seen hanging up in the Chapel for years. The tour was nothing short of fantastic. After every performance people we'd never met came up to us to express their delight. It was wonderful.

The *pièce de résistance* was Mass at the Vatican. It's hard to put into words exactly how that felt but, 15 years later, the signature tune – John Rutter's 'For the Beauty of the Earth' – still brings me out in goosebumps. Yes, it's right up there with the Exhibition Weekend anthem 'Tell Out My Soul'.

Before I left Rome I threw a coin into the Trevi Fountain, so am assured that one day I will return.

NATALIE PEREZ

1993–1994

I came to New Hall for a year to learn English. Fortunately it was a language which my parents didn't speak so I was able to 'translate' my school report to them – I could tell them I was excellent at everything.

It was not only the language that was new to me. I remember being taken over to the Chapel on my first day in a bright blue overall, thinking I was going on a tour of the School – and then being told to dust the benches. Going to bed at 9.30pm – before I would even have eaten supper in Spain.

What else did the Spanish 'Little Flea' (as S. Moira called me) get up to at New Hall? Passing Spanish written notes in Geography lessons which Mrs Strudwick and Mr Davies could never understand. Going to visit my friend's rat at Pets Corner (she told me it was a hamster, as it didn't have a tail, but I still think it was a rat!).

THE NICHOLLS FAMILY

Jenny Nicholls (1992–1999)
Feeling both nervous and privileged at meeting Lord Longford.

Caroline Nicholls (1994–2003)
Looked forward to 'Away Days' at the Barn, where I enjoyed the team-building games and a treasure hunt in the meadow.

Louise Nicholls (1991–1998)
When my sister Caroline joined the Prep School I was excited to have my two younger sisters at school with me at the same time.

After leaving New Hall, all three of us went on to study at Newcastle University before travelling round the world. Caroline did a degree in Agriculture then went on to work for the cereals and oilseeds division of the Agriculture and Horticulture Development Board (AHDB), where she is still working as a Research Manager. Jenny is a Senior Biomedical Scientist and the Training Officer for the Histology Department in Basildon Hospital. Louise qualified as a Chartered Accountant at Deloitte and now works for an investment bank in London.

ANNABEL BROWN

Pole 1993–1998 and Staff 2005–2011

I vividly remember walking down Aloysius Corridor in my first term and reading the quote from St Augustine on the Choir noticeboard: 'The one who sings, prays twice.' Music and singing were central to my time at New Hall and looking back it is extraordinary just how much we did.

I eagerly joined the Choir and Orchestra (on trumpet) in my first term at New Hall. It was after getting told off for chatting by Mr Fardell that I was told to stand up and sing the soprano line on my own. I was terrified, but I stood up and did it. A week later I sang my first solo, the psalm 'Centre of my Life', in Assembly. It was the start of my exciting musical life.

On the Lourdes Pilgrimage with Ampleforth (assisting S.Moira and S.Margaret Mary) the first solo I sang was also 'Centre of my Life', which felt very fitting. I worked hard and played hard that first year in Lourdes and S.Margaret Mary still has the evidence – a photo of me, slightly the worse for wear, propping myself up on my trumpet during Mass. (I have been back to Lourdes every year since.)

I spent hours in Walkfares with my friends writing our first musical (sadly as yet unpublished!) and many occasions in Poles and Mores singing along to the hits of the moment. Take That's 'Relight My Fire' will always remind me of the red Choir robes which were surreptitiously stolen to use in the dance routine choreographed during Easter weekend, and 'Love Shack' was definitely a Poles House favourite to dance to – I still know all the moves!

Other things that remind me of school: housework, especially the purple fluff under the bed that seemed to reappear every morning no matter how many times you swept; Liturgical Dance (still known as doing a Wendy Wong today); the Good Shepherd Fair; avoiding the Octagon during study; merits, and more often than not, demerits; the pool changing-rooms with millions of daddy-long-legs; making fudge in the House; water fights; apparatus rounders; forgetting my Exeat card; hiding in friends' wardrobes after lights-out and picnic lunches on Exhibition Weekend.

Choir with Andrew Fardell conducting

After I left New Hall in 1998 I studied for a BA (Hons), always maintaining strong links with New Hall via the Lourdes Pilgrimage and as a Committee Member of the OFA. At one OFA meeting Mr Fardell invited me to join the Choir on a tour to Rome. Little did I know how much it would change my life. I shared a room with the new Headmistress, Katherine Jeffrey, who encouraged me to apply for the role of Housemistress.

I started back at New Hall in April 2005 as Deputy Housemistress and moved to the full-time role of Director of Marketing and PR in 2007. It was great to be back and singing remained a part of my life there. I used to find index cards in the music filing system written in my scrawl from when I was Choir Prefect and it would bring a smile to my face.

It was a privilege to be a part of New Hall and to help give back just a small amount of what I was lucky enough to receive as a student there. Never did I feel more proud to be a New Hall girl than when we were blasting out the descant to 'Tell Out My Soul' on Exhibition Day every year.

I left New Hall in 2011 and I am now Marketing Manager at St George's School, Ascot.

SARAH FRUCHARD (née Hamlyn)

Southwell 1994–2001

It doesn't take much effort to conjure up images of us running to our cubicles after lights-out with Mrs Murray close on our heels, or having our photo taken by tourists in Rome as we wandered the streets of the Vatican City in our Choir robes.

There is one memory which is especially worthy of recollection – an annual character-building exercise, which went by the name of Parents' Day. This was the most torturous Saturday in the academic year.

To know that there is a date firmly in the diary when one is to be the topic of discussion is hard enough, but to have to sit in that third chair in front of the teacher and be privy to their candour is surely a tad too painful. The torture was not confined to one spring Saturday but began a week before as we entered into open competition with our classmates in order to secure the most strategic schedule of appointments with our teachers. It took us just one Parents' Day to realise that the only way to survive was to shun the school lunch, organise back-to-back appointments and be out of the school gates as quickly as possible. The appointment slots directly after Mass were hot commodities, with bartering and underhand negotiation all being part of the game. The general advice from teachers was, of course, to leave some room between meetings to allow time to get from one to the next – advice that was rarely heeded. Instead, we pushed our parents through a fast-forward version of the year's events. Within half an hour my mother had a headache and my father had no idea which subject was being discussed, while I merrily ticked off meetings. The one fly in the ointment was the danger of being stuck behind the sort of chatty parents who took Parents' Day as an opportunity to reminisce with teachers about their own misadventures in the Physics Lab or how they scraped through their Maths O Level – which only raised the possibility of the minute-perfect timetable being thrown off course.

Somehow I always managed to persuade my frazzled and confused parents to take a slight detour on the way home via the nearby McDonald's drive-through. A treat of saturated fat and fizzy e-numbers seemed to be an appropriate tonic at 2pm on Parents' Day. I have not visited a McDonald's drive-through in the ten years which have passed since my final Parents' Day. I can only assume that there haven't been any adequately stressful occasions since.

I took a degree in Theology and Education at Cambridge University. After graduating in 2004 I moved to London to join a Global Investment Consultancy where I am still working today as the HR Adviser in its London office.

LIZ WELSH-SMYTH

1995–2000

Random memories include: Hawley housework duties resulting in bin-bag throwing competitions outside PE2; regular visits to the Wilderness for a cigarette – carefully avoiding S.Patricia and her torch; roller-blading trips to McDonald's after lights-out; very nearly being thrown out of PE1 for painting my nails during my Physics GCSE; buying peach schnapps with some others on the school trip to Venice, coming back to the hotel a little the worse for wear and trying to pass it off as sunstroke; S. Patricia's threat to start dancing on the tables to convince us that Bible Studies was interesting; a midnight feast in the nuns' Refectory with some others and unwittingly getting the entire Sixth Form grounded for a weekend (retrospective apologies); Pledge and Gumption placed in every cubicle at the beginning of every term without fail; winning the dustpan-and-brush for the messiest cubicle of the term.

VICTORIA BACON

1996–2003

My interview for New Hall was with S. Margaret Mary, Headmistress at the time – and I didn't want to be there. But she welcomed me on the first day and I felt overwhelmed. She read my project on 'The Philippines' and then we drank tea. S. Margaret Mary gave me the much needed opportunity of a government-assisted place. At the time, I was far too young to appreciate this but her faith in me is now one of my fondest memories.

MARIA ADEY

1996–2001

Sneaking out of cubicles after lights-out involved mastering the art of the silent dash from one cubicle to another without hitting the curtains, which would give away your whereabouts. The most agile among us discovered the technique of scaling the cubicle walls as a means of escape.

Cleaning the cubicles was a ritual after which stringent checks were made by the Housemistress, and she would never fail to find some out-of-reach spot we hadn't managed to polish. And Gumption – I've never seen it anywhere else on this planet.

Lucy Gosling, Danielle Hake and I were playing outside Beaulieu on the grass, perfecting our cartwheels, handstands and handstands into bridges, when we heard a rustling in the hedge. Shockingly, it was a young boy. Our Deputy Housemistress at that time was an ex-army officer and she sprinted outside to chase the boy and his bike down. But he had a head start and a bike so she retreated to call the

Aerobics

Chelmsford Police, who scrambled a helicopter, with infra-red tracking equipment. He was wanted by the police but we never found out why or if he was caught, but I'm pretty sure he didn't venture into New Hall's grounds again.

In the second-hand uniform shop, S. Magdalen John picked the items that you didn't want – like the longest possible school skirt (never the daring knee-length one) or the faded school jumper. I never got anything new because I had my mum's uniform from her days at New Hall, which shows how little it had changed. I just got new name tags put over the top of hers. As I spent most of my days doing gymnastics on the grass and falling into ponds it was probably for the best.

NATALIE SHARROCK

1996–2002

My favourite memories of New Hall tend to involve some aspect of dressing up. Whether it was randomly putting on Halloween masks and singing hymns with my friend Billie in the Quad (it wasn't Halloween) or bounding into S. Moira's tutorial at 8:30am wearing reindeer antlers and a red nose (it was Christmas). I think the best memory has to be a certain Biology lesson when my friend, Gemma, and I paired up to do a presentation about global warming. For some reason we decided to do it from the point of view of two sheep. This entailed wearing dressing-gowns and baaing our way through (probably an extremely rubbish) presentation culminating in our singing (or rather baaing) Michael Jackson's 'The Earth Song'. We then decided we were quite comfortable in our dressing-gowns and thought it would be funny to wear them for the rest of the day. This lasted all of 10 minutes as we were denied entry into the Refectory unless we took them off; hunger prevailed.

I attended Wolverhampton University where I studied Drama, specialising in Scriptwriting and Stand-Up Comedy. I had a short Stand-Up career during which I was presented with an award by Frank Skinner. I am currently a Business Development Manager for Extra Personnel.

LUCY DORMANDY (née Crick)

1996–2002

My time at New Hall was an absolute joy. It was a place of nurture, encouragement and fun. Whether we were sporty, academic, musical or theatrical, there was a way for all gifts to be recognised and we grew in an atmosphere that made us feel we belonged.

The opportunity to get involved with NHVS and have input from the community, and the provision of regular reflection days away from usual lessons, set New Hall apart as a school experience. It meant that our education wasn't just academic, but much more rounded, and ensured the sort of holistic development which is so important in those formative years.

There are so many happy memories – school trips, plays, assemblies, Exhibition Days, Foundation Days, as well as the variety of lessons and gossip-filled break-times. An H.E. class when a friend set fire to her wok stir-fry; a drama lesson with the stalker from the famous Alan Partridge series (who was a pupil's dad); and an anatomy class where

New Hall Voluntary Service (NHVS)
Clare Devanney and Jo McQueen, with Jim McGhee
as escort to Babs Chapman

we each got a pig's eyeball and heart to dissect – there was rarely a dull week at New Hall.

It was also a place where special friendships were forged. Not having boys at the school seemed like a disaster at the time but, in retrospect, I think having the chance to grow up free of the complications of in-school relationships helped us to develop friendships that were not a prey to hormones or jealousy. Now we are grown-up, having gossiped at break-times about boyfriends we've loved and lost, how special to see friends walking up the aisle or find ourselves moving in with 'the one' that we had been trying so desperately (and, unsurprisingly, unsuccessfully) to find at 15!

LUCY GOSLING
Hawley and Pole 1996–2001

I couldn't believe how long the drive was, when every Sunday night, as my dad drove me back to school, I tried to count the number of trees, but failed every time.

On my first day at school a nun said to me, 'You must be a Gosling,' recognising my aunty (my father's sister) in me and not my mum, Brenda Ludlow.

I dreaded the closed weekends but going to Sainsbury's was the highlight (who would have thought that a supermarket could attract so many excitable girls?).

Housework and the blue overalls that also got used for Science classes, the 'high-drys' and Gumption (does Gumption actually exist in real life? – I still haven't found it).

Falling head first into the school pond with Maria Adey while doing pond research for Biology. Being marched up to the Infirmary, where I was petrified by S.M.Matthew's talk of Weil's disease.

I remember thinking I was going to become a nun in Year 8.

I have such fond memories of S.M.Christopher, who gave us Elocution lessons before we had to speak in Chapel. She had a powerful aura around her, which I cannot explain, and as a 12-year-old girl I found her strangely fascinating.

Going to collect the House tea for Hawley with Lara Carew-Jones and hiding about four cakes each up our sleeves for eating later in the afternoon.

The revolving lunch-tray machine that became a challenge if the only space to put your tray was about to whizz around into the kitchen; you had to place your tray with great care to avoid disaster.

The Ha-Ha, Hawley, Dennett, Mores, Gumption, cubicle, Six Acres, Plant Prefect (surely unique – Danielle Hake was the best Plant Prefect I remember), Pets Corner, Refectory, merits and demerits.

Running away from school with Danielle Hake; we got as far as the exit gate when we got stopped by a teacher asking us where we were going. 'We're running away,' I replied. He said, 'Good luck,' which so perturbed us, we turned and walked back.

We were not allowed to read or listen to music after lights-out but, as I couldn't sleep well, I used a small light to read and covered my Walkman in about three pillows to muffle the whirling sound it used to make. I was so scared of getting caught I don't think I ever heard any music and just ended up getting boiling hot trying to read under the covers.

One day Maria Adey, Danielle Hake and I discovered a boy hiding in the bushes in the school grounds, near Beaulieu. We told our Housemistress about this fascinating event and the next thing we knew

*A visit to
S.M.Matthew in
the Infirmary*

we were being hurried inside, all doors were locked and two police cars turned up. A helicopter circled the school. Unforgettable. I'm still not sure whether he was caught.

I attended Ampleforth Sixth Form College (from convent to monastery!) then taught and travelled in Africa for six months, got a BSC Honours in Geography from Newcastle, did a rally, driving 10,000 miles across 16 countries from London to Mongolia for charity, and spent two months as a charity relief worker in Sri Lanka after the Tsunami hit. Now I am living and working in London as a TV Associate Producer for shows such as The X Factor, Britain's Got Talent *and* The Voice.

CELESTE IRVINE

1996–2001

My memories range from my first Prizegiving in 1996, when I was awarded the Susan Hawley Scholarship, through to my last summer at New Hall helping the NHVS with the annual holiday for disadvantaged children.

Of them all, however, my fondest memory is of the countless hours I spent with the Debating Society, valuable experience which helped me in deciding to become a barrister. I remember the dedication of S. Moira and Mrs Webb, who taught me how to argue persuasively and gave me the belief that I could be good at it. All the hard work paid off in 2001, when we won the Knights of St Columba National Debating Competition. To this day, whether I am on my feet in Court or in my room at Goldsmith Chambers in London, I thank the staff at New Hall for giving me that first taste of success.

LINDSEY REDGWELL

1997–2004

Joy Palit running down the path outside Campions and splatting straight into the window of Mr Calendar's office. The bemused look on his face as she peeled herself off the glass was classic!

On the school trip to Normandy I bought a novelty stress-ball which turned out to be a balloon filled with flour.

The many hours in the Sixth Form spent sitting in armchairs on Mores landing chatting with friends.

A bunch of us going for milkshakes after receiving our GCSE results.

Alishia Patel covering my GCSE history folder in doodles during each class – by the end of the year it was a thing of beauty.

CHARLOTTE SPEAKMAN

1997–2003

I remember all the little moments when I made people laugh (and sometimes scream!). In the Sixth Form, jumping out at people from different doorways never failed, along with the challenge in Year 7 of attempting to fit myself into the green lockers.

Eating snails on the Normandy trip, which did not give me a taste for snails.

Trying to get everyone to do Christmas housework in Mores with Christmas music blasting out.

The best thing was the friends I made, especially during my time boarding in the Sixth Form.

FRANCES THOMAS

1997–2004

Among the best opportunities provided by New Hall were the overseas trips. How many can say that they rode camels through the desert in Tunisia, sang to the Pope in the Vatican and struggled through snow and ice in Russia?

The most memorable was our trip to Russia: travelling on an overnight sleeper (not much sleeping went on); celebrating someone's birthday by decorating their room with toilet tissue (there was nothing else to be found); visiting a Russian school where the children could speak English just as well, and some of them better, than we could; drinking the vodka offered with every meal and in every shop when we thought the teachers weren't looking.

My favourite image of this trip is of a random moment in Red Square. Having been both horrified and fascinated by the perfectly preserved corpse of Lenin, and after taking numerous photographs of the surprisingly graceful onion towers topping St Basil's Cathedral, Joyeeta and I decided that no trip to Moscow would be complete without a photo of us with a soldier. Having stalked, stopped and coerced a typically Russian (and fairly good looking) soldier, Joyeeta and I posed proudly for the picture. Unfortunately, the rest of our friends spotted what we were doing and gate-crashed the shot, stealing our moment entirely. When I look back at the picture I am glad they did. The resigned look of amusement on the soldier's face at being mobbed by a group of English schoolgirls always makes me smile.

RUTH MANNING

1996–2003

Hanging out with S. Diana in the Tuck Shop. Table football with S. Moira in France – I think she beat Camilla! Music lessons with S. Patricia, who was a bit scary. Wondering how S. Anne-Marie knew everyone's name. Drinking wine with S. Diana and Mrs Hopkins at the end of a long day in Mores. S. Diana's tortoise. Our Sixth Form Leavers' Ceremony, the candle, necklace and the nuns' anointment and

Army challenge

blessings. They gave us a tour of their Community quarters and the attic where the New Hall Archives are kept, which was a very special leaving present.

LAYLA JONES

1997–2004

During our GCSE years there was a custom of sticking sellotape from one side of the door, across the entrance, to the other, so that when anyone walked through the door they would get stuck to it – including teachers. A silly joke, but it never got old and gave us loads of laughs.

RIO ALI

Red pants also known as PE knickers.

I'm writing a fashion feature on the wonder that is Kate Moss, and way back in the day when she used to be a fresh-faced, drug-free teen and *The Face* was still in publication, she did her most famous photo shoot to date called 'The Third Summer of Love'. Take a look at these photos: I do believe that she is wearing some pants that seriously resemble the New Hall PE kit!

MARGARET McGHEE

Member of Staff from 1979

My first visit to New Hall was for Midnight Mass one Christmas in the late 1960s. In those days cars had to pass over a level-crossing before being able to enter the grounds of New Hall. The Chapel was quite dimly lit and very cold. Fortunately I had been told to 'wrap up warm'. The crib was a work of art, filling the rear bay-window area and carefully assembled by S.M.Joseph. She told me in later years it could take her up to a week.

The Community entered in pairs, about 48 nuns in full habit, including wimples. The singing was perfect. After Mass we were invited to join the Community in their Refectory for hot soup and warm mince pies. The nuns were very welcoming and to this day there is nothing like a New Hall Welcome.

My first daylight visit to New Hall was in 1979, when I went for an interview, with S. M Thérèse. As I drove up the Avenue two girls were galloping their horses down. I got the job and stayed for over 30 years and S.M. Thérèse became a dear friend.

In all, eleven members of my family worked for New Hall, including my husband, who helped rewire the Chapel.

An amusing episode I remember well could be called 'The Case of the Anorexic Nun'. I cannot recall the exact date but sometime in 1987 a member of staff went into the Ladies and received a great shock: sitting on a loo was a skeleton. In its mouth was a cigarette, on its feet were a pair of nun's sandals and by its side was an empty bottle of wine! Everyone laughed. Surmising that the culprits would be hovering in the corridor outside to note the reaction of staff, we had to play them at their own game. Staff exiting the Ladies behaved as if they had seen nothing amiss. We planned to put the skeleton back in the Lab while the girls were at night study. Everyone agreed the plan but it did mean that the skeleton had to hang on a hook next to the wash-basins for the rest of the day. Well, it was a good talking point.

Teaching staff kept their ears open and names were mentioned. S. Margaret Mary sent the parents one of her special letters saying something along the lines that while she admired the ingenuity of their daughters in carrying the skeleton over the roof, it was a dangerous thing to do and the skeleton was expensive. But no heads rolled.

My own memory of an Easter at New Hall is of when in 1997 my seventh grandson, Callum, was given the honour of being baptised at the Easter Mass. What an emotional experience.

The family drove up the Avenue to be greeted with the bonfire blazing in the paddock and the Comet Hale-Bopp shining brightly over New Hall. The Community, staff and girls were singing around the bonfire and after the short service we all moved in procession to the Chapel, which was in darkness. As we reached the entrance we were all presented with a lighted candle so gradually the Chapel filled with warmth and light.

The service was very moving, Fr Jim Clarke was at his best, the Community and girls sang beautifully and Callum behaved impeccably. He was baptised with water brought back from the River Jordan. I often remind Callum what a special event it was.

FR JIM CLARKE

Celebrant (Easters) 1990s

During the 1990s I had the privilege of coming into contact with New Hall School after a Caring Church Week when I was asked to come and facilitate a CAFOD 'Justice and Peace' Day with the Sixth Formers. That was the start of a fantastic relationship which lasted up until my departure for Brazil in 1999.

During that time I celebrated many Easters with the Sisters and the School community. Easter at New Hall was something special. The liturgies were creative and lively. Lots of preparation went into them and Easter really became a celebration of life. Aligned with the Easter liturgies there were so many activities, events and workshops which gave a real flavour of the New Hall Community but which also celebrated the youth, vigour and energy of the young people. Easter at New Hall was a powerful moment of spiritual deepening and communal living. In sharing fun, friendship and faith we glimpsed the real Easter message of life in its fullness. One minute I was nervously singing the Eucharist Prayer and the next I was puffing and panting after an hour of aerobics. It was a real body and soul workout!

Apart from Easter at New Hall, I also visited various times to celebrate Eucharists at special events. I was the principal celebrant at Prizegiving and at the final Mass of the Sisters' presence at New Hall. All were powerful moments of God's presence and celebrations of a faith Community at work.

Exhibition weekend dancers in 1998

I have been truly blessed with the friendships and fond memories of the New Hall family. Ministry is a mutual experience and I know I probably gained far more than I ever gave.

One lasting memory is standing in a paddling pool on the staircase baptising a Chinese student during the Easter Vigil. Strange things happened at New Hall, but we know that our God is anything but conventional.

LESLEY BOWLES

Member of Staff 1990s

Oh my dear, I have so many happy memories of my time with you. Since I worked with Magdalene, I felt that I belonged and you were all part of my family. I started off as Lesley, went into the School as Mrs Bowles, especially with the Sixth Form I soon became Aunty B, then over the last three years I was promoted to Nanny B or Nanny Bowles. Wonderful, isn't it?

While I was working in the Infirmary in the spring of 1990 with S.M.Matthew and Mrs Linda Bacon we noticed a duck waddling on the roof; we could see her out of the Dispensary window and yes she had built a nest. Mother duck sat on her eggs and eventually they hatched but to our surprise all eight ducklings went one by one down the drainpipe. Immediately, nurses to the rescue, downstairs we rushed. No ducklings had appeared, so we rang Tony La Roche who came straight away and located the drainpipe they had vanished into and removed the bottom section. He put his hands up the drainpipe and, guess what! they were all huddled together on a ledge. After getting in touch with S.Diana (who always cared for animals in Pets Corner) Tony lifted each duckling to safety, one by one, and put them in the box she had provided. Then they were taken to the Lab to be put under an infrared light by S.Diana and a lab technician to get them warm and over the shock of falling. When they had recovered S.Diana brought them down to the Quad, lifted them out and put them on the grass; we were very worried that Mother Duck would reject them, but after a few chirps she returned to them and led them off round to the pond for a safer place to sleep. A very happy day for everyone involved.

2000 Onwards

What's going on in the world during the 2000s

War on Terror / Rise of digital media / Emergence of China / Climate Change becomes major concern / Economic downturn sparks global recession / Reality TV / Sat Nav / Facebook, Twitter and YouTube / Crocs & Ugg Boots / Skinny jeans

2000 Dot com bubble bursts / George W. Bush becomes 43rd President of the US / Tate Modern and London Eye open / Ken Living-stone becomes London's first elected mayor / Paris Concorde crash / Atomic Kitten 'Whole Again' / Eminem 'Stan' / U2 'Beautiful Day'

2001 September 11th terrorist attack on the World Trade Centre / US, UK, Canada and Australia invade Afghanistan to oust Taliban / Netherlands legalise same-sex marriage / New-generation Mini launched / Dido 'Thank You' / Stereophonics 'Have A Nice Day'

2002 Death of the Queen Mother / Queen celebrates her Golden Jubilee / Will Young wins *Pop Idol* / Girls Aloud 'Sound Of The Underground' / Avril Lavigne 'Sk8er Boi' / The White Stripes 'Fell In Love With A Girl'

2003 Invasion of Iraq / Space shuttle *Columbia* disintegrates on re-entry / Human Genome Project completed / Europe hit by 40°C heatwave / Apple launches iTunes / 50 Cent 'In Da Club' / Black Eyed Peas 'Where Is The Love' / Outkast 'Hey Ya' / Beyoncé 'Crazy in Love'

2004 Indian Ocean Boxing Day tsunami / Fox hunting outlawed / Facebook launched / EU accepts 10 new states / Razorlight 'Golden Touch' / Snow Patrol 'Run' / Gwen Stefani 'What Are You Waiting For' / Kaiser Chiefs 'I Predict A Riot' / Keane 'Everybody's Changing'

2005 London bombings / New Orleans hit by Hurricane Katrina / Pope John Paul II dies / Prince of Wales marries Camilla Parker Bowles / Harold Pinter wins Nobel Prize for Literature / Sugababes 'Push The Button' / James Blunt 'You're Beautiful' / Pussycat Dolls 'Don't Cha' / Arctic Monkeys 'Bet You Looked Good On The Dance Floor'

2006 Saddam Hussein executed / *Top of the Pops* shown for the last time / Scissor Sisters 'I Don't Feel Like Dancing' / Take That 'Patience' / Amy Winehouse 'Rehab' / Gnarls Barkley 'Crazy'

2007 Gordon Brown succeeds Tony Blair as PM / Fidel Castro resigns / Benazir Bhutto assassinated / Last Harry Potter novel published / Mika 'Grace Kelly' / Rihanna 'Umbrella' / My Chemical Romance 'Teenagers' / Muse 'Invincible'

2008 Barack Obama elected President of US / Mumbai bombings / Beijing Olympics – Usain Bolt breaks 3 world records / CERN's Large Hadron Collider completed / The Ting Tings 'That's Not My Name' / Leona Lewis 'Bleeding Love' / Duffy 'Mercy'

2009 Swine Flu pandemic / G20 replaces G8 as main economic council / Michael Jackson dies / *Slum Dog Millionaire* wins eight Oscars / Lady Gaga 'Poker Face' / Florence and the Machine 'You've Got The Love' / Cheryl Cole 'Fight For This Love' / Dizee Rascal 'Bonkers'

Over: The Choir in St Peter's, Rome

What's going on at New Hall during the 2000s

The change to a new Millennium saw significant changes for both the School and Community.

In the early years of the decade, the Community recorded a CD of their sung music from all the liturgical seasons, aptly called *Eternal Light*. The CD became a big seller and went to number 2 in the Classical Music charts, which meant that New Hall became inundated with TV cameras and crew, journalists and photographers. Different members of the School were interviewed for their reactions to this sudden rise to fame!

In 2001 when S. Anne-Marie's Headship came to an end, she was replaced by the first Lay Head, Mrs Katherine Jeffrey, and this change was one of great import both for the Community and for the future of the School.

Following lengthy deliberation, the Community announced their decision to transfer the School to a Lay Trust, and later, their decision to leave the New Hall campus and root their lives elsewhere.

The Community launch their CD Eternal Light *which got to Number 2 in the Classic Charts in 2003*

The New Hall School Trust was set up in 2005 and the last members of the Community left New Hall in 2006.

Under Katherine Jeffrey's leadership, the School faced these challenges with great courage and vision, and soon made the announcement that the School would become co-educational, following the diamond model, and New Hall first opened its doors to boys (Year 7 and Year 12) in 2006.

Uniforms changed, buildings changed their usage, cricket and rugby pitches were laid, and following a five-year change-over period the School became fully co-educational in 2010.

A bold period of development was undertaken with the building of the all-weather pitch, the conversion of PE1 to the Eton Theatre, the building of Priory Court and the Fitness Centre, the opening of a Pre-Reception department for three- to four-year-olds, additional Science Labs and a further refurbishment of the Chapel.

Numbers grew throughout this period, and waiting lists were the order of the day, both for day and boarding places, and at the time of writing, there are 1,150 pupils on the School roll, aged between three and 18.

Katherine Jeffrey – the first Lay Principal

Joy Hopkinson – Head of Senior School from 2011

ANDREA HARRIS

Member of Staff 1990s to date

Whenever there's a reflection on change – from the perspective of one on the threshold of old fogeydom (some would say it has already been crossed), the mood that dominates is usually nostalgia.

The landscape as it used to be was more rural and the grounds dominated by horticulture rather than rugby culture. There was no Beaulieu Park, no Sainsbury's, no traffic lights on Generals Lane, and no barriers in or out of car parks. The swimming-pool was a modest open-air affair with changing rooms that were once set alight by some opportunistic Sixth Form students having a surreptitious cigarette during study time. The blaze was visible from what was then the Staff Room and resulted in the hasty departure from the meeting that was going on. S.Margaret Mary was not amused. Subtlety was infinitely more chilling than the direct methods that we tend to use now.

There were, of course, fewer buildings then. Walkfares opened in the early 1990s: Lord Longford officiated at one of the ceremonies. A further celebration of the Drama and English wings involved the late Sam Wannamaker of the Globe project being entertained by senior students' enactment of scenes from various plays by Shakespeare. We had the partition of Lear's kingdom, witty banter between Ganymede and Orlando in the Forest of Arden and the thumb-biting exchange that kicks off the street brawl in *Romeo and Juliet.* This was accompanied by a Year 11 performance of Tom Stoppard's thirteen-minute *Hamlet* as well as a rendition of *Brush up your Shakespeare.* The great Sam was gracious enough to seem impressed; in fact, in retrospect it was impressive – a tribute to Brian Harte, the Head of Performing Arts, and the incomparable Head of English, Joan Jones.

In 1994 the Preparatory School opened: a gamble that not all members of the school thought would pay off. As the parent of a four-year-old, this I found a merciful deliverance from juggling nursery pick-up times and paying extortionate childcare fees. When the first Preparatory Head realised that there was only one boy registered in a school we were keen to present as co-educational, he doubled the stakes by enrolling his own six-year-old son. Over the next decade and

342

a half the popularity of New Hall Preparatory School was reflected in additional classes, waiting lists and, eventually, a healthy transition of boys and girls from Preparatory to Senior School.

To do justice to the various leaders of New Hall School would take a David Starkey or a Simon Schama. As they will all read this and I am still employed, the extended version will have to wait.

S.Margaret Mary was the incumbent in January 1990 when I attended my first assembly. She spoke passionately about her hopes and fears for the next decade: an independent-school Headmistress with a social conscience and a concern for the environment surprised me – rather blinkered state-school teacher that I was then. I had not appreciated the practical aspects of the school's ethos: the Justice and Peace Society, the CAFOD lunches (held weekly) and NHVS. Political discourse was a feature of Staff Room conversation; assemblies regularly made reference to topical issues, always from an uncompromisingly humane, even radical perspective. There is less time for talk now and many of us rarely use the Senior Common Room; the outreach work, however, continues: in NHVS, in the Romanian Shoebox Appeal and in supporting Amnesty International and the Rwandan Literacy Centre.

This seemed to be a period of prosperity for New Hall: the year

Dance production

groups were large and evidence of wealth and plenty was conspicuous at Exhibition Weekends as gleaming Bentleys and Rolls-Royces lined the Avenue and luxurious picnic hampers were arranged by butlers in white gloves. Perhaps I made up the last bit . . . S. Margaret Mary presided over what seemed to be a most secure and privileged girls' boarding school. An abiding memory is of her indefatigable hand-shaking after tea on Exhibition Sunday as every member of the School trooped by – many of them sobbing at the thought of leaving for the summer holidays (those leaving for good were often prostrate).

S. Anne-Marie had attended New Hall as a Sixth Former. After graduating from Cambridge she taught both Classics and History and managed to look not much more than twenty when elevated to the Headship. If Margaret Mary was the charming and skilful manager of people, Anne-Marie was the intellectual ascetic who sacrificed her health to make the school profitable. It was rumoured that she lived on black coffee and chocolate: she replied to notes immediately, would run from one side of the school to another to speak to a colleague and was, despite her trim and efficient exterior, a most approachable leader who welcomed debate – even when her opponents were quite out-spoken.

The decline in boarding numbers had resulted in a cultural shift within the school. More prominent were day girls and the need to market the School more aggressively was addressed by more meetings, more Open Days and more initiatives to attract local families who would replace the dwindling numbers of boarders from farther afield. It was also a time of dwindling numbers for the Community, which had lost several of the elderly Canonesses who had been such vital presences in various parts of the school in 1990. Perhaps the decision to move out of an active role in the school should have been less shocking than it seemed at the time. The early twenty-first century brought the most far-reaching changes to date.

It is difficult to write about Katherine Jeffrey without listing achieve-ments. Having determined that it was time for a Lay Head, the trick was now to find one with courage and vision. Turning the oldest Catholic girls' school in the country into a mixed school on the diamond model and making her staff – including the diehards like myself – believe in it, was quite a feat. Within a decade the School has

344

swept triumphantly into a new era with Katherine presiding as Principal over two separate Headteachers, Sarah Conrad and Joy Hopkinson. Examination results, sporting achievements, economic turnover, successive inspections and a reputation both local and national will ensure that New Hall's success will be long-lasting.

But has it changed? Of course, to an extent . . . but although the people within a School will always move on, there is still that spirit of unsquashable exuberance and humanity – not just on Foundation Day or in Chapel assemblies and celebrations, but in classrooms, on the sports fields and in corridors.

Most of us, whether staff or students, love being here. Perhaps it is that lingering influence of all those great and committed women who put in place the values that continue to make New Hall a great school!

STELLA BEER

Preparatory School Teacher 1995–2009

Even with my eyes shut I'd recognise the familiar wump, wump, wump of air batting between the tree trunks. That heartbeat of a sound marks a visitor's progress up the mile-long avenue of limes and oaks leading to the School. It's the first thing you hear as you approach New Hall. From Easter 1995 to Christmas 2009 I taught in the Prep School; confining my memories into a few paragraphs is like trying to fit an elephant into a teacup.

When I think of New Hall I think of change. Hogwarts has its moving staircases but New Hall has its moving walls. I don't think I ever returned from a school holiday and found the walls where I left them. There was always something new being built or something old being altered as though the whole site was alive – and it's still evolving.

As well as the lively walls I remember the lively parents, those wonderful people who helped on history days when whole year groups became Ancient Egyptians or Victorians, and the hall was littered with bodies from the Battle of Balaclava. They made hundreds of costumes for Nativity Plays and their assistance on school trips and support during charity events was constant and generous. Then there were the staff. I have never worked with such an amazing bunch of characters. They were and are conscientious and clever, very hard working and above all fun. If all this sounds rather rosy, remember I'm retired now, so I can tell the truth. I don't have to be polite, after all what are they going to do? Fire me?

The reason New Hall exists is because of the children and one child's imaginative viewpoint of the School has always stayed with me. I was standing in the Nuns' Cemetery at the end of a sunny afternoon, surrounded by History Club members, when a delightful eight-year-old with flame-coloured hair looked up and said, 'You know, Mrs Beer, I think if it snowed, the snow that fell in here would be softer than the snow that fell outside.'

When the Time Team visited in 2009 they unearthed a small piece of flint which they said indicated that people had been living and working in this place for over five thousand years – and that tradition goes on. The buildings may be stunning but it's the people who make New Hall what it is because without them New Hall couldn't be New Hall.

I retired from New Hall a year early due to a series of foot operations. Since then, I have seen Venice in the rain, queued outside the National Gallery in the middle of the night, taken up t'ai chi and indulged my twin loves of history and writing.

'Time Team' visit in 2009

CATE BEAVIS
Southwell and Campion 1995–2004

Memories: The old outdoor swimming-pool on Six Acres, with the foot-bath and the spider-ridden changing rooms.

Moving to Beaulieu into Campions, with a chain of girls handing things down the hill from one to another

Always forgetting to move my Exeat card until about lunchtime

Celebrating in 1999 the 200th Anniversary of the school moving to the campus at New Hall with a Turn-Back-The-Clock-Day, with every-one dressed up in old-fashioned clothing – and even an old menu was followed for lunch, which didn't go down very well with everybody.

I did a BA in French then an MA in Translation at Leeds, and I'm now a Translation Coordinator for a company which translates medical questionnaires.

CELINA RUGHANI
Hawley 1995–2004

When I think back to my time at New Hall, I have images of vast amounts of greenery and the long and never-ending drive (especially when we had to run up and down it during Games).

Having done nearly the whole nine years at New Hall, my childhood memories are from various events: from closed weekends, fun filled with activities and late-night chaplaincy, to trips to Moscow, Prague, Bordeaux, Ypres and Stuttgart. New Hall was always a place for opportunities, whether it was entering into the Music competition, being an active member in the Voluntary Service, taking part in the Debating Society, joining the Choir or being a member of the many sports teams. There was never the opportunity to say, 'I never had the chance.'

In Senior School, I remember trips to musicals in the West End; Monday-morning Chapel assemblies; making things in Pottery class which were completely unusable; after-school dance classes; the various Drama performances, including *Joseph and the Amazing Technicolor Dreamcoat* and *Godspell*; numerous sports matches – with one hockey match in particular when the ball hit me directly on my mouth, from which I still have a small scar; doing the annual Hawley Secret Santa; S. Moira's love of *Tintin*; Mrs Murray's hatred of us turning up to class in our sports kit; the numerous fire-drills, with us all lining up outside the front of the Main Building and cheering as the local fire-brigade drove past.

Sixth Form was just as active: more free periods; lounging around in More playing pool and watching an endless succession of chick flicks; taking on Prefect roles; taking part in Children's Holiday; doing mock interviews with Dr Williams and Mrs Hopkinson for university entrance; attending the Ampleforth Ball, boys standing on one side of the hall and girls on the other; flexi-boarding and spending most of the evening in the TV room dancing away to MTV; lots of us learning to drive; and being so happy when Sam Devereese was one of the first to pass her test and get a car, as she would drive us to Sainsbury's so that we wouldn't have to do the long walk down the drive; the Sixth Form Leavers' Dinner – when I was in the Lower Sixth and actually ended up waiting on my sister and parents; the winter when we had a heavy snowfall and all went out to the bunker to make snowmen.

POLLY GLASS

1995–2006

It's strange to think of New Hall as a non-convent, co-educational School, where students wear chic blue business suits, go on skiing trips and swim in a swishy indoor pool. As someone who attended the school through an era of nuns, red uniforms and (for a while) a very past-it outdoor pool behind a creaky wooden fence at the corner of Six Acres, the experience was somewhat different.

Contrary to the current cosmopolitan state of affairs, our School involvement with boys consisted largely of debates with Westcliff Boys' High School and a couple of similar others. Lunchtime and after-school debates were always open to all, but the queues outside More's Debating Hall tended to be a little longer on these occasions . . . In the Sixth Form they developed into rather grandly named 'Debating Dinners', for which we, the Westcliff lot and our respective debating bods (aka teachers) would head for the Staff Refectory, engage in a 'serious' debate first (featuring the two from each school soon to be competing in an external competition), have a nice meal with wine, get a bit tiddly and then progress to a silly debate involving the Eurovision Song Contest, the moral standing of Homer Simpson or something of that ilk. We repeated the process at their school as well, driven in a minibus – as to all debating events held elsewhere – by S. Moira (bat out of hell behind the wheel), and later Mrs Clark.

Really though, now I think about it, it was one of the happiest times of my life – an enormous confidence booster for someone who was essentially extremely shy.

I remember Public Speaking coaching with S.M.Christopher, who was very old and quite deaf and used to position herself right at the back of the chapel while you recited to her from the front. She was extremely keen on steady pace and clearer-than-clear pronunciation, and never withheld her views on what you were saying. I still hear her voice in my head when I realise I'm talking too fast.

I remember putting on the first Fusion concert – not a smooth ride to get there but I was so happy with the final outcome and with how genuinely good all the performers were. A common memory for everyone is singing 'All Are Welcome'. Because we sang it. A LOT. With Mr Fardell robustly leading the way. We probably all claimed to be sick of it at some point, but it's a beautiful song.

There was a time when we had swimming lessons, in all weathers, in a tiny outdoor pool (complete with local aquatic life, no joke), with rickety wooden changing cubicles and an even more rickety fence around the edge. Oh, how we laughed . . . possibly more so now than then. But it had its charm, albeit in a roundabout sort of way.

There are fond memories of playing the old grand piano in the Debating Hall in the evenings. This would be followed by curling up in one of the bouncy chairs on More's landing, with a mug of hot Ribena, surrounded by my fellow Sixth Form boarding lot. Heavenly!

CATHERINE WILLIAMSON (née Beatty)

Owen 1997–2004

My mind is flooded with memories of firm friendships, merry mischief and fun. I am perpetually amazed by the number of people I meet who profess to have hated their schooldays. How could times like these be anything but the best days of one's life? There were days filled with playing sardines, picnics by the lake and music-making in Walkfares. How can any school that hosts a trip to another far-off city every term, on a vague pretence of the destination holding some educational value, be anything but wonderful?

My fondest memories of New Hall fall neatly into three categories – the place, the people and the trips. First of all, there are the day-to-day memories of the School and the surrounding grounds. From my first ever visit, I was captivated by the Avenue – the way that, as you approach, the trees appear to part, as if in deference to the exquisite buildings of the School itself. Over the years, as driving down the Avenue becomes part of your daily routine, you forget how spectacular it is. It's not until you return a few years after leaving, perhaps with a friend or relative who has never seen the School before, that their astonishment reawakens you to the spectacle you beheld every day for seven years without a second thought. It's not just the façade of the School that I loved – the Chapel, the Library, Mores, Dennett, the Refectory, even the Octagon! all hold special memories of good times.

Of course, the School is more than the buildings and grounds – it is most importantly about the people within it. I wish I could pay tribute to all of the brilliant teachers we had, but space does not allow. There are a few whose lessons (and personalities) will remain with me for ever – Mrs Murray (Mathematics) and her post-Chapel-assembly Monday-morning lectures on everything from squirrels to God; Mr Davies (Geography), with the permanent chalky spot on top of his head; S. Moira (French), with whom I will for ever credit the only French I can remember, as it started every lesson: 'Asseyez-vous'! I still blame Mr Evans (English) for my lack of tolerance of unjustified text and my hatred of indented paragraphs in typed prose. And, of course, it wasn't just the teachers – I've been lucky enough to

Kenya World Challenge 2002, on top of Mount Kenya
Including: John (group leader), Rachel Smith, Liz Cole, Sam Devereese,
Jenny Rumsey, Francesca Read, Catherine Beatty, Charlotte Speakman,
Katie Phillips, Julia Westnedge, Natasha Brooks

leave the school with a host of friends whom I know I shall still be in touch with in twenty years' time. There were so many things we got up to – pancake-making, racing demon, shaking our booties to 'Hey Ya', trips to Sainsbury's (the ultimate in privilege and independence when boarding).

And finally, the trips. It seemed we went everywhere – from Bradwell Power Station and Maldon, to Kenya, Russia and Tunisia – all were amazing in their own way. One of my favourite memories, not just of the School, but ever, is standing at 5.30am on the top of Mount Kenya, at minus 15 degrees, with ten other New Hall girls, waiting for the sun to rise.

I studied Medicine at Birmingham, and have remained in the West Midlands training to specialise in Paediatrics. I married Kit Williamson in September 2011.

EMMA ROSE

1997–2004

There was a group of us Sixth Form boarders who regularly took trips to Sainsbury's to pick up ingredients to make pancakes at night in the little kitchen in More while dancing to 'Hey Ya' by Outkast. It was hilarious trying to figure out quantities without any measuring equipment. They were brilliant evenings – being with friends, laughing and dancing and learning that pancakes are good even if the mix isn't quite perfect!

A superb part of New Hall was being in the Choir. In the Sixth Form we went to Rome. Apart from a great memory of Mr Fardell pretending he wasn't lost trying to find the 'best coffee shop in Rome', the best was being able to sing in St Peter's, which was incredible. Dressing in the red robes with rolled-up jeans and black tights underneath – so fashionable.

At the end of Sixth Form, a group of us performed in Chapel in front of friends and family. Although I was passionate about music, I never wanted to perform in front of people. But with help from Mr Fardell, Mr Wenden and friends the concert was the first time I sang and played the piano in front of a larger group. I'll never forget it and finding my confidence was something that New Hall enabled me to do. The experience has helped me significantly in the years since I left.

GERALDINE CABANERO

1997–2004

From the grand School entrance at the end of the unforgettable drive to the dreaded Octagon study hall, every part of New Hall conveyed a striking sense of character and history.

As a nervous Year 7, I was intimidated by the size of the School and I remember, during my first week, wondering how I was ever going to get to grips with this maze. But, as the years flew by, the grand buildings became a comforting second home.

The place that I remember most fondly is Walkfares. My favourite subjects all housed in one building, a Performing Arts hub that encouraged and nurtured creativity.

BETH TURNER

1997–2004

I remember rushing out at the end of a Psychology lesson with Mrs Wintersgill to hide in the wardrobe of the room I shared with Jessica Shrimpton and Lauren Wenden, and then waiting very patiently for Jess to come back from the same lesson and jumping out with a big, 'Raaahhh!' and scaring her half to death.

I remember spending hours and hours after school in the Rock Room in Walkfares desperately trying to teach myself bass guitar, then forming our 'band' and writing rubbish songs; singing 'Fields of Gold' at our Leavers' Concert and crying during the last chorus; spending time using our modular Biology lesson to perfect our Tippex graffiti skills, until at the end of term my GCSE Biology folder was more Tippex than paper; the brilliant Sixth Form Halloween Ball – dressing up for it and being allowed to invite boys; throwing Ms Brady a birthday party – sneaking in early to decorate the classroom, and Charlotte Speakman baking an awesome chocolate birthday cake and getting out of doing any actual English work for the whole lesson!

JOYEETA PALIT

1997–2004

It was easily the most grown-up decision of my life. As a 10-year old I had been relatively untroubled by any real responsibility, but choosing my secondary school was a decision that felt palpably adult. Not only had I been excused for the day from primary school but I was even allowed to sit in the front seat of the car.

On the way, that first day, we took a wrong turning and, after a brief tour of Hatfield Peverel, I was very relieved to see the sign for New Hall. As we entered the gates, I looked eagerly for a glimpse of the building, but there was no school to be seen, and I began to wonder if we had lost our way again. Then we turned a corner, and all at once there was a definite air of anticipation as into view came the strong leafy trees that stood guardsmen-like, dappling light across the drive, heralding the fact that there was definitely something ahead.

New Hall School slowly revealed itself – a building so beautiful I could hardly believe it functioned as a school. I remember the unexpected jolt of the first speed bump. In later years these little punctuations became so routine they hardly registered.

We were now waiting at the striped barrier and I had already made up my mind – I just *had* to come to New Hall. I would never have thought that the School, which to my 10-year-old self looked so stately and imposing, would one day feel so homely, and that the drive down the Avenue would become such a natural journey to make.

REBECCA HARVEY

1997–2005

One of my happiest memories of New Hall actually starts off with me being not so happy at all. I was always a fan of my sleep, particularly in the morning. Every year, on the last day of term before Christmas, the Upper Sixth boarders would get up at about 6am and come outside the Houses and carol-sing at the *top* of their voices. Now as an angsty teenager, this was the worst possible thing to contend with – there was no sleeping through it, and the Housemistresses actually seemed to enjoy it. You just had to allow the inner Grinch in you to stay cool.

By the time I got around to being in the Sixth Form myself, however, my opinion had entirely shifted. This was the greatest tradition and I would not let it die on my watch. I dutifully got all of my friends out of their beds on that cold December morning, checked the batteries and CD in the CD player, and traipsed round the school displaying my Christmas joy for all the younger students to scowl at. The stars were the Housemistresses, who brought us out cups of tea and joined in.

The best thing that New Hall provided was the feeling of community. It is all very well achieving good grades, being on sports teams, being in orchestras, but when something awful happens to you, you need a community of love to help you through, and that is exactly what I found at New Hall. When I was 15, my friend passed away after a two-year battle with cancer. I can remember very clearly how my School friends and my teachers supported me through this, by allowing me to organise a mufti (non-uniform) day in memory of my friend and to raise money for the Teenage Cancer Trust. The memory of that time, which could have been so hard, is one of love and support, and I really thank New Hall for that.

LAUREN BOTT (née Wenden)
1997–2004

I remember being impressed by the mile-long Avenue, which culminated in the stunning vista of the Tudor palace across the Ha-Ha. The Ha-Ha was something of great mystery in my early days at the school; I remember being distinctly disenchanted to learn that it was in fact just a ditch.

Aside from the building itself, I remember the people. First, friends – many of whom are still close companions today. Then the staff, several of whom were inspiring and taught me a lot more than just their subjects. It is safe to say I left New Hall a completely different person, confident and equipped for the future and a long way from the shy girl that started in Year 7. Four years later my sister followed in my footsteps; I was always very quiet at school, quite unlike my sister who, in the scathing words of my Mathematics teacher Mr Hill, made more noise in one lesson that I had in my entire two years in his class.

SARAH ORMES
1997–2004

The memory that sticks in my head the most is the Spandex débâcle: I believe it was Rebecca Coxshall who shoe-horned me into a canary-yellow Spandex jumpsuit and then led me to believe it would be a smashing idea to 'streak' through the school. Off I streaked – only to be met by a very bemused Mrs Wintersgill. Oh, and the rather handsome painter.

355

ARABELLA GORDON

1998–2006

New Hall holds so many memories for me, right from my first day when I came to school crying, until my last, when I left the school crying! Among the tears and anxiety over work and the teenage years, there were plenty of smiles and lots of laughter. I felt 'at home' at New Hall – it was a real community. I particularly liked boarding and being able to be around friends constantly. I also loved the food (even if I am the only one). I missed the syrup sponge when I went to university.

That I am still really close friends with many of the people I met there is testimony to the strong community spirit.

I was part of the last year of all girls and the last year of the red uniform. I remember the outdoor swimming-pool, with its disinfectant and really rough sides. The indoor one was a blessing.

Playing pool in Mores was a favourite. Mr Fradley was often drawn out of the Physics Department for this treat.

Going to Lourdes for the first time is something I will never forget. I

On the Ampleforth–Lourdes Pilgrimage

had not planned to go, but Annabel Brown and S. Pauline persuaded me one afternoon. It was the best week of the year.

I enjoyed Mrs Cooper's Psychology lessons. Always so entertaining, especially when a friend had taken Night Nurse for her cold and had to struggle to stay awake for the rest of the lesson.

Another memorable moment was when I was caught chatting in the Hawley toilets after lights-out and sent back to bed by Mrs Murray. Looking back on this experience was salutary when I was the Hawley Prefect, although, of course, everyone had rooms by then – rather than wooden cubicles – so it was a lot easier to hide.

My final summer at New Hall (2006), I took part in a World Challenge Expedition to Honduras. In September 2006, I began my studies at St Andrews University, where I read Theology. Currently, I am working in London for the Ministry of Justice.

JENNIFER (Jenny) CLANCY

1998–2005 Campion and Hawley

I remember well the trips to Sainsbury's at the end of the drive, singing all the way as if we were in *The Sound of Music*. Then we'd all get together in the TV room and watch *Anne of Green Gables* over and over.

Mrs Bright ensured we didn't take too long in the showers by using her infamous whistle and barking instructions as to which part of the showering process we should be on.

Mrs Murray and her weekly House assemblies would not have been complete without the warning, 'All actions have consequences.' As a spotty, hormonal teenager, I couldn't see the point but now I am beginning . . .

This was the era of 'rug surfing' when you stood on one end of the rug and a friend would drag it around the room by the other end, perhaps adding in a few spins along the way. It was the age of cubicles, and once about 14 of us squeezed into one comfortably (well, as possible) and slept there until morning.

There was rounders in the Quad after supper, and fire-alarms at silly hours – which had us waiting in keen anticipation by the Ha-Ha as the fire-engines roared up the drive, actually too far away for us to get a proper glimpse of a man in uniform.

In Mores, the landing became the place to be and many a night would be spent there chatting, debating, generally developing our own opinions about current topics, along with a glass of wine or two.

After leaving New Hall, I studied Paediatric Nursing at Canterbury Christ Church University, and I'm currently working on the children's ward at Darent Valley Hospital in Kent, as a staff nurse. I also work part-time at a Children's Hospice. I still live in Essex.

JESSICA SHRIMPTON

1998–2004

Locker-room and hockey stick (least said about that one the better); hiding in wardrobes to avoid teachers; and other people hiding in cupboards to make me jump. The endless games of pool in the House and of course the hours and hours spent on the 'landing' in More playing card game after card game.

My Christmas tree has to be given a special mention – as do our attempts at making pancakes. What fun times we all had sharing the laughter and the tears and helping each other through the good times and the bad.

REBECCA COXSHALL

Hawley 1999–2004

Now I love the red woollen uniform with its heavy pleated kilt and bright itchy jumper, and the red sports knickers for Athletics. I wasn't so enamoured at the time, freezing in the open air, waiting to sprint 100 metres like a madman. But oh, how I wish I could still fit into them now!

New Hall was a turning point for me, no boys to worry about impressing, no make-up, no hair doing . . . just simple school and friends. However, there were squabbles and squeals. I fear my treasured tutor, S. Moira, may say that I was involved in many of them! She spent much of her time trying to get me out of trouble and defusing the situations. Sometimes I wish she was still doing that for me today . . .

New Hall was an encouraging and caring environment where I learned a lot and changed a lot.

I went to Colchester Royal Grammar for Sixth Form then on to University to read Finance and Accountancy. I started working life with Sunseeker Yachts, London.

ELEANOR SHIPLEY

1999–2011

I was at New Hall School for twelve years. I can remember my first day, in my tiny red blazer and pigtail plaits. As the years went on, there were more memories and stronger friendships. I always felt part of the community and there was always someone I could turn to for support.

Being at New Hall made possible so many achievements. I received some amazing Music results as well as doing well in my academic classes. It also gave me lots of opportunities, among them starting new sports and going abroad on a French exchange for a week.

ALISON POTTER

2000–2004

One of my happiest memories of New Hall was a trip that a dozen of us girls took to Kenya. It was a wonderful and unique expedition. A highlight was the visit to Lake Nakuru National Park, where we encountered the local Masai warriors. We visited their village, saw their huts and learnt about their various trades, and the male warriors performed the traditional dance in which they chant and jump progressively higher. We trekked with them in the Masai Mara, getting close to much of Africa's wildlife (including a leopard) and camping out on the grassy plains. In the evenings we sat around a campfire under the stars, listening to the Masai warriors tell us tales of lion-hunting with just a spear, a knife and a shield. It was amazing to see first-hand a completely different culture and it will be one of the most unforgettable experiences of my life.

ALEXANDRA MARLER

2000 to date

New Hall School has been such a key part of my life. The many memories of all that I have shared with my friends at New Hall I will treasure for the rest of my life. The School community has supported me throughout my time and I can truly say some of the best years here have been the best in my life (well so far anyway!).

ALEXANDRA VAN HELFTEREN

Pole 2001–2008

Having had an Old Fish for a mother (Claire Van Helfteren), I was slightly daunted at the idea of seven years at New Hall. I tried to leave after five years but, with a bit of scholarship incentive, I decided to stay on for Sixth Form. These were probably the best two years. I was in the first year of the co-educational Sixth Form, which made the girls behave somewhat erratically. However, I really enjoyed the experience and ended up being House Captain.

Pranks carried out in the Sixth Form included telling the staff by letter that they were no longer allowed to use the Staff Room due to its untidiness, placing a speed camera down the Avenue and, in our final week of term, deciding to hide all the cutlery from the Refectory on the roof (this involved climbing through windows and evading terrifying guard dogs).

I have subsequently graduated from Sheffield University with a 2:1 in Geography and I am off travelling around South America for five months before returning to find a real job!

SOPHIA MILLER DE VEGA

2002 to date

Throughout my years here at New Hall, I have witnessed great changes, the biggest was the intake of boys. The 'diamond' system has been beneficial academically and socially, giving us the opportunity to socialise without interfering with each other's academic work.

Whilst boarding at a young age seemed like a massive sleepover, I soon came to realise that along with privilege came responsibility. Something that I have valued the most from being a boarder is the relationships that I have built over the years. Some of the staff have known me from the beginning and have always been there through thick and thin. Being a boarder has taught me the values of trust and respect of others and has also made me a more independent, self-reliant and organised person.

The experience of going to southern Peru with World Challenge was unforgettable. The community work was incredibly rewarding, especially because the local people appreciated our efforts in building their shelter. My favourite trip was a History trip to Ypres in Belgium,

Children's Holiday in 2002

where we visited the Somme battlefield of WWI and the famous Canadian Memorial. This was a very moving experience.

I have fond memories of working with NHVS. As well as helping our local communities, as a school we also supported communities abroad. We raised money for an adult literacy centre in Rwanda – £7,000. The Religious Community, who are closely linked with this project, came to talk to us about Rwanda's brutal history, to raise awareness of the situation in Rwanda.

Through thick and thin, staff and fellow students at New Hall always helped me to explore both academic and creative talents and always supported me throughout. The New Hall community has provided me with a sense of trust and security and I believe that New Hall has given me a great start in life.

EMILY CRISP

Pole 2003–2008

When my interview day for New Hall dawned, I was adamant I didn't want to go. By the end of the day I asked my dad whether I could board.

I remember being read to on the landing by S. Ann before bed. She had a robot figure that sang and danced. We always looked forward to her visits.

Because it was such an old building, ghost stories were rife, often being spread through the boarding houses like Chinese whispers. The best stories, however, were told by the nuns. With historic 'fact' to back them up, they kept us constantly wondering.

I joined the Army's sixth form college, Welbeck, which marked the start of my military career. I am currently studying Mechanical Engineering at the University of Birmingham as a British Army Officer Cadet, and hope to take my place at the Royal Military Academy Sandhurst after I have graduated and join the corps of Royal Electrical and Mechanical Engineers.

ELODIE PENDRED

2004–2007

My most vivid memory of my first day at School was of driving down the magnificent tree-lined Avenue and being promptly shown to my 'bedroom'. With a curtain for a door and walls that didn't reach the ceiling it looked more like a dilapidated cattle stall than a 14-year-old's bedroom. Upon close inspection there wasn't even a plug for my radio – disgruntled doesn't even cover it. Luckily, I was soon ensconced it what can only be described as the unique New Hall ethos of NHVS and community spirit and my last day proved more emotional than my first.

Exhibition Day . . . one of the most memorable days in the New Hall School calendar. Parents busy creating the picnic to beat all others, teachers scrutinising every inch of each pupil's uniform. As the concentration spans fade and hands grow tired from clapping, there is a growing sense of anticipation from within the Upper Sixth crowd. As the Upper Sixth were called to centre stage, our hearts sank and heads bowed in fear of catching the teary eye of a close friend. I remember everyone forming a circle and holding hands before the distribution of candles. Silence reigned over the Hall for the first time as a candle was lit and given to the Head of School to send around the circle. I remember lighting my candle and then turning to my best friend to light her candle and all composure went out of the window, the silence only broken by those unable to control their sobs. Looking back it is a wonder that such a ritual was allowed to take place year on year, surely health and safety would now rule that hysterical crying and candles are a dangerous combination.

The emotion conveyed on this day is unlike any other I have experienced, even university graduation didn't elicit the same response; which is indicative of the special place that New Hall was, and remains.

I studied Sociology at the University of York. After an internship at the British Red Cross and the NSPCC, I am working at Teens Unite – a charity that supports teenagers with cancer and other life-limiting illnesses.

JAMIE HARRIS

2006–2008

I can describe my days at New Hall as some of the best days of my life; they have shaped me into who I am today. My first real memory is of the boys' induction day in June 2006. We were sitting in a circle out by the Ha-Ha, playing one of those 'interesting facts about me' games. My now very good friend Tristan took his go: 'Hi, I'm Tristan, and I'm single.' Needless to say, the Year 13 Prefects were clearly a little taken aback.

Break-time in Mores gave us the opportunity for complete carnage, with anything from pool competitions (which seemed always to involve accidentally breaking the cues) to a heated debate over the *Jeremy Kyle Show*. Come Year 13 and some of us were starting to pass our driving tests, and as an immediate result learning how to sneak off to McDonald's by claiming we had a doctor's appointment.

Being the first Head Boy at New Hall was an honour. I loved every second of it and I'll never forget Mrs Hopkinson turning to me, after I bowed out on Chapel for the first time, and saying, 'You're the first boy ever to have done that, you know.'

Exhibition Day was great but hard; the thought of leaving what feels like a family behind is difficult and I spent half of my gap year trying (and succeeding) to find excuses to come back. I had the time of my life at New Hall and being part of the first cohort of boys was brilliant.

IMOGEN OVENDEN

2006 to date

I must have been four or five years old when I first came up the New Hall Avenue, and I remember being amazed by all the trees on the Avenue and the size and architecture of the buildings. I started boarding in Year 9 and it was in boarding that I developed some of my strongest friendships and learned a lot about developing independence. I will always remember Mrs Mingham, someone anybody could talk to at any time about just about anything. Mrs Mingham, Dr Wheadon, Dr Thomas, Mrs Helliar and Dr Shaw were all absolutely fantastic teachers.

My year group was the first to be joined by boys in the Senior School, and this made for healthy academic and sporting rivalry between the boys and girls. In the world, there were natural disasters and terrorist attacks and the New Hall Community took action to raise money to help the people directly affected.

Specific memories, such as the annual madness of Foundation Day and Sports Day and the drama of accidentally flooding the corridor in the boarding house, will stay with me for a long time. Any school could have taught me what I am and what I can achieve in life, but New Hall taught me who I am and how I can achieve it.

JAN NEDVIDEK

2010–2012

On my first day at New Hall, I was stunned by the beauty of the campus. Boarding was a completely new experience for me.

The emphasis on academic excellence is a very distinct feature of New Hall, expressed through the scholarly habits. However, it is not all about academic development. The School ethos of trust, support and friendship goes very well with the values of the Catholic faith that New Hall seeks to promote.

In my time at New Hall, I have been involved in a number of chaplaincy activities. With Mrs Hopkinson and Miss Tait, we organised a morning prayer group called the Oratorium, which involves a gospel reading and a reflection upon it.

Unfortunately, I have been unable fully to appreciate the sporting facilities at New Hall – my sporting career finished almost as soon as I arrived, when I was disqualified in swimming races because I dived too early.

Nevertheless, I have made a contribution to New Hall music. Mr Fardell, Director of Music, leads our School Choir, which has an excellent record of many concerts and foreign tours, and I have fond memories of the trip to Bologna and Florence. We also performed regularly with musicians from outside the school; for example, we sang Rutter's 'Gloria' with a brass ensemble from Chelmsford.

I have also been fortunate that, as an organ player, I could make use of the recently renovated three-manual organ in our beautiful Chapel. I have enjoyed the fact that I can play it whenever I want to. By doing this, I was able to achieve Grade V, having played for only two years.

DANIEL MULLENS

2006 to date

Having joined New Hall School in Year 7 as one among the first cohort of boys, I have witnessed key changes; not only time's passage among my peers, but the growth of the School as a whole.

Sixth Form at the beginning of the twenty-first century

New Hall has introduced me to the Classics; I have lasting memories of long, ritualistic Exhibition Days; and I have enjoyed all the other quirky yet fantastic traditions of this hallowed place. My most vivid memory is of the History trip to the Battlefields of WWI.

CATHERINE LEIGHTON

2006–2011

Following my arrival in Year 7, I made some lovely friends and had many enjoyable experiences. My best memories are of the Choir trips, but I will take away a whole host of memories of New Hall and my friends.

NADIA WHEALON

2006 to date

New Hall School is a great community with a fantastic ethos, which has sustained me through my five years here. The students create a friendly atmosphere and are always willing to offer advice and to cooperate with each other. The teachers give inspired lessons, which makes learning so much easier.

Facebook

Fishes from all ages and continents shared their memories of New Hall on Facebook and here is a small selection.

Earliest or most vivid memories

Alli Roberts – The endless Avenue and imposing frontage of New Hall on day 1. Later, awful blue aprons for housework, putting the duvet out in the corridor first thing and kneeling on a stone floor for prayer, being dared late at night to walk through the ref to the corridor outside the chapel to hear the horses and see [the ghost of] Queen Mary. Signing my name on a brick on the outer wall in front of the school (smoking circuit). Ordering chocolate rice krispie cake from the Refectory for birthdays and dressing up and dancing in Fisher's common room.

Annabel Harris – I've got some photos of me and my Fisher friends wearing those awful blue aprons. Nicking Alpen from the Refectory (probably shouldn't mention that one!!)

Gillian Erdil – Red knickers and brown shoes!

Annabel Harris – I remember crying when my parents drove away and left me there! It didn't last long, soon made some friends and settled in. I liked the cubicles but not the early nights and stripping the bed *every* morning, pulling the chair out of the cubicle and kneeling for prayer!

Sarah Jane Carroll – Exeat cards, smell of linseed oil from rows of lacrosse sticks, S.M.Thérèse in The Shop, polished tiles of Ambulacrum . . . Branflakes and Alpen at breakfast . . . bathtime rota!! No bubbles allowed! . . .

Cate Beavis – I remember starting at the prep school in its second term in a class with Years 3, 4, & 5 in it. I think Mrs Manning was my teacher.

Elizabeth Smith – Milk machines in the kitchenette, fresh buns for tea

(if you got there first), toast machine in the Refectory – just toast with butter and sugar on top for breakfast, housework and Southwell's weekend talent shows (or lack-of-talent shows!).

Amy Mathews – Endless corridors!

Lucy Mitchell – Going up to Libby Searle Knight and Charlotte Campbell and saying, 'Hi, I'm Lucy, can I be your friend?'!

Caroline Hoefter – First Day of School was One Day After Princess Diana died!! I remember also how much I was crying when my parents left! But I had the Best Time in New Hall!

Gig Moses – standing in a line waiting to go into the Refectory and being told to stop talking at least 3 times by Francesca Bedford who I subsequently discovered was the Head Girl! Camel coat, brown shoes and my red beret.

Alicia Guinness – Being given hot chocolate by S.Magdalen John to cheer me up. Later discovered this was something we could only get in the last year at Fishers as a privilege! I remember those ghastly brown lace-up shoes and Aertex shirts . . .

Raquel Anstee de Mas – Green curtains lining the dorm, bare cubicle, lots of smiling faces, S. Margaret Mary and the feeling of nervousness and excitement on that first night when lights went out – start of a new life . . . I found it very strange when S. Margaret Mary came in

New Hall students competed for their Pony Clubs at the 2010 Gosling Cup

to say goodnight as I thought she was bending down to give me a goodnight kiss, instead she made the mark of the cross on my forehead!

Jessie Bird – I remember my first day at New Hall in Chemistry class with Mrs Wall. She took one look at me and said, 'You'd better come and sit at the front in case you don't understand the English.' This is before even asking me if I spoke English . . . I was actually born in Chelmsford!

Helen Hingston – My first day at New Hall I remember being greeted by Miss Morrow in Owens. I was then informed I needed to check what my housework duty was. I discovered it was cleaning the loos. My big sister thought this was hysterical!

Michelle Hunt – Foundation Day, being up on stage performing dance was so scary but such good fun, and after having a picnic with friends and family on the grass in front of the main building.

Amanda Waite – . . . and of course TAGs! The netball team that entered in the Chelmsford Women's League and won League 7 in our first year. We were trained by Miss (Terry) Cox and TAGs was short for 'Terry's All Golds!' I still have my netball skirt, although sadly it will now only fit one thigh!

Clare Petre – . . . crème eggs and plastic cups of cider after midnight vigil at Easter . . . Fr Leslie coming up the avenue with little white pony Peter Blue as we all waved palm leaves at him . . . Mr Fardell losing it during mass one Sunday and lazily biting his conductor's lectern thing . . . S. Pauline on roller boots in the quad . . . Help the Homeless sleepout . . . PE1 sit-in protest at the stables' closure . . . the fear and smell of the Infirmary steps . . . Midland Bank accounts . . . 80p a week in school shop where we queued from the moment the bell for the end of study rang . . . feeding tea-time currant buns to cows in Class 1 . . . Races across the library on the wheely steps (that got us banned) . . . smoking on the roof of PE2 . . . and *that flipping clock chiming every seven and a half minutes*!!

Jacqui Murphy (née Heuer) – Chapel chairs, Jacqui, chapel chairs.

Amanda Waite – My memories are of NH girls' hair – always a long fringe being flicked from side to side and looking dishevelled. Girls excitedly waiting for their parents in flowery, Laura Ashley dresses followed by picnics on Six Acres at Sports Day, Exhibition Weekend, horses occasionally bolting from stables area and people running after them! PS on the hair front there was always an Alice-band nearby which would be applied with a flick of the hair and then pushed forward to create a bouffant fringe. Then pluck down loose, straggly bits of fringe to complete the look, yah!

Swimming in the 1990s

Vanessa Martin (née Money) – Does anyone remember engraving their name in the perimeter wall? I wrote mine about 20 years ago and as my son is now at New Hall took the opportunity to find it one afternoon – and did!! When asking around about 6 friends that I am still very close to no one remembers doing it! Was I the only vandal?? [No Vanessa – see Alli Roberts above. Ed.]

I still have my wooden cross that was made from the cedar tree that fell in front of the school in the hurricane in the 80s. The whole school was given one. It is very treasured.

Housework

Elizabeth Miller – Always managed to get Stable Duty for housework – it was great!!

Amy French – Always got the loos!

Marta Goulão de Sousa – Housework was tedious, I remember the cubicle inspections!

Neela Cleary – Loved the housework! Is that saaaad?

Michelle Hunt – cubicle inspections and the long line to wait to get your book signed so you could leave.

Book Week in 1994

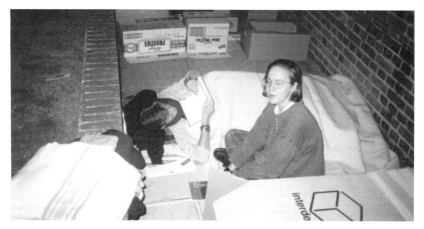

Shelter Sleepout in 1996 – L. Lawrence, S. Wagner

Katha Wood – Housework for me was at the stables! Phew! What a relief!

Clare Devanney – Gumption . . . cubicle inspections . . . worst housework was the sanitary towel bins!

Karen Holt – Housework – what fun – I was in charge of ensuring no harm came to the new Nilfisks [vacuum cleaners].

Alicia Guinness – Can we still get gumption? Also wish schools could continue to get pupils to do housework!!! Maybe fees might be reduced!!

Raquel Anstee de Mas – blue overalls, gumption, toilet duty not good but chapel duty an excuse to natter – end of term major clean.

Amanda Waite – never understood why day girls had to do housework, as we didn't live there. Had to do two lots, home and school!

Tessa Wilson – Carousel, Refectory, Gumption, Mass, Walkfares, Beaulieu, Campion and, best . . . Uniform, nuns' Refectory, the home . . . overalls, it all seems very strange now I am in the real world!! Loved it tho', specially stables' housework.

Janina Tonks – I'd forgotten how fab stables housework was . . . I remember I had Arty and Star at some point . . . Your list sums it all up perfectly, Tessa, that . . . gumption! . . . I also remember all the subtle (!) groups going out 'to the back fields' for a packet of fresh air after supper . . .

Pet's Corner

Anna Latimer – Oh yes, a rabbit called Cotton Tail, who had a dog-carrier to bring him home each half-term. My friend Emma had a Russian Hamster who gave her some kind of lice!

Kate Marriage – I had a rabbit called Hazel who had a nasty habit of depositing things on people as they walked into the rabbit hut. S. Diana bore it with incredibly good grace!

Television documentary

Rebekah Cambridge – back in the 80s I remember a documentary made about New Hall, there were film crews everywhere . . .

Annabel Harris – was it about 1982? I think I was in Lower Six, Mores, and can remember walking across the landing and being filmed!

Raquel Anstee de Mas – . . . it had been made by the BBC before I joined. It was interviews with the Nuns about how they balanced their lives within the convent and running a school. They filmed quite a bit in Fishers – showing the getting up (duvets on chairs and saying a prayer!) and the going to bed and lights-out.

Annabel Harris – I remember the blooming duvets over our chairs every morning outside our cubicles! Anyway, I was definitely filmed in Mores (had a hideous 80s perm at the time!)

Easter

Marta Goulão de Sousa – Easter was great, loved all the choir gearing up for the finale . . . and in the pre-buffet days, Easter lunch was a real treat, I remember those!

Elaine Coulthard – Fr Jim leading an aerobics class at Easter . . . Quality!

Sascha Williams – I'd forgotten about the Easter aerobics with Fr Jim! Priceless!

Raquel Anstee de Mas – Easter for me is choir practice, Teze, dancing in the Refectory and sewing with Mrs Turner.

Memories of the Community

Sister Moira – awesome French teacher! / Sister Angela and her brilliant RE lessons, talk about trendy nun! / Sister Magdalen John in the second-hand uniform shop! / Sister Mary Ignatius in Geography. Bad move having a walk-in cupboard in the classroom! / Sister Margaret Mary – awesome faith, awesome love and awesome ability to make you feel secure even on the roughest of days / Sister Patricia, during RE and was near end of the day we were all tired and she told the class that she will get up on the table and dance to wake us all up! and with no delay she got up on the table and started to dance. All I can say is it did the trick. / Sister T. She was just rock and roll!!! Oh and Sister P holding lots of beers for the sixth form BBQ very funny! / Sister Mary Therese – tuck shop provider and community service angel / Sister Mary Mark for the time and patience she put into my time in Owens / Sister Mary Therese who led the Voluntary Service with her true heart of gold! / Sister Magdalen John for her continual friendship and links with my family. I used to love helping her arrange flowers for the church – always a good excuse for a natter . . . / and S.M.Elizabeth for her passion in describing Mrs Bennett in *Pride and Prejudice* / Chrissie of course! / S. Anne-Marie for her dedication, and Sister Mary Matthew for keeping us all alive on Strepsils / Sister Mary David for letting us listen to Simon and Garfunkel etc (Bridge over troubled waters) in her room for hours on end and creating a warm and friendly house atmosphere . . . / Sister Mary Stephen her calmness and talent / MO'S always has a special place in my heart / Sister Margaret Mary a very astute Head, and a wise and humble person . . . she helped carry up a fridge to the out quarters flat when I was a newly wed Deputy Head / Also Sister Teresa who inspired me so much as an RE teacher and as my Housemistress in Mores later on. All the community really / Sister Stephanie – she had great patience with me (and an incredibly quiet voice) / Sister Teresa who was always up for a laugh in Mores, MO'S, Sister Mary Stephen, Sister Pauline . . . it was the nuns that made the school what it was . . .

Acknowledgements

The Contributors – without whom we wouldn't have a book!
In particular those who attended our Photo ID reunions,
which got the ball rolling and Old Fishes connecting.

Pauline – who has co-ordinated us all, juggling all
the 370th Anniversary events and people

The Book Group – Rachel (and her patient pooch Kali) –
co-ordinating editor and consultant (patient,
encouraging and motivating);
Henrietta – editor and sensitive telephone interviewer;
Juliet – excavator of photos and OFA files from the New Hall cellars,
copy editor and editor of histories;
Joan Jones – ever the English teacher, correcting our grammar,
the ultimate copy editor (pen and paper!)
Claire Merry – organiser of the Launch, hosting Photo IDs
and rallying people to take part;
Teresa and Moira from the Community, who inspired
the project and steered the ship

The Readers – Paula Leydon and Veronica (Ronnie) Wald –
who read the text (in tight time), seeing the big picture

S.M.Magdalene – for her indefatigable work of research
and discovery in the Archives

The Community – for their elephantine memories of
generations of people and dates

New Hall School – for helping us put together the last chapter

The Old Fishes' Association and Libby Searle – for helping
us contact Old Fishes

St Bernard's High School, Westcliff (Pat Barron and Mo Ruston)
for the initial inspiration and advice

Cover photograph – Chris Beech, Van Cols Ltd

THE BOO HAu: AN IN-DEPTH LOOK BEHIND THE LEGEND

PORSHA GARRETT

PROLOGUE

At the heart of this cultural mosaic lies a legend, whispered in hushed tones around flickering fires and shared through generations. It is the tale of the Boo Hags, a haunting presence that creeps within the shadows of the night. To fully comprehend the origin of this spectral folklore, we must journey back to the distant shores of West Africa.

Across the vast expanse of time and oceans, the enslaved Africans carried with them a tapestry of stories, a mosaic of spirits and creatures that populated their imaginations. In the realms of their folklore, malevolent spirits and supernatural beings reigned, shaping their understanding of the unknown. These tales of caution and wonder merged with the experiences of their new reality, blending with whispers of European folklore that wafted through the air.

Today, the legend of the Boo Hags stands as a testament to the enduring power of folklore. It serves as a guardian of the Gullah community's cultural heritage, a whispered reminder of their ancestral ties to a distant land. As we embark on this journey into the heart of this spectral tale, let us peer beyond the veil of time and immerse ourselves in the world of the Boo Hags, where shadows dance, and the echoes of the past resonate in the hearts of the present.

For within these pages, the legend comes alive, bridging the realms of myth and reality, inviting us to explore the depths of our own imagination and uncover the truths that lie hidden within the folklore.

Welcome to the world of the Boo Hags.

Chapter 1

INTRODUCTION: THE GULLAH PEOPLE AND THEIR CULTURAL TAPESTRY

In the heart of the United States' southeastern coastline, stretching from the northern part of Florida to the southern reaches of North Carolina, a rich cultural tapestry has been woven over centuries. This unique cultural blend belongs to the Gullah people, a resilient, vibrant African-American community whose roots run deep into the soil of their coastal lands and the turbulent waters of their history.

The story of the Gullah people begins with the transatlantic slave trade, which spanned the 16th to 19th centuries. Enslaved Africans from a variety of ethnic and cultural groups, primarily from West and Central Africa, were forcefully brought to the coastal areas of South Carolina and Georgia. The geographical isolation of these coastal and island plantations, often called the Sea Islands, created a unique environment that allowed for a distinct cultural identity to form—the Gullah culture.

The Gullah people managed to preserve an astonishing amount of African cultural heritage despite the horrors of slavery. This resilience is a testament to the strength of human spirit and the power of cultural identity, as well as a reflection of the unique geographical circumstances of their communities. Because of the deadly mosquito-borne diseases prevalent in these coastal regions, plantation owners often retreated inland during the warmer months, leaving the enslaved Africans largely unsupervised. This relative isolation allowed the Gullah people to maintain their African languages, folktales, music, craftsmanship, and culinary traditions.

Although the Gullah culture is a vibrant blend of various African traditions, it is not merely a carbon copy of African cultures. It is a unique evolution, a new cultural synthesis shaped by the blending of diverse African ethnic groups, the experience of enslavement, and the influence of the indigenous American and European cultures they encountered. The Gullah language, for example, is an English-based Creole language that incorporates words and grammatical structures from various African languages, creating a unique dialect that has survived centuries.

The Gullah people's spiritual beliefs and practices also reflect this cultural fusion. Many Gullahs practice a form of Christianity infused with African spiritual traditions, creating a unique syncretic faith. This amalgamation of beliefs is reflected in their religious ceremonies, which often combine Christian practices with African rituals, songs, and dances.

Through the lens of the Gullah people, we see the power of cultural preservation under the most adverse conditions. Even when faced with the brutalities of slavery, displacement, and cultural erasure, the Gullah people held tight to their African roots, weaving them into the fabric of their new circumstances to create a vibrant, unique culture. Today, their cultural tapestry continues to provide a rich source of study for historians, anthropologists, and linguists, and a source of pride and identity for the Gullah people.

In the following chapters, we will delve deeper into the fascinating world of the Gullah culture, exploring its unique language, spiritual practices, arts and crafts, cuisine, and more. We will also examine the challenges the Gullah communities face today, such as land loss and cultural erosion, and the efforts being made to preserve and celebrate this remarkable cultural heritage.

Chapter 2

THE ROOTS OF THE BOO HAGS: WEST AFRICAN FOLKLORE

In the rich cultural tapestry of the Gullah people, certain threads stand out for their vibrant colors and intriguing patterns. The legend of the Boo Hags is one such thread, a tale of supernatural creatures that has, over centuries, become deeply entwined with Gullah folklore. In this chapter, we will trace the roots of the Boo Hags back to their origins in West African folklore, exploring the cultural currents that carried these tales across the Atlantic and into the Gullah oral tradition.

The tale of the Boo Hags is a chilling one. These creatures are said to be malevolent spirits that, according to Gullah tradition, slip into the homes of living beings at night to ride their victims, leaving them exhausted and breathless by morning. This concept of the nocturnal, life-draining witch is not unique to the Gullah culture. It has parallels in numerous cultures worldwide, especially in West Africa, the ancestral home of many of the enslaved Africans who came to inhabit the Sea Islands.

West African cultures are rich in folklore, with countless stories of spirits, both benign and malevolent, that interact with the human world. The Ashanti people of Ghana, for example, have legends of the "asumansu," a malevolent spirit that attacks people in their sleep. Similarly, the Yoruba people of Nigeria tell tales of the "aje," witches who can drain the life force from their victims.

Such tales were likely carried over to America with the enslaved Africans. Amid the horror and hardship of their new lives, these stories provided a link to their homelands, a way to make sense of their experiences, and a form of resistance against their oppressors. Over time, these tales melded with indigenous American and European folklore, as well as the lived experiences of the Gullah people, to form new narratives. The Boo Hags is one such narrative, a uniquely Gullah tale that nevertheless carries within it echoes of its West African origins.

The Boo Hags, like their West African counterparts, are often seen as metaphors for oppression and exploitation. They can be interpreted as a symbolic representation of the enslavers who drained the life and energy from the enslaved Africans, leaving them exhausted and depleted. This interpretation underscores the depth and complexity of Gullah folklore, revealing it to be a rich source of historical and cultural insight.

The survival of stories like the Boo Hags is testament to the resilience of the Gullah people. Despite the attempts to erase their African heritage, they managed to preserve and adapt their ancestral folklore, creating a rich oral tradition that continues to thrive today. In the next chapter, we will explore how this tradition is kept alive, and how it continues to shape the identity and worldview of the Gullah people.

Chapter 3

THE BIRTH OF THE BOO HAGS: A NEW WORLD OF FOLKLORE

As the transatlantic slave trade expanded from the sixteenth to the nineteenth centuries, enslaved Africans were transported to the New World, taking along with them their rich tapestry of cultural beliefs and traditions. These beliefs were as varied and diverse as the African tribes from which these enslaved individuals hailed. They included a profound respect for the power of the spirit world, ancestor reverence and the existence of supernatural beings. In the crucible of their new, harsh reality in America, these traditional beliefs, borne from the heart of Africa, would intertwine with the elements of European folklore and the experiences of their new environment to give birth to unique local mythologies. One such mythology that emerged from this fusion in the American South was the folklore of the Boo Hags.

The Boo Hags, as per the Gullah culture of the South Carolina and Georgia Sea Islands, are nocturnal creatures, skinless, and able to squeeze through any crack or crevice due to their lack of skin. They were said to ride their victims at night, leaving them exhausted and bruised by morning. These malevolent spirits were believed to be an explanation for sleep paralysis, a phenomenon that was not well understood at the time and thus attributed to the presence of evil spirits.

The concept of the Boo Hag finds its roots in Central and West African mythology, where the belief in night witches and malevolent spirits was widespread. However, the Boo Hags were not simply a continuation of African folklore. They were the result of a cultural melding that occurred when African beliefs met European myths and local environmental factors.

European folklore was replete with tales of witches, vampires, and spirits, themes which resonated with the African belief in the spirit world. The idea of the Boo Hag, a skinless being that could slip into homes unnoticed, paralleled the European vampire, a creature of the night that feeds off the living. The Boo Hags, however, were more akin to spiritual parasites than bloodsuckers, feeding off the energy or breath of their victims.

The harsh realities of the enslaved Africans' new environment also played a key role in shaping the Boo Hag folklore. The slaves were forced to live in poor conditions, often in confined spaces, leading to various health problems. The Boo Hags' ability to squeeze through any space, no matter how small, would have been a terrifying prospect to people living in such close quarters.

Moreover, the Boo Hags became an expression of the enslaved Africans' experiences. The concept of a creature that drained one's energy while one slept served as a metaphor for the draining, grueling labor that the enslaved Africans were subjected to. The tales of these creatures, while terrifying, also served as a form of resistance, embodying the harshness of their lives in the form of a tangible, albeit supernatural, enemy.

The birth of the Boo Hags in the New World was a testament to the resilience of the human spirit under oppression. It demonstrated how cultural traditions and beliefs could survive, adapt, and merge to create new narratives that reflected the experiences of a displaced people. The Boo Hags, thus, while being creatures of nightmares, were also symbols of cultural survival, adaptation, and resistance.

Chapter 4

THE BOO HAGS: A CAUTIONARY TALE

The Boo Hags, as they emerged in the folklore of the Gullah culture, were a terrifying manifestation of the enslaved Africans' fears and hardships. These beings were no ordinary witches or spirits, but skinless, vampire-like creatures that preyed on unsuspecting victims in the dead of night.

In their true form, Boo Hags were a sight to behold, a horrifying spectacle that could turn the bravest man's blood to ice. Their skinless bodies, raw and glistening in the moonlight, revealed a grotesque display of pulsating muscles and throbbing veins. Devoid of skin, they were the very embodiment of vulnerability, yet they wielded a power that was as terrifying as their appearance.

Boo Hags had the unique ability to steal the skin of the recently deceased, using it as a disguise during the day. This allowed them to blend in with the living, undetected, a chilling thought that instilled fear and caution within the community. At night, they would shed their stolen skin, revealing their true form, and seek out the living, slipping through the smallest cracks and crevices to find their victims.

Once a Boo Hag had selected its victim, it would 'ride' them while they slept. Unlike the bloodsucking vampires of European folklore, Boo Hags would drain their victims of their breath or vitality, leaving them exhausted and withered by morning. This ongoing loss of energy was said to lead to the victim's eventual death if the Boo Hag wasn't stopped.

The legend of the Boo Hags was more than just a tale of horror; it served as a cautionary tale, offering guidance on how to protect oneself from these dark forces. Various protective measures were handed down through generations, providing practical advice wrapped in the cloak of folklore.

One such preventive measure was to sprinkle salt or pepper around the bed, as Boo Hags were believed to be compelled to count each grain before they could attack their victim, thus delaying them until dawn. Blue paint was also often used on window frames and doors, as it was believed that a Boo Hag would mistake it for water and refrain from crossing it. Brooms were also placed by the door, as the Boo Hag would feel the need to count the bristles, keeping them occupied until sunrise.

The story of the Boo Hags also served to reinforce societal norms and values. It encouraged vigilance, community solidarity, and respect for the dead. The practice of 'sitting up with the dead', a tradition where family members would stay awake with a deceased person until they were buried, was not only a sign of respect but also a way to protect the deceased's skin from being stolen by a Boo Hag.

Thus, the tale of the Boo Hags, while terrifying, served a dual purpose. It was a form of entertainment, with its chilling tales told around fires or in hushed whispers before bed, and a cautionary tale offering practical guidance on protection against unseen forces.

It was a reflection of the cultural resilience and adaptability of the enslaved Africans, who used their folklore and beliefs to navigate the challenges of their new environment.

Chapter 5

THE EVOLUTION OF THE BOO HAGS LEGEND

The evolution of the Boo Hags legend is a fascinating journey into the realm of folklore and mythology. As with many cultural narratives, this legend has been shaped by a myriad of influences over the centuries, evolving and adapting as it passed through generations. The Boo Hags, as they are known today, are a product of a rich tapestry of tales dating back to the times of African shape-shifting spirits, European vampires, and witches, which have all contributed to molding the current narrative.

The origins of the Boo Hags can be traced back to the African diaspora, specifically to the West African and Central African regions. African folklore is rife with stories of shape-shifting spirits and creatures that could transform into different forms. The Boo Hags, with their ability to shed their skin and take on the appearance of ordinary people, echo these ancient African narratives. They are thought to be akin to 'Soucouyant' in Trinidad and Tobago folklore, a creature that sheds its skin at night to suck the blood of its victims. The presence of such elements in the Boo Hags legend indicates a strong African influence.

As enslaved Africans were transported to the Americas during the Transatlantic Slave Trade, they carried their myths and legends with them. The new environment, however, forced them to adapt their stories to make sense of their new circumstances. This is when the European influences, predominantly those of vampires and witches, began to shape the Boo Hags narrative.

The European vampire, as popularized in legends and literature, is a nocturnal creature known to drain the life force of its victims, usually in the form of blood. This trait is evident in the Boo Hags, which, according to the legend, ride their victims at night while they are asleep, sapping their energy and vitality. The parallels between the two creatures highlight the vampire's influence on the evolution of the Boo Hags legend.

Witches, on the other hand, have been a staple of European folklore for centuries. They were often depicted as malevolent beings with the power to manipulate and bewitch innocent people. The Boo Hags, with their cunning ability to blend in with humans and their malevolent intentions, show strong similarities with the witches of European tales. This aspect of the Boo Hags legend illustrates the fusion of African and European folklore, creating a unique blend of horror and mysticism.

The evolution of the Boo Hags legend didn't stop with these influences. As the story continued to be told and retold, it further adapted to the cultural and sociopolitical contexts of the time. For instance, during periods of social unrest or hardship, the Boo Hags were often portrayed as more malevolent and terrifying, perhaps reflecting the collective fear and anxiety of the community. Conversely, during more peaceful times, the narrative might focus more on the Boo Hags' cunning and trickery than on their malevolence.

In conclusion, the evolution of the Boo Hags legend is a testament to the enduring power of folklore and mythology. It is a mirror reflecting the fears, beliefs, and values of various cultures over centuries. From African shape-shifting spirits to European vampires and witches, the Boo Hags have incorporated elements from various sources, evolving into the fascinating, multifaceted legend that continues to be a part of cultural discourse today.

Chapter 6

THE BOO HAGS TODAY: PRESERVING THE GULLAH HERITAGE

The Boo Hags legend holds a significant place in the Gullah community, not only as a captivating tale but also as a powerful symbol of their cultural heritage and resilience. Today, the story continues to be passed down through generations, serving as a testament to the enduring spirit of the Gullah people and a reminder of their African roots.

The Gullah community, residing primarily in the coastal regions of South Carolina and Georgia, is comprised of descendants of enslaved West and Central Africans. Despite the hardships they endured during the era of slavery and the subsequent challenges of segregation and discrimination, the Gullah people have demonstrated remarkable resilience in preserving their unique heritage and cultural traditions. The Boo Hags legend plays a vital role in this preservation.

The story of the Boo Hags serves as a link to the African roots of the Gullah people. It reflects the shared beliefs, mythologies, and folklore that were brought from Africa and adapted to the new environment. By maintaining and passing down this legend, the Gullah community keeps alive a connection to their ancestors and the cultural practices that have been an integral part of their identity for generations.

The Boo Hags legend also serves as a reminder of the struggles and resilience of the Gullah people. The tale depicts a constant battle between good and evil, where the Boo Hags represent the malevolent forces that seek to drain the life force of the innocent. This metaphor resonates deeply with the experiences of the Gullah community, who have faced and continue to confront systemic injustices and challenges. The perseverance and strength exhibited by the characters in the story mirror the resilience of the Gullah people in overcoming adversity.

Furthermore, the Boo Hags legend acts as a unifying force within the Gullah community. It is often shared through oral traditions, storytelling, and cultural events, bringing people together and fostering a sense of shared identity and pride. The storytelling traditions surrounding the Boo Hags allow for intergenerational connections, as elders pass down the tales to younger generations, ensuring the preservation of their cultural heritage.

In recent years, there has been a renewed interest in Gullah culture and heritage, both within the community and in the wider world. Efforts to preserve and celebrate Gullah traditions, including the Boo Hags legend, have gained momentum. Cultural festivals, art exhibitions, and educational initiatives have emerged, providing platforms for the Gullah community to showcase their vibrant traditions and share their stories with a broader audience.

In conclusion, the Boo Hags legend holds a special place in the Gullah community today, representing a living testament to their resilience and the preservation of their African roots. It serves as a reminder of the struggles faced and overcome by the Gullah people, while also fostering a sense of unity and cultural pride within the community. By continuing to pass down the story, the Gullah community ensures that their heritage and traditions remain vibrant and relevant, enriching not only their own lives but also the broader cultural landscape.

Epilogue
THE ENDURING POWER OF LEGENDS

Throughout history, legends and folklore have played a crucial role in preserving cultural heritage, history, and the collective memory of communities around the world. They are the threads that connect us to our ancestors, our roots, and our shared humanity. The Boo Hags legend, explored in this book, exemplifies the enduring power of such stories and their ability to transcend time and space.

Legends are not merely tales of the past; they are living narratives that evolve and adapt with each retelling. They are passed down through generations, carried by the voices of storytellers who weave the fabric of traditions and beliefs. The Boo Hags legend, originating from the fusion of African shape-shifting spirits, European vampires, and witches, has survived the test of time, reflecting the complex tapestry of cultural influences that have shaped it.

Legends like the Boo Hags are not confined to a single community or culture. They are universal in nature, transcending geographical boundaries and connecting people across different societies. These stories address fundamental human experiences and emotions, such as fear, love, and triumph over adversity. They provide a shared language through which we can understand and relate to one another, fostering empathy and cultural exchange.

Moreover, legends serve as vessels of cultural heritage and historical memory. They carry within them the wisdom, values, and traditions of a community, providing a link to the past and guiding the present. The Boo Hags legend, for instance, serves as a testament to the resilience of the Gullah people and a reminder of their African roots. It encapsulates the struggles, triumphs, and enduring spirit of a community that has faced numerous challenges throughout history.

In a rapidly changing world, where cultures and traditions can be easily diluted or forgotten, legends act as anchors, preserving the essence of a people. They are a source of pride and identity, grounding individuals in their cultural heritage and fostering a sense of belonging. Legends provide a foundation upon which communities can build and grow, nurturing a collective consciousness that transcends generations.

The enduring power of legends lies in their ability to adapt and resonate with new audiences and contexts. As time progresses, these stories continue to evolve, incorporating contemporary themes and concerns. They are not frozen relics of the past but living narratives that speak to the present and shape the future. Legends have the power to inspire, challenge, and provoke thought, inviting us to reflect on our values and beliefs.

In today's globalized world, where cultures are increasingly interconnected, the importance of preserving and celebrating legends and folklore cannot be overstated. They offer a counterbalance to homogenization, celebrating the richness and diversity of human experiences. Legends promote cultural understanding, bridging gaps between different communities and fostering appreciation for the complexities of our shared human tapestry.

As we conclude this exploration of the Boo Hags legend, let us recognize the intrinsic value of legends and folklore in preserving cultural heritage and history. They are the living threads that connect us to our past, illuminate our present, and guide our future. By embracing and cherishing these stories, we honor the resilience, wisdom, and beauty that reside within the collective soul of humanity.

ABOUT THE AUTHOR

My love affair with writing began at a tender age, around 10 years old, when I discovered the captivating allure of crafting stories. Armed with my typewriter, I embarked on a journey of creativity, weaving tales that danced with the darkness of the human psyche. It was during this time that I found solace in the works of R.L. Stine and Christopher Pike, masterful authors who effortlessly wove webs of spine-chilling horror. Their stories awakened a passion within me, and I realized that the genre of horror held a special place in my heart.

However, my love for writing extends beyond the realms of fear and terror. With a background in children's education, I have cultivated a deep appreciation for the power of storytelling in nurturing young minds. This has inspired me to explore the creation of notebooks, journals, and children's books, crafting worlds that blend imagination and learning seamlessly. The joy of penning tales that not only entertain but also educate and inspire young readers is a feeling like no other.

Printed in Great Britain
by Amazon